African-Australian
Marriage Migration

Studies in Critical Social Sciences Book Series

Haymarket Books is proud to be working with Brill Academic Publishers (www.brill.nl) to republish the *Studies in Critical Social Sciences* book series in paperback editions. This peer-reviewed book series offers insights into our current reality by exploring the content and consequences of power relationships under capitalism, and by considering the spaces of opposition and resistance to these changes that have been defining our new age. Our full catalog of *SCSS* volumes can be viewed at https://www.haymarketbooks .org/series_collections/4-studies-in-critical-social-sciences.

New Scholarship in Political Economy Book Series

AFRICAN-AUSTRALIAN MARRIAGE MIGRATION

An Ethnography of (Un)happiness

HENRIKE A. HOOGENRAAD

Haymarket Books
Chicago, IL

First published in 2021 by Brill Academic Publishers, The Netherlands
© 2021 Koninklijke Brill NV, Leiden, The Netherlands

Published in paperback in 2022 by
Haymarket Books
P.O. Box 180165
Chicago, IL 60618
773-583-7884
www.haymarketbooks.org

ISBN: 978-1-64259-794-3

Distributed to the trade in the US through Consortium Book Sales and
Distribution (www.cbsd.com) and internationally through Ingram Publisher
Services International (www.ingramcontent.com).

This book was published with the generous support of Lannan Foundation and
Wallace Action Fund.

Special discounts are available for bulk purchases by organizations and
institutions. Please call 773-583-7884 or email info@haymarketbooks.org for more
information.

Cover design by Jamie Kerry and Ragina Johnson.

Printed in the United States.

10 9 8 7 6 5 4 3 2 1

Library of Congress Cataloging-in-Publication data is available.

For my parents

Contents

Acknowledgements

This study would not have been possible without the assistance of a number of people—to all of whom I am extremely grateful. I want to take a moment to thank a few of them in particular.

First and foremost, I extend my greatest thanks to all the interlocutors of this study. I am extremely grateful to the men and women who shared their life stories, their feelings and their time with me. I thank them for their hospitality, for trusting me, and for opening up to me. Not only would this research not have been possible without them, their stories and experiences also taught me about love and marriage, and about the journey of migrating for love. Their recollections and our conversations have been very helpful in my own personal circumstances of starting a family abroad.

In addition, I want to thank those in Australia who helped me to get my research started. I am grateful to Mzee Sossy Msomi, Valerie Gatabazi, Tanya Lyons, Gido Mapunda, Sukanya Das, and my second cousin once removed Eva Rennie for welcoming me, for making me feel at home, for inspiring me and motivating me, and for introducing me to interlocutors.

Within the Departments of Anthropology and Development Studies and Sociology, Criminology and Gender Studies at Adelaide University, I want to thank Susan Hemer for advising me and for believing in me from the start, and I am grateful to Rodney Lucas, who helped me get ready for my fieldwork. I also thank Richard Vokes, for supervising me during the first years of my research. His knowledge of literature and his original thinking has positively influenced the study's directions. I also want to thank the late Graeme Hugo, for his initial interest in my research plans, and his encouragement to move to Adelaide to conduct this research.

I am extremely thankful for my postgraduate supervisors Georgina Drew and Pam Papadelos. Their knowledge, precision, encouragement, patience and kindness have helped and inspired me tremendously. Both have taught me so much about researching and writing. Georgina's sharpness and skillfulness, and her ability to help me focus—not to lose sight of my arguments and not to get lost in all the interesting theories and approaches—were among the many things I am grateful for. Pam, with her knowledge of the Australian context, of gender, femininity and masculinity, her careful reading of my drafts, as well as her kindness and support were particularly valuable. I feel very lucky I had both of them as my supervisors. In a way Georgina and Pam never stopped supervising me, as they continued to guide and support me during the preparation of this manuscript, by offering me practical advice, proof reading chapters, and through our valuable discussions about my work.

Other colleagues have also provided me with valued advice and support. I am particularly grateful to Tess Geraghty, Nadine Levy, Maryke van Diermen, Ruthie O'Reilly, Nathan Manning, Megan Warin and Tanya Zivkovic. The coffees and conversations that we had, as well as just knowing that they were in close proximity and working hard in their own offices motivated me significantly. I want to express great gratitude to Concetta Scarfiello, with whom I had countless conversations analyzing love, romance, and intimate relationships. I also thank her for our friendship, for being there for me, and for being patient with me. Her unconditional support has helped me feel that I belonged in Adelaide.

The University of Adelaide has supported me in numerous ways during the process of the research, the writing of the dissertation, and during the process of converting my dissertation into a book. I thank the University of Adelaide for the Adelaide Scholarship International that has supported me throughout this study, and the Department of Anthropology and Development Studies for providing the additional funding for fieldwork. During the last phase of preparing the manuscript, I was supported by the School of Social Sciences by providing me with office space with a beautiful view. I was also supported by my employment at the Department of Sociology, Criminology and Gender Studies.

I want to thank my Brill editors David Fasenfest and Alfredo Saad-Filho for their valuable comments on the manuscript and for guiding me through the process of publishing my work. In addition, I also thank John Liddle for his help copyediting my work. With his help, the accuracy and clarity of the study increased significantly.

I also thank my supervisor for my BA degree at Utrecht University, Geert Mommersteeg, and my supervisors for my MPhil degree at the African Studies Centre, Leiden University, Eileen Moyer and Rijk van Dijk, for inspiring me and encouraging me. They taught me about anthropology in general, my topics in particular, and encouraged and supported me during earlier fieldwork in Zanzibar, Tanzania. This book would not be here without them.

I further want to express my gratitude to the amazing team at Goodstart Melrose Park and the educators at the Pilta and Kuula rooms at the Childcare North Terrace. Their continued dedication and love for my children is truly invaluable.

I am grateful for my friends in the Netherlands, who—sometimes reluctantly—accepted my move to Australia and always encouraged me to follow my dreams, and are still there for me. Fenna, Annechien, Janna, Eline, *dank*! I thank my sister Josine and her husband Gerard for their support and encouragement. I am honored to name and to express thanks to my partner Kassim.

I thank Kassim for being patient with me, and for his unconditional love and support. With Kassim, Zeles came into my life and motivated me through her own passion for storytelling. Later, Francis and Hassina joined. I am extremely grateful for the children as they bring so much lightness, joy and purpose to my life. Kassim and the children have made me a home in Adelaide, and seem to never stop believing in me.

Finally, to my parents, Hans and Francine Hoogenraad-Rosier, who passed on before I could finish this work. My parents taught me to be curious, to be active and to keep learning. They introduced me to the world through literature, music, art, travels and food, and their own careers and awareness for social justice serve as an inspiration for me. I believe it is their influence that led me to choose anthropology. I am exceptionally grateful for their generosity, their love and support. I know they would have been, or are, the proudest of all. I dedicate this work to them.

CHAPTER 1

Introduction

This study examines cross-border couples' journeys of love and marriage migration to Australia. It narrates how for couples consisting of an Australian woman and a man from the continent of Africa, journeys of marriage migration are "happiness projects" leading to a good life. For the interlocutors of this study, happiness is connected to dreams for enduring partnerships that are located in Australia. After romantic first encounters and a period of dating, couples embark on their journeys to everlasting happiness by applying for a Partner visa. This study follows such journeys until well after couples settle in Australia. While there are moments of joy along the way, happiness is often an aspired state rather than an achieved goal. Despite the best of intentions, couples face multiple obstructions to their sought-after happiness. Government bureaucracy, institutional and everyday racism, and unrealistic expectations of romance often prevent the hoped-for happy endings. I argue that such pressures significantly affect partnerships. Initial hopes for lasting love and happiness deteriorate, and are replaced by emotional, mental, and physical duress. The personal experiences of such obstructions to happiness are the focal point of the book.

In the Australian media, international love and marriage migration are often sensationally described as insincere and even as a sham. Such news items are not fully representative of cross-border love and relationships as success stories are generally ignored by the media. Stories of sham marriages, chain migration, and fake love abound. Such stories describe how vulnerable white Australians fall victim to predatory foreigners that would buy and cheat their way into obtaining permanent residency in Australia through marriage migration. For instance, in the Sydney Morning Herald, Australian women described as "vulnerable" and "disadvantaged" are reported to be targeted by a "global syndicate" between India and Australia (Rawsthorne 2019). An article in the Australian *Herald Sun* newspaper uses the terms "foreign fraudsters" and "bogus relationships" that the writer claims are "being uncovered at an alarming rate" (Galloway 2018). The controversial Australian right-wing politician Pauline Hansen is quoted in an article in the *Herald Sun*, describing marriage migration as "a free ticket to enjoy our lifestyle" (Masanauskas & Minear 2017). Further, the Australian Competition and Consumer Commission (2015) reports that in 2014, a total of almost 28 million Australian dollars were lost to romance scams by just over a thousand people. Of those Australians that sent money to what turned out to be scammers, 81 lost over 100,000 AUD of their savings.

One news story was particularly dramatic as it described how an Australian woman paid for cross-border love with not only her life savings, but also later with her life. The Western Australian woman in her late sixties had travelled to South Africa to meet her 28-year-old Nigerian fiancé Mr. Omokoh and was found dead in a Johannesburg rental apartment. All her belongings, her passport, laptop, jewelry, and credit cards were missing. Before her trip to South Africa, she had sent her fiancé well over 100,000 AUD over the period she had been in contact with him online. While her children warned her not to trust this young Nigerian man, the woman insisted they had a good relationship and that he was trustworthy. The news article quotes the woman's son, who states that she was obviously blinded by love and who describes how she would not listen to anyone warning her that she may have been the victim of a scam. He explains that his mother's loneliness is what brought her to the online dating site where she met her fiancé. While South African police say it was Mr. Omokoh who reported finding the body and that it was too soon to conclude it was murder, for the woman's family and for Detective Martin from the Western Australian Fraud Squad, it seemed clear she fell victim to a scammer. The latter half of the article is devoted to the words of Detective Martin, who explains that this woman is not the only one getting tricked into a romance fraud. He warns people, especially those of middle-age and over, of the dangers of meeting partners online, of traveling overseas to meet someone they have never met before, and of sending money to someone they have not met face-to-face (Powell 2013).

In another instance, a news article reports how an Adelaide-based woman fell victim to a man from the Democratic Republic of Congo, who she says only married her for the visa. They had been married for a few years and had a child together before he came to Australia on a Partner visa, but after only ten weeks of living together he left her and now lives in another city. She had spent over 10,000 AUD on him and even though they are no longer together, and the visa has been cancelled, he is still receiving Centrelink payments.[1] The woman is quoted as claiming that he should have no such rights after his deception and feels that "the only interest he has had in his child is for his plan to stay in the country" (Littley 2012). Similar to the aforementioned story, the newspaper article portrays the Australian woman as a victim of trickery, and the

---

1   Centrelink is the Australian body delivering social security services and payments to its citizens and residents.

Congolese man as a perpetrator. As in many other cases, citizen spouses are depicted as naïve, while foreign spouses are distrusted as they are accused of having reasons other than romantic ones for marriage. As a result, a private matter becomes subject to public opinion.

It is within such a suspicious, derogatory, and often racist context that binational couples have to navigate their marriage migration journeys. Cross-border relationships are readily considered as fake while migrant men are seen as untrustworthy, and their sponsoring partners are seen as naïve (Andrikopoulos 2019; Brettel 2017; Eggebø 2013; Constable 2009; Beck-Gernsheim 2007). Such attitudes reflect a general fear that due to geopolitical and economic hierarchies, individuals from poorer non-Anglo-European countries may use their western spouses to gain citizenship and/or to profit financially. Such sham marriages—marriages of convenience that are supposedly entered into solely for the purpose of a monetary advantage and/or for a visa—are seen as a cautionary tale in popular discourse. Increasingly, they are also a point of concern for the governments of countries with majority Anglo-European populations (Neveu Kringelbach 2013). Australia is no exception. The country's so-called "non-discriminatory" immigration policy is welcoming to those who can contribute economically but limits the movement of people without skills. An indication of this is that Partner visas are subject to critical inspection, as marriage migration is seen as a weak link in Australia's migration policies (Jupp 2002). The primary narrative that emerges is a warning that there is little that is romantic about cross-border marriage.[2]

This work upsets an unfounded narrative that migrant men from various parts of Africa engage in relationships with white Australian women for the sole purpose of obtaining a visa. It does this by looking at the experience of sponsoring women and migrant men based in Adelaide, and in a few cases in Melbourne. This scam artist narrative generalizes male marriage migrants and their sponsoring partners, and it also overlooks and obscures the very difficult process of crossing borders, both physical and intimate.

The central assertion of this monograph is that migrant men and their spouses experience numerous challenges to overcome both everyday and institutional racism in their daily lives, as well as gendered obstructions generated by the process of marriage migration. As sincere as these relationships are initially, such challenges can cause tensions that jeopardize the intimate relationships and undermine their success.

---

2 Various news articles cover stories on visa fraud and marriage scams. See for instance Acharya (2017).

To underscore this assertion, the book explores the many ways that men from different parts of Africa are regulated and policed at multiple stages of the migration process as well as exposed to different registers of racism in their new lives in Australia. Also explored are the ways that expectations and aspirations for good, happy lives in Australia are subject to additional stress due to different norms around masculinity and femininity in their cross-cultural pairings. It is under the strain of these pressures that many of the relationships that initially promised love and happiness crumble, causing emotional, mental, and physical hardship.

1 Conceptualizing Marriage Migration

In this study, I use Lucy Williams's (2010) definition of cross-border marriage migration, which she defines as: "Migration that results, at least in part, from a contractual relationship between individuals with different national or residency statuses. Cross-border marriage either changes the immigration status of one partner ... or it enables one partner to enter and to set up home as a non-citizen spouse in a country foreign to them" (Williams 2010, 5). I want to add that the "contractual relationship" Williams speaks of can be either marriage, or a *de facto* relationship, so long as the couple is settling in one partner's home country through obtaining a Partner visa. Despite the legislative and therefore simplistic character of this definition, for partners and couples, marriage migration is complex and has multiple meanings (Williams 2010, 8).

Cross-border marriage migration is among the most popular streams of regulated migration globally, and recently, research on cross-border marriage migrants has bloomed. Various terms are used to describe cross-border marriage migration, and two streams have become common (Williams 2010, 9). The term "transnational marriage" as used for instance by Alison Shaw & Katherine Charsley (2006), Charsley (2005), and Elisabeth Beck-Gernsheim (2007), describes marriages "within established, transnational, ethnic communities" (Williams 2010, 9). Such transnational marriages are among the various transnational practices that preserve family and kin-based relationships. Research on transnational marriage migration is often ethnographic, emic, and nuanced, describing how and why people marry, and how marriages fit within individual as well as communal life courses (Williams 2010, 53; see also for instance, Charsley 2005; Gallo 2006; Gardner 2016.

Another body of research focuses on *difference* among couples. Terms for describing cross-border marriages with this emphasis, as summed up by Williams, are: international, intercultural, intermarriages, cross-cultural marriages, and mixed marriages (2010, 9). As Joelle Moret et al. (2019, 5) note, "studies on 'mixed' or 'binational' couples may assume that national or ethnic differences between the two partners—and not, for instance, the difference in their legal status—are the central elements worth studying." Such terms indeed "emphasize a cultural, ethnic, religious or social *difference* (italics in text) between the marriage partners regardless of other commonalities that may exist" (Williams 2010, 9). I concur with Williams as she notes that the term "cross-border marriage" is relatively neutral and therefore "avoids value judgements or reference to social or ethnic characteristics" (2010, 9; see also Moret et al. 2019). Throughout the study I use the term "cross-border" to describe couples.

For long, studies on such exogamous relationships often related marriage migration to labor migration, and many of those studies focus on marriage migration in the East Asian region (Williams 2010, 53). More recently, studies on intercultural relationships and marriage migration are taking a broader perspective. Important works are, for instance, the research undertaken by Helene Neveu Kringelbach (2013) on marriage migration among intercultural couples in France; Nadine Fernandez' (2013; 2018; 2019) work on Cuban-Danish marriages in Denmark; the study by Jennifer Cole (2014) on relationships and marriage migration among French-Malagasy couples; and that of Apostolos Andrikopoulos (2019) and Anne Lavanchy (2014) on binational marriage migration in respectively the Netherlands and Switzerland. As Stephan Scheel and Miriam Gutekunst (2019, 852) note, a "tendency of the existing literature on marriage migration concerns its mostly one-dimensional preoccupation with ever more restrictive legislative frameworks and administrative hurdles." This means that, in turn, the ways in which cross-border couples maneuver such legal restrictions, their "border struggles" (Scheel and Gutekunst 2019) are paid less attention (exceptions are, for instance, Cole 2014, Fernandez 2013 and Wagner 2015). Moreover, this focus on the legal aspects of marriage migration also means a tendency to focus on a particular moment in the marriage migration journey: the period in which couples navigate visa applications. By doing so, other—equally valuable—dimensions of marriage migration, namely the couples' journey *towards* the visa application, and their experience of marriage migration *post* settlement, are overlooked. By looking at the sweep of journeys of marriage migration, at marriage migration as happiness projects among male migrant spouses and female citizen spouses in intercultural relationships, this work contributes to a growing body of ethnographic studies on intercultural marriage migration. It aims to add a narrative that explains how marriage migration is practiced, for what reasons, what such journeys mean for couples and how it affects them.

Further, while the body of anthropological work on cross-border marriage migration is growing, much of this work focuses on migrant women in relationships with male citizens (but see Charsley 2005 and Gallo 2006 for accounts of transnational male marriage migrants). And while many of the studies on cross-border marriage migration almost exclusively focus on the migrant spouses and their migration journey (but see Cole 2014 and Fernandez 2013), this discussion focuses on the experiences of the journey of marriage migration of both the migrant partner as well as the citizen partner.

There is a vast body of literature on multiculturalism in, and immigration to Australia (e.g. Betts 2003; Moran 2011; Noble 2005), but only a relatively limited number of studies focus on marriage migration. As research that does focus on marriage migration mainly deals with family reunification and intracultural marriages (e.g., Khoo 2001; Shabbar 2012), still little is known about intercultural marriage migration. Exceptions are studies focusing on so-called "mail-order brides" from Asian countries marrying Australian men (e.g., Robinson 1996); these often have as their central topic power relations and the image of relationships in popular discourse. Furthermore, the book *Mixed Matches: Interracial Marriage in Australia* by historian June Duncan Owen (2002) provides an overview of the experiences of cross-border couples in Australia. The book provides a thorough timeline of Australia's policies vis-à-vis marriage migration policy, but does not inform on significant details of the personal journeys of marriage migration. Another interesting study is that of Carmen Luke and Allan Luke (1998) on cross-border families from Anglo-Australian and Indo-Asian backgrounds, describing couples' experiences with racial difference and everyday life. Fatin Shabbar's (2012) work focuses on the experiences of individuals with marriage migration policies specifically, as it describes the experiences of Iraqi spouses on Australian temporary Partner visas. Nevertheless, research is sparse and relatively dated. With this study, I also hope to add contemporary insights into couples' migration journeys in Australia.

2   Marriage Migration as a Happiness Project

2.1   *Dark Anthropology and an Anthropology of Happiness*

For the cross-border couples I worked with, the popular belief that marriage migration is often for reasons other than love, and that therefore these relationships are a sham, placed their narratives of love in a rather dark setting. Alongside the gendered difficulties couples faced because of their journeys of marriage migration, such assertions created an environment that was rather harsh and suppressive, instead of featuring the optimism and positivity couples initially had envisioned. In this book, I combine a dark perspective with a lighter or positive anthropological focus on happiness. I look for ways in which individuals search and aim for a happy life, despite the obstacles that may be against them. While describing obstructions to interlocutors' happiness, I emphasize that interlocutors faced such challenges because of, and *en route*, to the happy life to which they aspired. Interlocutors of this study thus were actively pursuing a life worth living, even though they faced the considerable constraints that shape the bulk of this monograph. And while the coming chapters describe suffering, harshness and disappointments that the journey of marriage migration brought them, all interlocutors were actively pursuing a better life. As a framework for this study, then, I combine a dark perspective with an anthropological focus on happiness. The paragraphs to come first explore "dark" anthropology, before elaborating on "good" anthropology, and more specifically, on happiness.

Couples' experiences with marriage migration could easily fit within a frame that Sherry Ortner calls "dark anthropology" (2016). Ortner focusses on the influence of both governmental as well as economic neoliberalism and its (darkening) effect on anthropological theory. Neoliberalism—as an economic system and as a form of governmentality—as well as its effects, became both "objects of study and frameworks for understanding other objects of study across a wide range of anthropological work" (2016, 51–2). She describes a turn to dark anthropology since the 1980s, focusing on power relations, exploitation, inequality and hopelessness. Such a turn came about, Ortner explains, after previous anthropological work mainly used a culturalist perspective, focusing on how culture provides meaning. Although this perspective was popular in the 1960s and 1970s, the latter decade also witnessed a new reductionist critique with a Marxist or political economy approach. Especially significant were postcolonial theories, feminist studies, and a bit later, racial critiques. These new points of departure, although often disagreeing amongst one another, did agree on one important thing: that attention needed to be shifted to inequalities and power relations, and by the 1980s they dominated anthropology. This became dark anthropology: "anthropology that emphasizes the harsh and brutal dimensions of human experience, and the structural and historical conditions that produce them" (Ortner 2016, 49).[3]

---

3   Regarding neoliberalism as an economic system, Ortner sums up studies such as Bourdieu's *The weight of the world: Social suffering in contemporary society* (1993) and James Ferguson's *Expectations of modernity: Myths and meanings of urban life on the Zambian copperbelt* (1999). Such studies focus on issues such as unemployment, disconnection, abjection, on the loss of optimism and on a growing insecurity about the present as well as the future

In many ways, dark anthropology takes a focus on the downtrodden populations of anthropological study. Joel Robbins (2013) describes how studies of the "suffering subject" build upon the foundations of the discipline's initial focus on the savage, the primitive, and the culturally opposite "other" to Anglo-Europeans (see also Trouillot 2003). In more recent years, and especially since the 1980s and 1990s, Robbins sees a renewed focus on what he calls the "suffering slot."[4] This emphasis was in many ways propelled within the social sciences and humanities by the work of scholars such as Michel Foucault and Edward Said. According to Robbins, who bases his elaboration on Trouillot (2003), such a shift to a new anthropological focus on the "suffering other" was "rooted in transformations in [a] broader symbolic organization that defines the West and the savage" (2013, 449). He goes on to argue that by the late 1980s, such transformations came about as "the narratives of development and progress that had driven western history were beginning to lose their power to organize our understanding of the world" (Robbins 2013, 449). In these new times, the other was no longer culturally a radical opposite, and the boundaries between "us" and "them" had become "blurrier than ever before" (Trouillot 2003, cited by Robbins 2013, 449). In the by now globalized world, the other now stood in a different relation to us. Whereas before the other was bounded by culture, they now had become the oppressed, marginalized, racialized, and discriminated other (Robbins 2013, 449).

For the last twenty years or so, anthropologists have used a dark perspective, focusing on suffering subjects. Robbins suggests that within the framework of dark anthropology, "trauma" became the bridge between cultures. This new focus on trauma, which "came to define a humanity without borders" (2013, 454) was the opportunity for anthropologists to let go of the notion of the other and to replace it with that of the suffering subject. Historical cultural and global transformations—inspired by globalization and neoliberalism, and amongst others through a focus on decolonization, cultural loss and humanitarianism—opened up a space for scholars to describe trauma (and thus suffering) as a universal commonality. While such studies provide a cultural context to some extent, much attention is given to general ideas of

---

(Ortner 2016, 53–5). Studies focusing on neoliberalism and Foucault's notion of governmentality, such as that of Foucault (2008) and Ong (2006) focus on for instance "ways in which society is being neoliberalized," the "regulation of populations," and the "precariousness of life" (Ortner 2016: 55–8).

4   Robbins bases this term "suffering slot" on Trouillot's essay titled 'Anthropology and the savage slot: the poetics and politics of otherness' (2003).

power and inequality, as well as the universal concepts of trauma and suffering (Robbins 2013).

Over recent years, a reaction to dark anthropology, with a renewed emphasis on the good, has become discernible. According to Robbins (2013), an anthropological focus on the good is apparent as anthropologists are exploring "the different ways people organize their personal and collective lives in order to foster what they think of as good, and ... [to] study what it is like to live at least some of the time in light of such a project" (457).[5],[6] The anthropology of the good, as Robbins sees it, focuses on "value, morality, imagination, well-being, empathy, care, the gift, hope, time and change" (2013, 457); see also Fischer 2014; Kavedžija & Walker 2016). Such works should be seen as reactions to both neoliberalism and dark anthropology, and offer a welcome positive counterweight to current darkness in both anthropology as well as and more importantly, global politics. Each perspective should not be seen as mutually exclusive or as completely opposite to the other but need to be integrated together (Ortner 2016, 58–60).[7]

One subfield of the "anthropology of the good" focuses on happiness. The idea of happiness is closely related to wellbeing, which has become a focal point of research (Ortner 2016, 58). In the introduction to the edited book *Values of Happiness: towards an anthropology of purpose in life*, Harry Walker and Iza Kavedžija state that "Insofar as the study of happiness necessarily draws together considerations of meaning, values, and affect, it could be seen to lie at the very heart of the anthropological endeavor" (2016, 2). Yet, it has been mainly other disciplines such as cultural psychology and economics that

---

5 He identifies three directions within an anthropology of the good: a) on value, morality, wellbeing, and imagination (see for instance Graeber 2001, Laidlaw 2002, Lambek 2010, Lohmann 2010, Mathews & Izquierdo 2009); b) empathy, care and the gift (see for instance Hollan & Throop 2011, Garcia 2010, Sykes 2005); and c) on time, change and hope (see for instance Deeb 2009, Smid 2010, Crapanzano 2004).

6 Another term for what Robbins calls "anthropology of the good" is "a positive anthropology," as coined by Fischer (2014).

7 Appadurai agrees with Ortner in incorporating anthropologies of both the dark and the good, as he writes: "These studies recognize that aspiration and hope, like despair and suffering, also have a cultural logic and are shaped by language, history and context. They contest the dominant developmentalist belief in the universality of ideas of the good life and of justice, freedom and equality. They also undermine the older modernization theory bias, which saw all human societies as heading towards a Euro-American moral consensus around ideas of equality, liberty and reason. These recent studies of the good life and its varieties thus also incorporate the Foucauldian fear of capillary governmentality, but they avoid the Foucauldian tendency to batten down the hatches and close the doors to resistance and change" (2016, 23).

have studied the phenomenon. One explanation, alongside the discipline's aforementioned focus on dark experiences, also has to do with a "certain suspicion of happiness as an essentially bourgeois preoccupation, increasingly associated with a neoliberal agenda, and potentially at odds with emancipatory politics" (Walker & Kavedžija 2016, 5; see also Ortner 2016). Another reason that anthropologists have not contributed much to the wider community of happiness studies is their different approach and methods. For anthropologists, happiness is not easy to define, and they do not share the more general quantitative approach to happiness and thus do not take part in measuring happiness levels (Walker & Kavedžija 2016, 5).

Walker and Kavedžija (2016) elaborate on the values of happiness. According to them, "How people conceive of, evaluate, and pursue (or not) happiness can reveal much about how they live and the values they hold dear" (2016, 1). There is no uniform "pursuit of happiness." but rather, happiness "means different things in different places, different societies, and different cultural contexts" (Mathews & Izquierdo 2009, cited by Walker & Kavedžija 2016, 7). Walker and Kavedžija emphasise that when studying happiness, attention should be given to the "social and cultural as well as moral and political dimensions of human experience" (2016, 8). Therefore, they find it important to relate happiness to values in three different ways. First, "happiness may not be an unquestionable good in every social context, let alone the ultimate good." Second, "happiness itself is intrinsically evaluative," and lastly, "happiness therefore cannot be separated from the spectrum of cultural values in relation to which it becomes meaningful, and which necessarily inform the process of evaluation" (2016, 8). Happiness within anthropology:

> figures as an idea, mood, or motive in people's day-to-day lives: how they actually go about making their lives happier—or not—whether consciously or otherwise, in ways conditioned by dominant social values as well as an array of aims and aspirations that are potentially conflicting.
> WALKER & KAVEDŽIJA 2016, 6

As Michael Lambek (2016) describes, happiness can be about one specific moment in time, or looked at over the course of one's life. Furthermore, he notes that the temporal dimension of happiness, and the evaluation of an individual's life can be either in the past (in memories and lived experiences), in the here and now, or in the future as goals to strive for. For Sara Ahmed, happiness is directed towards the future, as "a wish, a will, a want" (2010, 2). Katy Gardner, in her work on happiness and suffering in transnational spaces of a Bangladeshi family in Britain and Bangladesh, describes how Ahmed's

(2010) notion of happiness projects helps to explain the emotional ambiguity of migration. Using Ahmed's (2010) conceptualization of happiness, Gardner argues that "Rather than seeking to describe what is at best a fluid and elusive state of being ... social scientists might profitably think of happiness in terms of what it *does*" (Gardner 2016, 193). She explains how objects, as well as projects, can become signposts of happiness (ibid.). Gardner goes on to argue that happiness is aspired to and sought after, rather than something actual. "Individuals" she continues, "face choices or paths that we believe will lead to happiness, the promised end point of our journey" (2016, 193). Gardner explains that while migration is often understood as a journey to make life better, it simultaneously leads to feelings of loss, sadness, longing, upheaval and rupture, separation and sorrow. Migration may thus make migrants (as well as those who are left behind, those who return, and those they will meet along the way) both happy and unhappy at the same time—depending on temporalities and perspectives. But to evaluate or try to determine levels of happiness is not so much the point. Rather, as Gardner argues, "By treating happiness as a project—an enterprise that projects people into the future—we focus on how it is imagined and the routes taken in order to reach it, both over the life course and over space" (2016, 194).

Ahmed's notion of happiness projects serves as a framework for the cross-border couples' journeys that are described in the chapters to come. Like Gardner's study, this work sees marriage migration as a happiness project that generates ambivalence, conflict, and suffering, but also hope and joy. For the interlocutors of this study, happiness is something that was experienced during the couples' first encounters, as they got to know each other and together enjoyed a period of carefree fun, romance and intimacy. Marriage migration is framed as a project that is taken on because it is an imagined achievement of everlasting happiness. Romantic partners, for a variety of reasons, connected such great expectations to these journeys. *When I marry, I will be happy. When we live in Australia, life will be good.* But as the happiness project was set in motion, it turned out that marriage migration had an insidious effect on aspirational happiness, the achievement and the promise of happiness that couples intended to achieve. By combining a dark anthropology perspective with an anthropological focus on happiness, the study aims to shed light on the series of regulations, institutions, sociocultural ideals, norms and practices, which come into play and make navigating journeys much harder than anticipated. Strict and elaborate visa regulations, the experience of everyday racism, and the often-negative effects of marriage migration on intimate partnerships all made the promise of happiness an unrealistic ideal. Since institutional and everyday racism are significant obstructions to happiness, I use a Critical Race lens to analyze such obstructions to marriage migration as a happiness project.

2.2   Critical Race Theory: A Framework for Obstructions to Happiness in Australia

Critical Race Theory emerged in the late 1980s in legal studies in the United States and has since been widely used in other branches of academia, such as anthropology, and on a global scale (Valdes et al. 2014, 1). Critical Race Theory materialized as a response to Critical Legal Studies' class-based analysis as it was deemed incomplete (Dixson 2018, 233). While not discarding class as an analytical factor, Critical Race scholars believe that the law reifies, and is often responsible for, racial subordination and inequality (ibid.). Critical Race Theory's main assertion is that the legal system—in the US, but also in other Anglo-European countries—is "structured to maintain white privilege" in ways that keep the "normative supremacy of whiteness" in place (Valdes et al. 2014, 1). Whiteness as subjectivity, Georgina Ramsay explains, is "shared, mostly unconsciously, by the descendants of European settlers in settler-colonial contexts as an often-institutionalized mode of, or assumed right to, sociocultural, political, and economic dominance" (2017, 172). Critical Race theorists aim to "expose and dismantle this social and legal status quo from an explicitly race-conscious and critical 'outsider' perspective" (Valdes et al. 2014, 1). Adrienne Dixon maintains that for Critical Race theorists, studying race and racism should not merely be an intellectual exercise but instead "must inform social actions that can lead to social change" (2018, 233).

Three assertions form the core of Critical Race Theory: First of all, the theory insists on race consciousness instead of "color blindness" to address racialization. Second, it asserts that structures, systems and institutions need to be scrutinized, rather than the actions of individuals. Lastly, Critical Race Theory insists on an analysis that is intersectional, or multidimensional, in order to take "into account the complex layers of individual and group identity that help to construct social and legal positions" and power relations (Valdes et al. 2014, 2). Multiple aspects of identity such as gender and class, theorists assert, need to be taken into account in order to safeguard "antiessentialism" (ibid.). Critical Race Theory is attentive to such dynamics in its focus on racial prejudice. One branch of Critical Race Theory is especially worthwhile to mention, namely Latinx Critical Race Theory (LatCrit) scholarship. Being particularly concerned with "a progressive sense of a coalitional Latina/Latino pan-ethnicity" (Delgado Bernal 2002, 108), LatCrit scholarship urges theorists to move "beyond the Black/white binary" (García 2017, 1). This binary limits "the understanding of how people of color experienced, challenged, and resisted racism and other forms of subjugation" (ibid.). LatCrit scholars emphasize how "racism, sexism, and classism are inextricably linked with other forms of marginalization based on phenotype, culture, sexuality, surname, linguistic accent, and immigration status" (García 2017, 2).

San Juanita García describes how Critical Race Theory addresses ways in which immigrants are racialized in host societies, by shifting "the focus from 'ethnic' descriptions of immigrants of color by bringing race and racism to the forefront" (2017, 1). According to anthropologists Deborah Thomas and Kamari Clarke (2013), notions of belonging and civilization are historically based and embedded in social hierarchies that generate and were generated by racial inequalities. Besides colonialism and enslavement, "Modern racism is frequently intertwined with both early and later stages of nation building" and Anglo-European (scientific) racism has had a huge impact on racial systems and projects elsewhere in the world (Mullings 2005, 672). Throughout history, the nation state as the hegemonic sovereign political actor always had the tendency to naturalize "national social formations as biological races into specific, bordered geographies" (Malkki 1992, cited by Silverstein 2005, 368). Faye Harrison notes that while "Racial meanings and hierarchies are unstable … this instability is constrained by poles of difference that have remained relatively constant: white supremacy and the black subordination that demarcates the bottom" (1995, 58–9; see also Glick Schiller & Fouron 1990).

While the term race may not often be used to describe difference, Harrison argues that, "Racialization, no matter how subtle and uneven, is an undeniable dimension of new immigrants' experience" (1995, 58). In the context of this study, this notion of racialization featured strongly. For example, male marriage migrants I interviewed all had countless examples of encounters with everyday racism. In a similar way, Ramsay (2017) explains by using a Critical Race approach how racism is part of migrants' lives in Australia. Based on ethnographic research, the author describes how Central African refugee women experience marginalization in their everyday life in Australia, through acts of everyday racism. She argues that "belonging in Australian society demands that resettled refugees demonstrate complicity with naturalized hierarchies of whiteness as an implicit basis of authority in Australia, and, conversely nonwhiteness as a basis of inferiority" (Ramsay 2017, 171). Ramsay illustrates how verbal harassment and name calling are part of everyday life for women from Central African countries, stemming from a continued acceptance and normalization of white sovereignty in which imaginaries of racial hierarchization are legitimized (2017, 172).

While Ramsay focuses on migrants' experiences exclusively, this study takes into account the experiences with racialization of not only male marriage migrants, but also among cross-border couples practicing marriage migration. Anne Lavanchy describes "how race matters" in the context of marriage migration to Switzerland. Borrowing from the fields of Critical Race and whiteness studies, Lavanchy explores how "nationality constitutes a legitimated idiom of racialization in a race-mute context and reinforces othering processes based on tacit racialized premises" (2014, 4). Nationality, the author points out, "seems to be an objective, race-neutral, non-discriminating and therefore legitimate way of categorizing people" (ibid.). However, nationality used in this way serves as a "euphemism for racialization" (Lavanchy 2014, 9), and visibly different immigrants are distrusted, as their reasons for marriage could be fake or insincere. In my research, for all partners that are or had been in a cross-border relationship, their difference first became palpable when applying for a Partner visa. The government's focus on "genuine" relationships in order to decide who is eligible for a visa, implicitly pinpoints race as a marker of difference. Hélène Neveu Kringelbach (2013) points out that binational couples (consisting of one non-EU partner) especially face internal as well as external boundaries. According to the author, French citizens feel that by scrutinizing their cross-border relationships, the state infantilizes them by deeming them "incapable of making appropriate life choices" (2013, 16). Foreign partners, in turn, are suspected of "emotional trickery for migratory purposes" (Neveu Kringelbach 2013, 11).

This work aims to illuminate how race and racialization serve as key themes in understanding why couples' journeys of marriage migration did not turn out to be as happy as previously imagined. Institutional racism—and consequently everyday racism—were part and parcel of cross-border couples' lives, and hence their experiences of marriage migration. The visible difference apparent in migrant (Black) men incited instances of both blatant and subtle racialization on an almost daily basis. But not only did couples and partners experience institutional racism and everyday racism in their interaction with others, also expectations about romantic partners were sometimes based on racialized and exotic imaginaries of the other. Race, thus, appeared to be obstructing happiness in various ways, and consistently emerged as a central theme when analyzing the happiness journeys of cross-border pairings. In the coming chapters, I focus on the various processes of racialization that obstructed the happiness to which cross-border couples aspired.

3   Overview of the Book

In the chapters to come, I describe the expectations of, and obstructions to couples' happiness from their romantic first encounters, to well after settlement in Adelaide or Melbourne. Each chapter focusses on specific imaginations and hurdles that are all, in one way or another, related to instances of racialization. By doing so, I aim to demonstrate that marriage migration is a journey that couples embarked on in the anticipation of happy lives, but one that involves various layers of disappointing realities and instances of racism that partners had not anticipated. To an extent, the chapters narrate such expectations of, and obstructions to happiness, in chronological order.

Before focusing on such hardships, Chapter 2 and 3 provide more context to the obstructions to happiness. Chapter 2 sets the scene by providing a sociohistorical context to (researching) marriage migration in Australia. This chapter elaborates on Australia becoming a "multicultural" country and also addresses the country's hegemonic whiteness. It further provides data on immigration to Australia from the African continent. The chapter also elaborates on the research that this book is based on, research methods, and researcher positionality.

Chapter 3 narrates the 'beautiful beginnings' of couples' romantic journeys. This chapter explains how the idea of romantic love serves as the foundation for journeys of marriage migration, and the start of happiness projects. It elaborates on the ways in which couples met, the first period of dating and long-distance relationships, and how couples decided to stay together and settle in Australia. In this way, the chapter demonstrates that romantic love guides movements, logistics, and financial decisions. At this stage, other than sometimes having temporary long-distance relationships that occurred before settling in Australia, couples do not meet any obstructions to their love and therefore are particularly positive about what the future holds for them.

Chapters 4 and 5 focus on institutional racism and everyday racism, respectively. In Chapter 4, a first hurdle on the path to happiness appears. The chapter discusses couples' and partners' experiences with applying for a Partner visa to settle in Australia. Because the application process has an administrative focus on genuine relationships, it becomes apparent that couples face several instances of institutional racism. The application process evaluates relationships by looking at their genuineness, from evidence of intimacy, companionship and equality. Partners perceived this procedure as indicating suspicion about their cross-border relationships. Such scrutinizing of relationships produces not only anxiety among couples, affecting couples' everyday experiences of love and intimacy, but the procedure also shifts the meaning and feeling of romantic love among couples. Thus, while the visa application brings couples closer to their desired happy ending, it also serves as a first obstruction to happiness. Chapter 5 focusses on experiences of everyday racism and everyday prejudice after couples settled in Adelaide and Melbourne. It gives examples of various encounters with racism and prejudice that influenced couples' everyday lives, and that caused significant feelings of discomfort and non-belonging. Such experiences were part of everyday encounters with strangers, as well as acquaintances, friends and family of both partners. Not only migrant men, but through their cross-border partnering, sponsoring women also faced instances of racialization. These negative experiences can be seen as another obstruction to their imagined happy marriages and happy futures together.

Chapters 6 and 7 each deal with the particular experiences migrant men and sponsoring women had with marriage migration, and both seek to answer how their journeys did not realize their dreams of living happily ever after. Chapter 6 narrates how for migrant men, happy journeys of marriage migration were obstructed by issues related to migration and masculinity. While men had imagined their journeys would only improve their quality of life, in reality, their new status as migrant men and dependent spouses influenced their lives significantly. Everyday dependency on their spouse, isolation and homesickness, experiencing downwards socioeconomic mobility in the new context, and difficulties finding respectable work and an income all affected men's sense of self significantly. Migrant men, then, while they had aspired to a good life, turned into unhappy husbands instead. Chapter 7 illustrates how for sponsoring women, marriage migration often countered the romantic expectations and hopes women had of their relationships. While women had hoped for companionship and intimacy, relationships often turned out to be not as good as they had hoped, due to false expectations and representations of their self and of their partners. Notions of femininity and the body, as well as imaginations of their migrant spouses, also interfered with their desired happy endings. In conclusion, Chapter 8 sums up the main arguments made in the chapters, and by looking at life after the migrant spouse's permanent residency is obtained, considers in what ways happiness is achieved, and in what ways happiness is obstructed.

CHAPTER 2

Setting the Scene

1   Introduction

It is important to understand the history of Australia's race politics to appreciate the experiences of male marriage migrants and their Australian sponsors. This chapter elaborates on Australia's cultural ideologies and policies from the arrival of the First Fleet, in 1788, onwards. Such ideologies and policies, it will become evident, continue to support a white cultural hegemony and is harmful for Indigenous Australians and non-white immigrant alike. I then shift the focus more specifically to immigrants from the continent of Africa. I provide a demographic overview of African immigration to Adelaide and Melbourne. Hereafter, I elaborate on Adelaide as the main setting of this study, as this is where the bulk of the fieldwork took place. I elaborate on the ways in which African immigrants are perceived in Australia, and in particular in Adelaide. I also provide a critique of such perceptions, and problematize the notion of 'African men'. I then move on to focus on the research that forms the basis of this book: the methods of data collection, the interlocutors, and finally, I reflect on my research positionality. This chapter, thus, provides the groundwork for the chapters to come.

2   From White Australia to 'Multiculturalism'

This study is grounded in a particular geographical and socioculturally dynamic place, which influences the nuances of what I will discuss in the coming chapters. Australia's history from white settlement onwards highlights the controversial yet prevalent presence of the concept of race and racial practices with regards to immigration as well as toward Indigenous Australians. The first fleet of European settlers arrived in Australia in Botany Bay in 1788. Based on the ideology of the superiority of the British white race, and a desire for Australia to be an hegemonically white and British locality, throughout time various strategies were carried out to ensure "whiteness." Before elaborating what this desire for a white Australia meant for Australia's immigration policies throughout history, it is important to draw attention to the structurally violent and racist policies directed towards Australia's Indigenous peoples. From the moment of settlement or invasion, European settlers forcefully and violently dispossessed

Aboriginal people from their land. Ever since, white institutions have regulated
and controlled Aboriginal populations often in horrid and disregarding ways.
Serious efforts have been undertaken to 'breed out' Indigenous Australians,
for instance through policies of absorption and assimilation (Jupp 2002; Hage
2002). One of the most well-known systematically oppressive policies is that of
the forced removal of Indigenous children from their families, and their place-
ment in institutions and foster homes. Removals mostly took place from the
beginning of the twentieth century up until the mid-1960s, but ultimately this
policy continued into the 1970s. As Jeffrey Dafler (2005, 138) explains:

> The policies of forced removal produced what Australians refer to as
> the "stolen generations" of thousands of indigenous children who were
> subjected to varying degrees of cultural "re-education", isolation, and in
> many cases physical and emotional abuse at the hands of white mission-
> aries and foster families.

Only in the 1960s, "political institutions dominated by the descendants of
… European settlers" made the citizenship of Indigenous people something
to be considered (Ramsay 2017, 172). Prior to a 1967 referendum, Indigenous
Australians had been excluded from the constitution. Yet, these same institutions, Ramsay argues, are responsible for the marginalization of Aboriginal
people today (ibid.; see also Moreton-Robinson 2000). As Eileen Moreton-
Robinson (2009, 62) notes:

> the 1967 referendum did not confer on Indigenous people citizenship
> rights. Instead, the Australian Constitution was changed to give the fed-
> eral government the power to make laws on behalf of any race and so
> Indigenous people could be counted in the census. The rhetoric of citi-
> zenship became a strategy by which Indigenous people could now come
> under federal government control instead of being primarily the respon-
> sibility of state governments.

Such federal control, Moreton-Robinson (2009) explains, only increased the
control over Indigenous Australians, whilst simultaneously producing a narrative in which now Indigenous Australians are pathologized and are themselves
seen as responsible for their structurally disadvantaged position.

Not only did the British settlers deem the presence of Indigenous Australians
undesirable as it prevented them from building a "white nation" (Hage 1998),
also non-British immigrants were unwelcome. Australia was first established
as a penal colony, but from the 1830s onwards, the number of free settlers

increased (Australian Government, n.d.). South Australia, with Adelaide as its capital city, never served as a penal colony, but aimed to plan the composition of its population carefully. The State's permanent European settlement began in 1836, starting with predominantly British economic migrants. South Australia remained largely populated by British migrants. Early minority populations included immigrants of German, Scandinavian and Italian descent, as well as other European settlers, and also Syrians, Chinese and Afghans. Such groups suffered considerable racial prejudice. As in Australia in general, non-British, and later non-white immigrants were discriminated against significantly (Richards 2015).

When Australia became a federation in 1901, the *Immigration Restriction Act 1901*, which became known as the White Australia policy, came into place, severely restricting entry to Australia for non-whites (Richards 2015). Preferring a national identity that was a "racially-based white British Australia," this policy aimed to ensure that Australians would be British, Anglo-Saxon, white, and Christian (Moran 2011, 2156). Various policies were in place to curtail immigration, one of them being a dictation test. This test, in any European language but the immigrant's native tongue, was provided to immigrants with (the impossible) passing of the test set as a condition for entry. The test was particularly useful as it freed the government from being selective (Bashford 2014, 32). This policy not only obstructed some immigrants from entering Australia, it also served as a tool to deport undesirable immigrants.

Nevertheless, some non-British, non-white immigrant groups remained in Australia, such as the Chinese (especially during the gold rush of 1850–60), as well as Afghani camel drivers in the second half of the nineteenth century. The latter group significantly helped to explore Australia's outback (Waxman 200, 55). Although there was a preference for British immigrants, migrants from European countries like Germany, the Netherlands and the Baltic countries were also welcomed as they were "typically young, white and healthy" (Moran 2011, 2158). After World War II, the need for non-skilled laborers as well as a fear of an "Asian invasion" made for the amendment of the White Australia policy, popularized by the phrase "populate or perish" (Meaney 1995, 177). Now, immigrants from the Southern European countries of Greece and Italy, as well as from Turkey and Eastern European countries were welcomed (Hage 2002). The growing number of immigrants to Australia increased the population's number from 7.5 million in 1947 to 12.7 million in 1971 (Jupp 2002, 13). From the 1960s onwards, a small number of Asian immigrants were allowed to settle, but it was only after the Vietnam War—in which Australia was involved—that Australia welcomed Asian immigrants in larger numbers by providing refuge to displaced Vietnamese people. Thus, after World War II, the Immigration

policy slowly became liberalized, and Australia embraced a policy of multiculturalism from the 1970s onwards (Moran 2011).

Australia's multicultural policies aim for the inclusion of non-whites,
yet they have "not challenged the dominant position of the white cultural
hegemony" (Ali & Son 2010, 419). Up until today, belonging, inclusion and
exclusion are based on whiteness. As Ramsay (2017) argues, from the colonial invasion onwards, in Australia modes of belonging are contested, and
politics of inclusion and exclusion are administered through predominantly
white institutions. Non-white migrants, in some ways similar to the experiences of Indigenous people, encounter assumptions of "difference and defi-
ciency" and therefore, Ramsay argues, "contemporary immigration policies
in Australia are ... deliberately designed in a way which demands that new
migrants conform to cultural and linguistic forms of whiteness" (2017, 172; see
also Ndholvu 2011).

Consequently, or rather simultaneously, assumptions of white superiority
and a "racialised hierachisation" serve as a "collective cultural mindset" generating everyday racisms impacting on non-white persons in Australia and
causing structural inequalities (Ramsay 2017, 173). Multiculturalism, Ghassan
Hage (2002) argues, may have become too uncomfortable for Australians over
the last decades. While it is deemed acceptable to have a normative Anglo-
Celtic culture and multiple additional cultures ("multiculturalism as cultural
government"), having the Anglo-Celtic domain transformed by other non-
Anglo-Saxon cultures ("multiculturalism as national identity") is a cause for
anxiety in an otherwise "relaxed" country (Hage 2002, 429; see also Noble
2005). Thus, while the *Immigration Restriction Act* was repealed in 1958, the
legacy of a white Australia has not been erased from public memory and
other less overt, but nonetheless pervasive methods of exclusion continue to
be practiced.

2.1   *Migration from the African Continent to Australia*

In this section, I briefly provide a historical overview of migration patterns
from the continent of Africa to Australia, and in particular, to Adelaide and
Melbourne. This part on demographics helps to understand the ways in which
race and instances of racialization and othering are related to the relative rar-
ity and novelty of Black Africa-origin residents in these cities.

African-born migrants have a long history in Australia that predates federation of the original states in 1901 and the White Australia Policy (Hugo 2009;
Clarke 2019). Aboard the First Fleet in 1788 were seven convicts of African
descent. They had come from the United States to London as refugees and
were later deported to Botany Bay (Pybus 2006). The largest proportion of

African migrants to Australia are South African, of predominantly European or British origin. In 1861, there were 1,590 African-born persons in Australia, and 56.6 per cent of that number were white South African-born. In 1947, almost 80 per cent of all African-born migrants in Australia were South African. The White Australia policy effectively prevented the immigration of non-Anglo-Saxon Africans. The number of African-born migrants in Australia increased significantly after the Second World War, mainly with the arrival of Coptic Christians from Egypt. Decolonization on the African continent also resulted in an increase in migrants of British and European origin. While the dismantling of the White Australia policy meant that discrimination on the basis of race was officially removed from government policy, this shift in policy did not necessarily generate a significant increase in the number of arrivals of African-born migrants (Hugo 2009). Nevertheless, by 1961, the number of Africa-born people in Australia had increased to 28,559, with 27.7 per cent of South African descent (Hugo 2009, p. 15). This increase can mainly be attributed to the arrival of students under the Special Commonwealth African Assistance Plan, mostly from Ghana and Nigeria (Hugo 2009).

From 1981 onwards, the Special Humanitarian Program allowed for Africans from other parts of the continent to immigrate to Australia. However, to qualify for this visa, immigrants were required to demonstrate they had suffered "substantial discrimination amounting to gross violation of their human rights in their home country" and were further required to obtain sponsorship from an eligible person already in Australia (Chen, Ling & Renzaho 2017, 2). According to Muchoki (2014, p. 238), "between 2001 and 2008, over 24,000 migrants with refugee backgrounds from Sudan, Somalia, Ethiopia and Eritrea, relocated permanently to Australia." All the while, Africa-born immigrants entered Australia on student, skilled and partner visas. In 2007–8, Australia's intake of Africa-born migrants consisted of 10,603 people, or just over 7 per cent of the total number of 149,365 new arrivals (Hugo 2009). Almost 50 per cent of the Africa-born migrants arrived as skilled migrants. Just under 20 per cent arrived through the family visa category, and 23 per cent through the humanitarian program (Hugo 2009).

According to the 2016 census, Australia counted a number of 317,183 residents born in Sub Saharan African countries, while a total of 182,499 residents claimed Sub Saharan ancestry. It is important to note that 162.450 of the Sub Saharan immigrants were born in South Africa, just over half of the total of migrants born in Sub Saharan Africa (ABS 2016a, b). While the number of Africa-born settlers is growing, they only made up 1.3 per cent of the total Australian population of 24.1 million in 2016 (ABS 2016c).

Focusing now on Greater Adelaide, out of the overall population of 1.3 million in 2016, 14,712 persons were born in Sub Saharan African countries, approximately 1.1 per cent of the total (ABS 2016d).[1] Of the Sub Saharan Africa-born population, 34 per cent entered as skilled migrants, 29 per cent as refugees or on humanitarian visas, and 12 per cent through the family visa stream.[2] A total of 1,179 Sub Saharan Africa-born migrants in Greater Adelaide came on Spouse or Partner visas (ABS 2016d). Greater Melbourne in 2016, by comparison, had a total population of 4.5 million, of which 63,919 were Sub Saharan Africa-born (approximately 1.4 per cent) (ABS 2016d).[3] Just over a quarter of the Sub Saharan Africa-born migrants in Greater Melbourne came as skilled migrants, 14 per cent through the family category, and 11 per cent on humanitarian visas.[4] 73 per cent, or 6,362 Sub Saharan African immigrants that arrived in Melbourne through the Family visa stream came as partners to Australian citizens or residents (ABS 2016d).

2.2   'African' Men in Adelaide

Because the bulk of the fieldwork was conducted in Greater Adelaide, I continue by providing an illustration of my own, and more importantly my migrant interlocutors' experiences in this city.

That (Black) migrants from the continent of Africa are relatively new to Australia, and in particular to Adelaide, only became evident to me when I first arrived in Australia in 2013. I moved to Australia to study African-Australian marriage migration after conducting research on cross-border love in Zanzibar, Tanzania.[5] In a sense, this study is a continuation of my previous research. While back then I looked at romantic relationships in Zanzibar, I also saw a number

---

1   In Greater Adelaide, 5,586 immigrants come from South Africa, making up 38 per cent of the total of Sub Saharan born immigrants.

2   This is based on information derived from the 2016 Australian Migrants and Census Integrated Dataset. The scope of the ACMID is restricted to people who responded to the 9 august 2016 Census of Population and Housing and who had a permanent migrant settlement record with a date of arrival between 1 January 2000 and 9 August 2016 (inclusive). The remaining 25 per cent of Sub Saharan Africans in Greater Adelaide are most likely temporary residents on temporary visas, such as student visas, currently hold bridging visas, or obtained permanent residency prior to 2000.

3   As in Greater Adelaide, the number of South Africa-born immigrants make up 38 per cent of the total of Africa-born immigrants, or a number of 24,167.

4   Other Sub Sahara-born residents of Greater Melbourne are temporary residents, holders of bridging visas, or obtained permanent residency prior to 2000. See footnote 3 of chapter 2.

5   In between 2010 and 2013 I lived on the East African Island for 18 months and spent most of my time studying relationships among European women and Zanzibari men. I first focused on the beginnings of such intercultural relationships, while later on I looked at "what happens next" when European women decided to settle in Zanzibar because of, or by means of, their romantic relationships with Zanzibari men.

of Zanzibari men moving away from their beloved island, mainly to European countries, but also to the United States, and in a few cases, to Australia. Men moved permanently and shared their lives and successes on social media. I optimistically and somewhat naively concluded that it must be because their relationships and those new places make them very happy. I therefore wondered: How are those Zanzibari men, who practiced marriage migration to be with their foreign spouse, faring? What is life for them like, as proud Zanzibari in their new host countries? It was from these initial thoughts that I started studying African-Australian marriage migration.

Coming from the metropolitan area of the Netherlands, which to me felt rather multicultural,[6] I was surprised to discover that the main demographic of Adelaide was predominantly Anglo-European. At first, this gave me concerns about whether or not my research would be feasible. To my relief, I soon found out that my worries had been unnecessary. It turned out that I was looking in the wrong places, like the city center and its mainstream shopping streets, and the popular beach of Glenelg. This became evident by an early encounter with a Rwandan man called Andrew,[7] who had come to Australia as a student and was now a permanent resident. I met Andrew at a café close to the university, where we initiated small talk about nightlife in Adelaide, or the lack thereof. Andrew noticed my accent and asked me what brought me to Adelaide. I explained my reasons for coming to Australia and expressed my worries about finding interlocutors. Andrew then offered to help me, by taking me to African events and functions. That following weekend, he invited me to join him at an engagement party of an African-Australian couple, where he introduced me to prominent Africans in Adelaide. This first outing formed my introduction to various African subcultures in Adelaide that previously had been hidden to me. It was with the help of Andrew—and later through various African community organizations—that I found out about the many and varied "African" spaces in Adelaide. An African Adelaide turned out to be alive and well with its African nightclub and African or country specific dance nights, the annual African soccer competition, African community organizations, shops and restaurants, and women's and youth events. It was just a matter of knowing the right people and knowing the right places.

Most interlocutors expressed the view that Adelaide would not be as cosmopolitan as for instance Melbourne, and that Adelaideans would not be as

---

6   This is not to say, however, that racism is not a problem in the Netherlands. See for instance Philomena Essed and Sandra Trienekens' (2008) article on Dutch 'whiteness' and contested identities. See also the works of Essed and Hoving (2014) and Wekker (2016).

7   As with all other names in the book, this name is fictitious.

used to or comfortable with Black Africa-origin residents. During my research I often encountered descriptions and opinions from white Adelaideans about Africans and in particular about "African men." When talking about intimate intercultural relationships, people more often than not used this category of African men. Especially when something bad or extraordinary was happening, it seemed easy to explain or categorize such events by blaming the specific migrant man, as "all African men would be like that." The sense of discomfort among Adelaideans with migrants from the African continent can be related to essentialistic ideas about Africa and African men, as well as a general unfamiliarity with Africa, apart from knowing about African refugees, who began arriving in the city relatively recently.

Africa is often seen as a homogenous place, either full of war, or drought or poverty, or as a place of crisis and problems. James Ferguson argues that even though it is controversial and simply incorrect to consider Africa as a "place"—if only for its enormous surface area, numbers of inhabitants, and variety of natural environments, histories, languages and religious traditions—there is a certain truth in it, too (2006, 2). As Achille Mbembe puts it: "Africa as an idea, a concept, has historically served, and continues to serve, as a polemical argument for the West's desperate desire to assert its difference from the rest of the world" (2001, cited by Ferguson 2006, 2). In Adelaide, African refugees and other African migrants that are considered to be refugees can be seen as the radical others "against which the lightness and whiteness of 'Western civilization' can be pictured" (Ferguson 2006, 2).

As Rachel Spronk (2014, 508) explains, the essentialized notion of "the African" is a result of the complex processes of, and connections between, "colonial racism, academic discourse, and African discourses on a singular Africanness." Such ideas about the African are also gendered. In everyday life as well as in academic discourse, an idea about men in Africa as particularly dominant and promiscuous persists. That such stereotypes remain present in academic writing is, in part, due to the particular research topics in African contexts—on social problems and on sexuality in a health framework. Scholars have addressed and criticized such ideas about men in Africa being hypersexual and actively challenged such stereotypes. However, these stereotypes seem so "intrinsic to our understanding of the social world, that we continuously need to be reminded of the fact that we are stereotyping" (Spronk 2014, 505).

I certainly formed the impression that Africa-born migrants do take part in mainstream and normative Adelaide culture. But, it became apparent that many first-generation migrants I encountered, and who came to Australia as adults, seemed relatively more comfortable around other Africa-born migrants. Migrant men also identified themselves as African men (this being one of the many ways they identified themselves). In Australia, regardless of their nationality or socioeconomic status, these men shared this common nomenclature imposed on them, and acknowledged and used the term themselves (see also Fanon 1986 on blackness and see Spronk 2014). However, when African men used the term "African men" among themselves, they implied a shared knowledge of the diversity this term carried, while often, when I talked with non-African people about Africa-origin men such heterogeneity was, with some exceptions, generally not implied.

I emphasize that this loose use of the term African men is a dangerous way of describing these men, as it runs the risk of instigating or underscoring stereotypes that I aim to problematize (see Spronk 2014). As a result, I will refrain from calling my interlocutors African men unless that is how someone other than myself labelled them. Instead, I will refer to my main demographic of study as "migrant men." Although it would technically be possible to associate specific men with the specific countries in which they were born, this also poses problems. Even though the men I interviewed and whose lives I studied came from Zambia, Ghana, Nigeria, Liberia, Sierra Leone, the Democratic Republic of the Congo, Burundi, Rwanda, Tanzania and Kenya—and even though I am highly attuned to the nuances associated with these nationalities—in this work I am unable to associate specific interlocutors with their countries of origin as this would greatly diminish their anonymity among Adelaideans who might choose to read this book. Specifying one country (or city or region) may lead to a failure to secure the privacy of those men and their families because the networks of migrants within Adelaide can be rather tight-knit. Since I will be layering into the discussion key details of my interlocutors' lives, these details along with mention of a specific nationality would in many instances "out" my interlocutors' real identities within Adelaidean migrant circles.

3   Methods of Data Collection

This research is conducted by means of qualitative methods of data collection. These are participant observation, informal conversations, in-depth interviews and group discussions. The methods helped me to provide a detailed documentation of not only how individuals and couples say they feel and do things, but also what they actually do, and how they act, re-act, and respond. These research methods helped me to understand three general aspects of my interlocutors' lives: the ways in which romantic partners maintain, negotiate and attune their identities and cultural practices; how they relate to various places, practice place making and experience belonging and relating; and how the obstructions to happiness that they meet make them feel, both within their relationship, as well as vis-à-vis the community and state policies. Fieldwork took place in 2014 and 2015 and lasted 16 months, with follow-up conversations over the course of 2016.

Migrant men, who came to Australia as a partner to a white sponsoring female, and their sponsoring partners (or ex-partners), were the main research participants. I conducted interviews and had informal conversations with individuals who were or had been in a heterosexual cross-border relationship. These included: 18 migrant men (of whom 15 were based in Adelaide and three lived in Melbourne), and 18 Australian women (16 Adelaide-based and two Melbourne-based women). These men and women were not necessarily each other's partners. In six cases, I spoke with both partners in cross-border relationships—totaling 12 individuals. I interviewed 6 partners that were together with their sponsoring or migrant spouse without also talking to their significant other. Half of the interlocutors had practiced marriage migration but were separated from their spouses. Among couples that had separated I only interviewed one ex-partner. I did not feel comfortable about asking the "other ex" for their side of the story as I did not want to jeopardize my relationship with the first ex-partner I interviewed, disrespect them, or create a conflict of interest.

Participants were between the ages of twenty and seventy. All migrant interlocutors had settled in Australia through their romantic relationships, on a Partner visa. Couples met in African countries, in Asian and European countries, online, or in Australia where migrant men had resided as students or artists on temporary visas. The relationships I followed were in different stages. I captured stories of couples that were still in the process of obtaining a Partner visa, couples that had just acquired residency for the migrant partner and couples that have been living together in Australia for ten years or more. Other participants used to be in an intimate intercultural relationship but were now separated or divorced.

The relatively small pool of interlocutors can be explained by the quantity of time I spent with them. I felt that due to the personal character of my research topic and questions, in order to collect detailed data, it was of utmost importance to create a relationship of trust with interlocutors. I therefore met with them as often as I could. While in rare cases I only met interlocutors once or twice, in general I had regular contact with most of the participants of this study. On average, I met with interlocutors between 3 and 15 times and our meetings normally lasted over an hour. I visited them for coffee at their homes, met in cafes for lunch or dinner and went to bars with them. I often "tagged along," by participating in their activities. Together, we sometimes visited friends, or we went out for an African event. Occasionally, we had contact through phone or social media. I met most of the sponsoring women and couples in private surroundings for in-depth interviews and life histories. Some migrant men I met in private for interviews, although due to the cross-gendered context and relational and gender norms, I often met them in public spaces rather than in their homes.

I also aimed to capture the social landscape in which the couples were positioned. I interviewed and had informal conversations with 14 people that were either couples' friends, acquaintances or fellow members of social clubs and African communities. It turned out that marriage migration and cross-border love was a popular topic, as well as a popular source of gossip. I had many conversations with women of Australian origin and women and men of African origin about cross-border relationships, often not initiated by me but by interested others.[8] Another way of collecting data on the social surroundings of couples was to attend African functions, and nightlife activities aimed at attracting an African crowd. I attended 29 such events. Not only did I get to know many people, I also learnt much about group dynamics, just by observing and participating in whatever was going on.[9] In general, in making use of events and participant observation, I have not used any personal information from people that were unaware of my research, unless I received a clear verbal consent from that person.

To broaden the dataset, I also interviewed one cross-border couple consisting of a migrant woman and sponsoring man, and one Adelaide man who has sponsored a migrant woman in the past. Additionally, I worked with six cross-border couples that did not apply for a Partner visa, as the male migrant partners were already residents. I also interviewed three couples of African origin who had practiced marriage migration and/or who moved to Australia together, in order to understand similarities and differences between the various relationships and journeys to and within Australia. I interviewed six employees, presidents and founding members of organizations such as the African Women's Federation, the African Communities Counsel of South Australia and smaller

---

8 Sometimes such conversations were frustrating and bordering on racist, but most of the times they were amusing and interesting, and always, no matter what my collocutor's opinion, they were instructive, as such more general notions collected in this way illustrate the social realties in which intercultural relationships are located.

9 I want to underscore, however, that some of these functions I did not attend as a researcher, but just as myself, as a friend of people there. Especially towards the end of my fieldwork, and at the time of writing, I attended events and gatherings as social outings for myself rather than for the purpose of research. The small talk I had with people at such moments are not included in this research.

African community organizations that are organized according to nationality, background, or ethnicity. Furthermore, I interviewed two migration agents with extensive experience guiding and advising cross-border couples about a partner's visa application. Additionally, I interviewed one counsellor of intercultural couples who has experience working with African-Australian couples, and one legal adviser for migrant women. Lastly, I had countless informal conversations with Africans who entered Australia as refugees, as students and as skilled workers. In total, I conducted interviews with 81 people, including the cross-border couples. The number of interviews totaled 231, of which 156 were with sponsoring women and migrant men.

As the research topic is highly sensitive and emotional, it was not always easy for interlocutors to open up about the most private and intimate aspects of their lives. While some did get uncomfortable due to my questioning, others encouraged me to write about what is happening, either to inform others or to protect others. Experiences and emotions were often inchoate, difficult if not almost impossible to turn into words. Sometimes interlocutors did not have the dexterity to express their emotions, while at other times interlocutors may have been too emotional to express themselves properly. It was a huge challenge to construct a "right" and respectful portrayal of such divergent experiences all surrounding one topic. Sometimes, the stories that men shared were completely contradictory to the stories that women shared. I chose to not aim for "the truth in the middle." but rather, to create a space for all the contradictory stories. The messiness of everyday life, and the emotional character of marriage migration are best illustrated by such ill-fitting accounts. I am extremely grateful to my participants for opening up to me, and I hope I have translated their stories in a most respectful way. In order to protect the participants, all names are fictitious.

3.1   Researcher Positionality

As a white and highly educated female from the Netherlands, in terms of privilege, the differences between me and interlocutors of this study was almost always present, albeit in different ways. Yet, often, similarities in life experiences and interests provided for mutual understanding. Often, friendships formed over the months and eventually years.

Being a migrant myself was greatly beneficial to this research. With fresh and critical eyes, I examined Australian history and politics, and roamed Adelaide's streets, beaches and hospitality. It was not hard to meet friends, as the *Aussies* I met were often friendly, and interested in me and what had brought me to Australia. Being white, I was not identified as a new migrant until I started talking and my Dutch accent became evident. In what I believe is a much-telling idea about how Australians perceive their own country as "the lucky country" (Horne 1964), I was often told that it was "amazing" and "fantastic" and "rad" that I moved here to "chase my dreams." Just so much is possible in Australia, people often remarked. I want to note that these Australians were generally white, and I often wondered if non-white migrants were welcomed just as warmly as I was. One evening, as I was waiting for the bus home after meeting a friend in the city, a conversation unfolded with an Adelaide man who had migrated from an east-African country, years before. During this conversation, we discussed how revealing it is that while I was very new to the country, due to my skin color, I looked more "Australian" than he did. Although I had an accent, this did not matter much either, we felt, as it was a European accent, which perhaps in Bourdieusian terms would mean being in possession of cultural capital aplenty. This man, on the other hand, who had been living in Adelaide for about a decade, felt that he was considered an outsider, a migrant, and sometimes a danger.

On another occasion, and after living in Adelaide for a few years, at a celebration at one of South Australia's many wineries located only a few kilometers away from the city, I got into a conversation with a highly educated white Adelaide male in his early thirties. He was curious what brought me to Adelaide, and so I explained about my research. When I later on in the conversation mentioned that my partner, whom I met in Adelaide, happened to be Tanzanian, he responded in a surprised way, and quite indignantly proclaimed "do you have a fetish or something?" Both conversations, at the bus stop as well as at the winery, indicate a presumed difference between Black Africa-origin Australians and other Australians, and between me as a white migrant as opposed to Black migrants.

Migration, though, was an experience that I shared with my migrant interlocutors. Of course, in many ways, our journeys and everyday experiences were vastly different. But still, the missing of family, being "new" in Adelaide, and the learning about Australian and Adelaide culture were commonalities. Further, that I lived in Zanzibar, spoke quite some Kiswahili, and that I was knowledgeable about marriage migration and cross-border relationships is what further seemed to be much appreciated by male marriage migrants. It is my understanding that interlocutors understood my Zanzibar experience and my knowledge on cross-border relationships as a much-appreciated effort to understand their everyday lives. Further, the fact that I am not Australian provided us, it seemed, with more of an opportunity to share negative experiences as there was no need to close each conversation with a concluding remark on being grateful to live in Australia (see Tilbury 2007).

The obvious common denominators between me and female interlocutors were our Anglo-European backgrounds and gender. Women, it seemed, generally found it easy to relate to me because I understood their ideas about intimacy and companionship, because of my knowledge about marriage migration, and, I felt, because I was there to listen. For both women as well as for me, it was helpful that I had this time to listen, and sometimes could provide them with advice. Due to my experience and knowledge, I could sometimes translate what was not always clear to women about the visa application process, and in a friendly manner challenge some stereotypical ideas about "African culture" and "African manhood" that seemed to obstruct communication with their partners. I want to note that sometimes such ideas were planted by women's partners themselves, in an attempt to, for instance, get out of cooking or other less fun household tasks. Whilst education and experience thus were useful in a way, there were differences between me and some women in terms of education and nationality and in our experience of everyday life and the habitus in which we were positioned.

Having a Black Tanzanian partner and meeting him during fieldwork without doubt also influenced my researcher positionality. In fact, having a Tanzanian partner influenced my research in ways that I could not have imagined beforehand. I have no doubt that some migrant interlocutors now saw their suspicions confirmed: that all this time I would have been, indeed, looking for a partner, rather than doing research. Some men suddenly were not interested in talking to me any longer, while others saw my relationship as another piece of evidence reflecting on my sincerity and my open-mindedness. Some women assumed that because we both had Africa-origin partners, we also shared relationships experiences, both positive and negative ones. Such assumed similarities in *doing* intimate relationships seemed to strengthen my relationship with most interlocutors: because of my own cross-border relationship, I was now one of them. And while on the one hand I find this category quite problematic, on the other hand, I also feel proud and lucky to "belong" to this group of individuals who share experiences of being in cross-border relationships, and have been so generous in sharing their experiences, their moments of happiness, joy, sadness, and insecurity with me. Both personally as well as intellectually, I have learned a lot from spending time with the interlocutors of this study— for which I am very grateful.

CHAPTER 3

Love, Romance and Happiness

1 Introduction

In this chapter, I describe romantic love as the foundation and initiation for happiness projects. More specifically, I elaborate on significant parts of the sweep of the couples' experiences and decision-making—including how couples met, how they decided to be together, and how partners chose to settle in Australia. In doing so, this chapter focuses on the ways in which love guides movements, logistics, and financial decisions.

This chapter narrates how, for the main interlocutors of this study, cross-border intimate relationships provided the means through which happiness could be imagined being realized. I describe how cross-border couples recollected, experienced and practiced their intimate relations prior to, and as a basis for, their journeys of love migration. Many partners and couples experienced their first encounters as exceptionally romantic. The seemingly perfect match was often experienced as too great to let go, which resulted in setting up a new phase of life: living together in Australia. Romantic love provided the opportunity for cross-border relationships and consequently marriage migration. At the same time, romantic love could not be separated from socioeconomic or financial spheres of life—perhaps even more so in this cross-border context. The decision to live in Australia, and couples' experiences with long-distance relationships both indicate how the desire for and the imagining of a "happily ever after" is not merely romantic but also social, economic and political in character. Such narratives help to understand the commitment couples have, even if only initially. They also indicate the decisions and sacrifices that were made in the name of love—and in the hope of happiness.

To initiate the discussion of romantic love as a ground for marriage migration, I turn to scholarship to outline the concept of (heterosexual) romantic love. Here I elaborate on how romantic love is universal yet culturally constructed. Hereafter, I narrate interlocutors' accounts of their first romantic encounters, how couples came to decide to settle together in Australia and how they stayed in touch over long distances. I want to stress that I am not looking to answer the question of whether partners *really* loved their significant other. Rather, I am looking at how love is *enacted* as well as how it is (potentially) *transformative*. By enacted, I mean the ways in which love, as Lieba Faier (2007, 149) describes, was "performed, professed, and made meaningful" by couples.

By transformative, I mean the extent to which cross-border relationships were able to significantly affect couples' everyday lives as well as the wellbeing of the individuals within the partnerships. More importantly perhaps, love was transformative as it served as the foundation for happiness projects. Before I turn to love as a cultural construct, the following narration of Jacob's love journey illustrates and is typical for how male migrants and sponsoring partners started their journeys of love and happiness.

2   Jacob's Love Story

The first interlocutor I met in Adelaide was Jacob, a man in his early thirties from a southern African country. It was Andrew who introduced me to Jacob a few weeks after we first met in the café. Andrew had known Jacob for a couple of months and was impressed by how Jacob had come to Australia, and what he had experienced. While he knew Jacob would be happy to talk to me, as he had already inquired, he suggested to me that I should first get to know Jacob a bit before I introduced my research topic. Andrew stressed that while male marriage migrants like Jacob were not necessarily scam artists, many of them would still feel they were considered as such. Andrew explained that Jacob should know first about my sincere intentions for him not to feel threatened in any sense. The right approach seemed essential. It was for these reasons that Andrew organized for the three of us to have informal drinks after work at a bar.

It was winter in Adelaide when we first met together, and it was already getting dark when I arrived at the bar. The hotel (as such establishments for dining, drinking and gambling are often called in Australia) was about twenty minutes on my bicycle away from home, but around the corner from where both Jacob and Andrew lived. After searching around inside I concluded I had been the first to arrive. Then Andrew also arrived on his way home from the city. About half an hour later, Jacob followed. In the bar area, we sat down on large stools and shared a jug of beer together. While I had been nervous to meet Jacob, as I felt much depended on this first encounter, I instantly felt at ease due to his relaxed and happy demeanor.

We chitchatted away for the first half an hour, as I had been instructed by Andrew. At one point, I explained to Jacob that I had lived in Zanzibar for a while, where I studied cross-border relationships between Zanzibari men and European women. Jacob seemed pleasantly surprised by the fact that I had lived in an African country myself, and identified me as "one of us" as I would "know what it is like in Africa." He also started to ask me curious questions about these cross-border relationships and whether they work. This was the time for me to tell Jacob about why I had come to Australia, and my current research on marriage migration. I explained that I was looking to hear about personal experiences of marriage migrants, and that in Zanzibar I had learned that such journeys, for both men and women, could be very hard and different from what couples had expected. Jacob agreed by nodding vigorously and offered to help me with my research. He suggested I should come over to his home sometime and he would tell me about his own story.

A week later, I rode my bicycle to Jacob's apartment. It was a relatively tidy place, with a few faux leather chairs and sofa. He shared the place with an Australian man who was out at the time. When I came in, Jacob just finished sending remittances home, and Lingala music videos played on the television screen. We sat down on the sofa with a South African cider that I had brought with me. I knew Jacob had lived in South Africa, and I imagined he would be happy with something from "home." Jacob then started his story of how he came to Australia. He had met his now ex-partner in his home country where he was working in a hotel bar. She had come from Australia to his country for a holiday and stayed at the hotel where he worked. But she had only stayed a few nights in this town as she was touring around a few different countries. They had a drink together on the day she arrived and ended up talking for hours into the night. Jacob recalled how their connection felt very special straight away. During the few days she stayed at the hotel, they spent much time together. Her next stop was Cape Town and Jacob spontaneously decided to visit her there. Again, the couple had a wonderful time together, and Jacob felt that they really matched each other.

Because they got along so well, after Jacob's partner had returned to Australia, she decided to visit Jacob again. As Jacob had found a job in a Cape Town bar, she came to visit him in South Africa. This was only a few months after they had first met. Jacob estimates she must have journeyed three or four times more just to see him. Every couple of months, she travelled back and forth from Australia to stay with him for a few weeks. I assumed that his partner had spent most of her salary and possibly savings just to visit Jacob. He explained that "she had gone back to Australia and worked a bit. She made lots of money, you know, and came over just to see me. I felt very special that she came over just for me."

Jacob then elaborated on their decision for him to move to Australia. Because they had liked each other so much, they wanted the relationship to keep going and to "just try it." Both knew it was going to be risky, because they had only known each other for a short while and only spent time together intermittently and for just a few weeks in a row. But neither of them wanted to "let go." Jacob wanted to move to Australia because he was not sure about their employment prospects in his home country. "She had a good job back home and I was not really attached to my home the way she was to hers, and I thought life in Australia would be good." For Jacob, Australia had much more to offer than his home country. After all, he himself had already moved to another country for a better wage. As Jacob explained: "I really thought money grows from trees in western countries, you see? I had only seen tourists going on safaris and living the life!"

To be eligible for a visa, the couple got married in Jacob's hometown. This was two years after the couple first met. It had been a small wedding, and more of a formality than a family celebration. Some of his family and close friends were there, but none of his partner's relatives or friends were present. According to Jacob, that did not matter much, because they planned to "celebrate big time" once in Australia. After the wedding and a short honeymoon in his country of origin, Jacob resumed working in South Africa until his visa was approved, and his partner returned to Australia. He explained that he often felt uncertainty and disbelief that his partner would go to such great lengths just for him. He said that it was sometimes hard, waiting for their reunion, but that "each time we would speak on the phone, I could feel my heart melt."

It had been four years since Jacob arrived in Australia, and unfortunately things did not go as planned. He separated from his partner after about two and a half years of living together. Jacob explained that the age difference—he is ten years her junior—and different preferred lifestyles were the main reasons for the split. According to him, his ex-partner did not support him sending remittances home to his family, as she instead preferred to spend their money on shopping. Jacob did not see the point of online shopping and buying unnecessary things and he felt that the money could be spent in much better ways back home in Africa. He had also been doubtful about her friendships with other men. Jacob thought she had been too close with some of them and wondered what she had been "up to" when he was still back home. To him, it seemed that she preferred not to be monogamous.

Over the next few months, Jacob and I met regularly. Sometimes I went to visit him at home, sometimes we went for a drink in the city. In fact, Jacob even spent Christmas at my house, together with other migrants without family in Adelaide (like myself). The more often we met, and the closer we grew, the clearer it became that Jacob, too, was not the commendable partner he portrayed himself to be that first time we talked about his life. While he portrayed his ex-partner as set in her own "Aussie" ways, I felt that he also had not been as empathic to her as he could have been. In the way he explained their conflicts, it seemed that he had not made much effort in communicating with her, but instead had often been blunt and unforgiving in his reactions. One night, when I was having a late dinner with my partner in a popular city establishment, Jacob had noticed us and came over to say hello. We asked him to join us, which he did, and he complimented us on our relationship. It was something that he wanted too, he confessed. But at the same time, he said that he did not believe in love anymore. Jacob also said that he no longer believed in monogamy. As he shrugged, Jacob shared that during his last relationship, the one that he had been so happy with at first and that brought him to Australia, he had been unfaithful. While Jacob had fond memories of the early days of his relationship, after settling in Australia he felt the relationship was mostly disappointing. However, he insisted that he did not regret his choice of pursuing love migration. "We just had to try," he often repeated.

3   Conceptualizing Romantic Love

Jacob's story reveals the initial enthusiasm and excitement that love brought, feelings that were shared among all migrant men and sponsoring women. Romantic love generated happiness and uplifting feelings and signaled beautiful beginnings. Simultaneously, the story illuminates how such perfect romances, when faced with hardships and conflicts, can be replaced by a rejection of love and a deep sense of loss. Such strong emotions correspond with popular beliefs regarding romantic love. Anthropologist Charles Lindholm studied love around the globe extensively (1988; 1995; 1998a; 1998b; 2001; 2006) and states that:

> According to the romantic clichés, love is blind, love overwhelms, a life without love is not worth living, marriage should be for love alone, and anything less is worthless and a sham. Romantic love cannot be bought and sold, love cannot be calculated, it is mysterious, true and deep, spontaneous and compelling, it can strike anyone—even the most hardened cynic can be laid down by Cupid.
>
> LINDHOLM 2006, 5

While this statement reads as culturally consistent with Anglo-European social mores, romantic love as a cultural construct is present around the world.[1]

---

1   For example, the presence and focus on romantic love is evident from the popularity of television shows such as "Married at First Sight" and "Farmer Wants a Wife". Both shows, saturated with ideals of romantic love, have a primetime evening viewing in Australia.

Studies show that young people all over the globe view romantic love as a basis for marriage, thus wanting free choice of partners instead of, or as a basis for, an arranged marriage (Hirsch 2003; Lipset 2004; de Munck 1988; Spronk 2002). While social and historical contexts differ, various studies suggest that throughout the world, couples talk about and negotiate emotional intimacy and sexual pleasure as important characteristics of a marriage (For example, see Spronk 2006; Rebhun 1999).[2]

But what is love? As William Goode (1959) notes, the meaning of love has been widely disputed. Eva Illouz (1997) explains that it is the unique character of romantic feelings that make them hard to define. They are therefore often merely assumed, rather than elaborated upon (Evans 2003, cited in McKenzie 2015, 12). For a long time, social scientists have avoided the concept of love as they deemed the topic lacked seriousness (McKenzie 2015; Lutz & White 1986; Svašek 2005). As Lindholm (2006, 8) describes, the "scholarly reluctance to study love is connected to the way romantic love has been imagined to be a transcendent experience that, by its very nature, resists any rational analysis." Anglo-European scientists often considered love to be disease-like, a sort of madness (see also Alberoni 1983). In particular, the discipline of anthropology for a long time almost shunned the topic of romantic love completely. According to Lindholm (2006, 7), this lack of interest stemmed from a fear of anthropology not being recognized as an objective branch of science. It was strongly discouraged from studying "soft" topics such as love, or emotions in general.

In the 1980s and 1990s, the newfound anthropological interest in the study of emotions meant that the concept of romantic love was put on the table. Since then, romantic love has received growing attention from scholars aiming to define and describe the concept. Well before his time, Goode (1959) explained that anthropologists focus on the emotions of romantic attraction and are interested in where and under what circumstances—both social and psychological—love occurs. He identified sexual desire and tenderness as key features of romantic love (Goode 1959, cited by McKenzie 2015, 13). But scholars do not all agree on whether sex and desire are part of romantic love. As Lindholm (2006, 11–14) observes, some studies point out that sex is often

---

2   The idea of romantic love is not simply a Western invention copied and pasted to other parts of the world. Both the local and the global have an influence on notions of marriage. Through media, foreign notions of love and romantic relationships have become available in many contexts and inform people about other ways of loving and marrying (Hirsch 2003).

regarded as outside of the romantic realm, and that marriage and romantic love do not necessarily go hand-in-hand (see Jankowiak & Paladino 2008; de Munck 1988). In their cross-cultural study of romantic love, William Jankowiak and Edward Fischer (1992) do include sexuality and sexual desire in their definition of romantic love. Their comparative study claims that romantic love is, in fact, universal (Jankowiak & Fischer 1992). Other scholars, such as Holly Wardlow and Jennifer Hirsch (2006), Lara McKenzie (2015) and Lindholm (1998, 2001, 2006) point out that love is practiced and understood differently in different social and cultural settings. Contemporary research demonstrates that romantic love is culturally constructed, and that there is a correlation between notions of love and cultural constraints (see for instance Abu-Lughod 1986; Lutz & White 1986; Rebhun 1999). As Faier summarizes, "sentiments [of love] are discursively produced and tied to sociocultural practices and processes" (2007, 149).

For the interlocutors of this study, while the course of love may have varied, all emphasized the exciting and romantic first encounters with their partners. For all interlocutors, love and intimacy were considered as the foundations for happy relationships and happy lives. As Ahmed (2008) explains, the ideas of marriage and family are seen as "objects" onto which happiness is projected. However, it is important to stress that Ahmed focuses on love in its heterosexual form, and that in non-heterosexual love, relationships that are not reproductive are the object of othering, instead of happiness (Ahmed 2010, 88).[3] These observations are important as the relationship between (hetero) sexuality, love and happiness is more complex than may have been assumed at first: that any love leads to happiness. While this to a certain extent holds true, it is heterosexuality as normativity that (as assumedly opposed to non-heterosexual love) inherently holds the potential for the ability for do the right kind of love: "straight," and with the potential of marriage and family *within* normative boundaries.

Love and heterosexuality indeed are inherently connected. The act of loving, Johnson (2005, 1) argues, "is enacted through a socially mediated set of beliefs and practices that reproduces a particular set of conditions—the conditions of heterosexuality." Love, thus, is culturally constructed, and culturally represented as hegemonically heterosexual. For instance, "love still draws on the 'traditional' scripts of marriage and heterosexual domesticity" (Johnson 2005, 15). While love, intimate relationships and marriage among interlocutors

---

3 Such processes of exclusion and othering, according to Ahmed, lead to the idea of the "unhappy queer" (Ahmed 2010: 88).

were "ingredients for a good life" (Ahmed 2008), this placed couples within the heteronormative sphere. This is particularly interesting since other constructions and intersections of race, gender and class, as we shall see throughout the coming pages, make both cross-border relationships as well as intimate partners as "others" to normative categories.

4   Cross-border Love Stories

4.1   *Recollections of Beautiful Beginnings*

The start of my interlocutors' romantic relationships was often described and experienced as a fairytale-like experience. It became evident that such early encounters were considered as the beginning of interlocutors' happiness projects. For me, listening to such romantic recollections of how couples met was the most enjoyable part of my fieldwork. Even though some couples had been separated for years by the time I interviewed them, all interlocutors had good memories of those beginnings, and most of them looked back to those weeks and months with warm hearts. In this section, I elaborate on those first encounters.

Interlocutors met their partners in various places and spaces: in 14 cases they met their partners in Australia, in seven cases partners met in third counties in Africa, Europe or Asia, and two interlocutors met their respective partners on online dating sites. In 15 cases interlocutors met in the man's country of origin in Africa. The sponsoring partners had travelled there for reasons related to work, study or holiday and consequently, met their future partners. These sorts of encounters are well observed in literature on romance and sex tourism. Such studies describe how males and females from Anglo-European countries holiday in tropical destinations, as for instance Jamaica (Pruit & LaFont 1995), Egypt (Jacobs 2009), Brazil (Carrier-Moisan 2015) or the Dominican Republic (Brennan 2004), where they meet romantic partners. Such romances can last for the duration of the holiday only, but in some cases, contact continues well after the tourist returns home. The now romantic partners stay in touch through phone calls, text messages and other media platforms. Often, tourists come back and visit their partners once or twice, invite them to visit their own home countries, and meanwhile send their partners gifts such as clothes and mobile phones, as well as money for themselves and their relatives. Sometimes, partners eventually migrate to live with their tourist partner in their Anglo-European country of origin. This body of literature on romance and sex tourism emphasizes tourists' racialized fantasies, and the ways in which love is "performed" by local hosts as a strategy for economic betterment.

While for my interlocutors the course of their relationships was similar, they expressed the view that their own intentions had simply been for love. For the Melbourne and Adelaide-based women I interviewed, falling in love "just happened" to them—they did not travel with the main intention of finding love or romance. And the Africa-origin men, likewise, asserted that their love had been accidental, rather than intentional.

Most women that would eventually sponsor their partners described a "magical" and liminal space they felt they were in when meeting their partner. The only exceptions to this were Charlotte and Zachary. The two had met in his hometown where she ran a non-government organization (NGO). The first time Charlotte had come to Zachary's country was on a holiday. While she had fallen in love with the country, she also experienced extreme poverty and decided to start an NGO there active in the field of education. After a few years of travelling back and forth to the country she met Zachary who by now worked for her NGO. As both of them were in relationships, neither had considered the other as potential romantic partners and they became good friends. However, after a while both their relationships ended. As Charlotte and Zachary found themselves becoming closer over the course of everyday contact, they eventually started seeing each other romantically.

Charlotte and Zachary's journey from being friends to becoming romantic partners is very different from the stories of other couples. Couples who met in a holiday context experienced love rather quickly and spontaneously, as Jacob's story above illustrates. The connection that Jacob described between his romantic partner and himself, was a feeling shared by many interlocutors. Anne, who visited an African country for a music course where she met her future husband, also described an instant connection. Anne recalled how she was "swept off her feet" by that handsome young man who was a relative of the guest family she was staying with. She described him as charming and "straight forward with confessing his love to me." He had come by every day making sure she was comfortable, asking if she needed anything, or if she had enough water. During those visits, he talked about marrying her. Although Anne had thought it was a bit early to talk about marriage, she also "loved his confidence and how he took the lead."

Jade had met her (by now ex-)partner Desmond on an international dating website.[4] A mutual friend, who had asked her whether she would be interested

---

4   While in public debates such instances of online "international matchmaking" are often considered as sham relationships pursued merely for visa or money, scholars such as Constable (2003) and Patico (2009) urge others to approach such relationships by moving beyond the simplistic binary of romance on the one hand and strategies for betterment on the other.

in being interviewed about her marriage migration experiences, had introduced me to Jade. Jade had agreed, after which she suggested to our friend that I should contact her by sending her a message. We wrote back and forth a few times as we organized a time and day that suited us both. Jade was busy with volunteering, but often had afternoons to herself and was happy to have me visit her. It was a cold and dreary day when I drove to her home in a suburb about half an hour from the Adelaide city center. She had just remodeled the house, as she felt it was time for her to focus on the future, instead of her time with Desmond. She had painted the walls, and decorated the house with colorful artwork, curtains and pillows. They had separated about a year before, and the break-up had been exceptionally hard on her. She was still happy to talk to me, as she felt it was a good method to help her achieve closure. While she was making me an instant coffee, she instructed me to have a look at their wedding photos that she had collected in an album. The small wedding took place in Adelaide, and most photos covered the reception they had celebrated with friends and family in her parents' backyard.

When Jade appeared again from the kitchen, she began her story. After a previous marriage, Jade had been single for a long period of time and friends and family had encouraged her to "get out there" again. For a long-time she had not felt ready for love, as her split from her husband had been difficult. They had been married for more than fifteen years and had two (by now grown up) children together, but his infidelity had caused the relationship to fail. Eventually, Jade decided to listen to her friends and family and subscribed to a dating site where she soon met Desmond. Desmond had approached her in a "sweet and funny" way, she recalled, whereas other men "could be very annoying out there, really pushy and nasty." Because "he was different" and because of his "extremely good looks" she had decided to respond to his messages. Desmond had been charming and had appeared to be interested in Jade. She also described him as "polite" and making her feel "comfortable and happy." She felt he was the "perfect gentleman." They started chatting daily, and eventually exchanged contact details and continued with texting and calling. At the time, Desmond was living in an Asian country for his studies, and Jade decided to meet him there. It had been her first time overseas, and she recalled "being nervous and excited at the same time." While looking back at her stay with him she could see many "red flags." But at that time, she recounted, "I really fell for him." While she still doubted whether their relationship could be long-term, as Desmond was much younger than her ("He could have been my son," she confessed), he had convinced her that it was not a problem. Jade vividly remembered, "He kept saying that love conquers all," which made her decide to give the relationship a chance.

Couples William and Lillian and Matthew and Emma had met in European countries. Both men had lived there for a few years by then, and the women had come for a holiday and travelling, respectively. For William and Lillian it had been easy, both of them recalled, as it had been "love at first sight" when they met, now over ten years ago. Both of them "just knew" they belonged together the moment they had met. While on her holiday they had spent as much time as possible together. A few months after her holiday, Lillian had returned to Europe for the two to marry. Matthew and Emma also explained their meeting as something that was meant to be. Emma had invited me over for dinner to talk about their love migration journey. She was very willing to talk about their experiences, as she felt it was time to hear some positive stories about marriage migration. When I arrived around 6 pm, Emma warmly welcomed me with a hug. As she was still cooking, she invited me to sit in the living area with Matthew, who was watching the news on television. She excused herself before disappearing into the kitchen for a few minutes, where she quickly put some dishes in the oven. Before returning to the kitchen to make the salads, Emma sat down with us to elaborate on their love at first sight.

Emma remembered the way she and Matthew met very well, as she found it particularly serendipitous. About 18 years ago, she had gone to travel across Europe for a few months. About a week before she was to fly back home, she was particularly ready to return to Adelaide. She had not liked the city she was in and stayed in her hotel room most of the time. One night, however, she had to go out for some food, and decided to walk into the main shopping street— something she would otherwise never do, as it was too busy for her. "Then I saw him." She remembered with a smile on her face. At this point in the story, Matthew was grinning and nodding. As Emma continued, she described the first time she saw Matthew: "he was busking, singing and playing the guitar." His music was so good that she decided to sit and listen for a while. Matthew had also noticed her, and after he finished making music, they started to chat. "From that moment on" Emma emphasized with a grand smile, "we were inseparable."

Sophie and Lucas were among the interlocutors who had first met their intimate partners in Australia, and had met through a mutual friend. Lucas had come to Adelaide as a musician on a temporary visa, and after a series of concerts, he was to return home. But he and Sophie had "hit it off" together from the moment they met, at the house of another cross-border couple. Their shared passion for music and a peaceful Rasta lifestyle made them realize they just felt good together, "like a very strong team." Sophie felt that she could "finally enjoy love, enjoy the peacefulness and bond of trust between two people." Soon after they met, Lucas moved in with Sophie (also, he did not have a place for himself in Australia yet) and lived with her until he had to return home. But for both of them it was clear: they were inseparable, and they would do whatever it would take to get him back to Australia.

Robert, an elderly man from an East African country had come to Australia as a student back in the 1980s. He was one of the first African migrants in Adelaide. He remembered the day he met his wife "like it was yesterday." Back then, Robert lived about an hour north from the city center, close to the campus of the university he was attending. He would only come to the city once or twice a month, as he did not own a car. One day he went shopping in the city center and had a short break to get a cup of coffee. There, in the café, he looked at the woman serving him, and "instantly fell in love with her." This woman, Jo, had noticed this man coming into the café, now and then, due to his different appearance but also because she "fancied him." They met up a few times after she finished her work and got to know each other better. And after months of dating, Robert proposed to her.

Such narratives of beginnings of relationships indicate that love, romance and intimacy are assumed "natural" bases for relationships (for example, see Vannier & O'Sullivan 2017). In various contexts, however, the shift to romantic love and intimacy as bases for marriage is relatively new. In the history of western marriage, this shift is only recent and gradual (Povinelli 2002, 2006; Coontz 2005). For hundreds of years until the beginning of the nineteenth century, marriages were shaped by economic, political and social factors. Often, bringing two people together was more about linking families, strategically choosing in-laws, and generating a move up the socio-economic ladder. Personal happiness and affection were possible pleasant side effects. It is only in the last two hundred years that people gradually began to see marriage as a private and personal matter, which should provide the couple with emotional and sexual fulfilment. Only after this view became the norm, did people start to choose their spouse based on free choice, instead of societal norms. Love became the basis for a successful marriage (Coontz 2005).

The term companionate marriage, originating from descriptions of social changes in western Europe and the United States between the eighteenth and early twentieth century, underlines affective aspects of a contemporary relationship (Wardlow & Hirsch 2006). Companionship, intimacy, and sexual pleasure between partners in egalitarian terms are of particular importance for a companionate marriage. Anthony Giddens (1992) argues that people form a companionate relationship based on choice and pleasure, instead of obligation and commitment. He sees these relationships as modern forms of kinship connections that are not based on blood but on emotional bonds.

Whether or not such relationships are marriages or de facto relationships, romantic love has become the basis for unions. In Anglo-European contexts, then, when love dies, there is no reason for couples to stay together, which is evident by the number of divorces, as well as a current trend of people to have multiple successive relationships either prior to, or instead of, marriage. Marriage as an everlasting union thus may have lost its significance. Yet, emotional intimacy is more than ever expected from a relationship (Coontz 2005, 278; see also Giddens 1992). Such trends in marriage, de-facto relationships, and divorce are also present in Australia (Simons 2006; van Acker 2003; Dion & Dion 1996).

An emerging body of Africanist studies focuses on intimacy, romantic love and gender dynamics. Such research emphasizes, that in African contexts, just as in many settings around the world, mutual sexual pleasure, trust, decision-making, and intimacy seem to be more valued and seen as bases of marriage than in the past (see, for example: Ahearn 2001; Cole & Thomas 2009; van Dijk 2015; Smith 2009, 2010). For young (urban) people in Africa, romantic love nowadays plays a large role in their ideas about and practices in relationships and marriage, as well as in their positioning of the self in a postmodern global world (see, for example, Spronk 2009a, 2009b). As Rijk van Dijk argues:

> The embrace of the romantic—in many cases by the younger generations in Africa—often runs as a culture of critique vis-à-vis their elders and the way they want to maintain certain traditions in, for instance, marital arrangements. Opting for romance often becomes an expression of protest; an act of deciding for oneself whom to marry or how to express affections. In a sense, the romantic then turns into a battleground of self-direction, self-styling and self-assertion.
>
> VAN DIJK 2015, 9

But while romance and companionship as foundations for lasting relationships may be particularly embraced by younger generations across the continent, numerous long traditions of romantic love exist—although not necessarily as bases for marriage—and are often recollected in poems, songs and tales. Coastal East Africans, for instance, have used, and still use *taarab* orchestral performances to express notions of love, longing, passion and heartbreak. Song and dance are in this way used not only to express romantic emotion, but also to rehearse and instruct in the ways of love (Fair 2009). And, for example in Nigeria, while people increasingly select their partner on the basis of love, Nigerians demonstrate a longstanding celebration of romantic love. As one

Igbo proverb reveals: *uto ka na iko*, which translates to "sweetness is deepest among lovers" (Smith 2009).[5]

The stories of interlocutors in this research reflect the current trend of placing love and intimacy at the heart of relationships and marriages. Romantic love appeared to be the most important factor for starting relationships and embarking on their journeys of love migration, their happiness projects. As Ahmed describes, "happiness is expected to reside in certain places" (2007/08, 9). For interlocutors of this study, love was the path towards happiness, and a happily ever after the object of desire.

Only one interlocutor said that love was not the foundation for her marriage. This final story of a relationship that started in Australia is that of Lucia, an Adelaide woman in her mid-sixties, and her ex-husband who she had met in the 1980s. Through her work at a music theatre, Lucia had often been in contact with African performers from all over the world, and as a result, became very much involved with the setting up of the first African-oriented organization in South Australia. I visited Lucia almost biweekly for a quick visit and a coffee. Due to health issues, it was hard for Lucia to leave the house, and so she was always happy to have people over. At almost each visit she reminisced about those days, when she met her ex-husband, which I came to understand had been particularly happy for her. She used to go to all the concerts and performances that were organized by African migrants in Adelaide, who in those days were mostly students. She felt that back then, because "there were not many Africans in Adelaide," there was a sense that, "we were all very closely connected." Dinners would be organized for students to mingle, for instance, and everyone would bring some food or drinks to share. Lucia had met her ex-husband through this community. She described him as a "good and friendly man" and "got along really well and were kind of close." Lucia agreed to get married because he wanted to stay in Australia, "and after a while, we got a divorce."

Lucia's story is atypical in the sense that she was the only interlocutor who described her marriage as a practical benefit for her then husband. The other accounts underscore the importance of romantic love for starting off

---

5   But while evidently romantic love has always been present on the African continent, scholarship on love in Africa has been patchy. The reasons for this include the discomfort of both anthropologists *as well as* interlocutors with romantic love and emotions as research topics and as a basis for marriage. Also, sociohistorical thoughts, processes and events such as colonial racist ideologies, decolonisation and independence, as well as the HIV/AIDS epidemic have all contributed to reducing the significance of love as a research topic (Thomas & Cole 2009).

relationships. Descriptions of experiencing deep connections, being swept of one's feet, excitement and passion, and the finding of one's soul mate all indicate how the model of romantic love is applicable to the first encounters between cross-border couples. The temporary nature of a romantic love-experience seemed to deepen the experience itself, as almost all couples knew the time together was short and limited, and thus was simultaneously to be considered as extraordinary and to be experienced even more passionately. Such romantic first encounters with love set off journeys that couples hoped would lead to their own happily ever afters.

4.2   Visions of Australia

This section illustrates how for a variety of reasons, most couples considered Australia as the best location for them to live their happy futures together. That couples felt that their happiness projects would flourish in Australia, rather than in the particular African country or the third country in which they met, indicates that romantic love is embedded in a broader socioeconomic and political context (Fernandez 2013). Not only were the anticipated socioeconomic opportunities a reason to settle in Australia; family and the desire to establish a home for the couple were also decisive factors. Such pragmatic, unromantic factors influenced the course of romantic journeys significantly. However, the move to Australia was not always a foregone conclusion and sometimes had to be negotiated, as not all partners were convinced from the start that Australia would be the best place for them to live.

A better quality of life was the prominent reason for most migrant men and sponsoring women to choose to settle in Australia. Many men considered moving to Australia as helpful to achieving upward socioeconomic mobility. Paul was one of the first male migrants that I met through the African Communities Council of South Australia, an advisory and advocacy body for migrants from the African continent. Paul offered to be interviewed because like Emma, he felt it was important for people to learn about marriage migration beyond the narrative of African men as scam artists. A flamboyant and energetic man, Paul was in his mid-thirties and worked at a construction site. Paul explained how he himself did not consider his home country as a settlement option due to perpetuating violence, safety issues, and lack of job opportunities. He was already in a third country, another African country, working as a security officer when he met his now ex-wife. This woman, who eventually would sponsor him to come to Australia, had been visiting a friend who lived in the area Paul patrolled. They met up daily and according to Paul, got along so well that at one stage they decided they wanted to spend their future together. He felt that both of them had better job opportunities in Australia, and that his partner simply preferred to live in Australia. When his partner got back to Adelaide, they started his visa application process.

Men often named opportunities, education, employment, income, and safety as reasons for seeing Australia as a better option than their home country. Men felt that in Australia there would be room for development, to become more successful than back home, where they felt such opportunities were hard to find.[6] The men who had not visited or lived in Anglo-European countries before, like Paul, especially felt that once in Australia, life would be good. Liam is another example. I met Liam through a country-specific African community organization a few months after he moved to Australia. During a community barbecue, he told me that while he had been living in his home country with his partner for a few months, he had been happy to move to Australia, because he thought there would be more opportunities there. Back home, he worked in tourism but did not earn as much as he thought he could earn in Australia. He explained that he had thought it would be easy to get a job, "I thought I could just start working the first morning I [would] wake up in Australia." Because of his experiences with tourists, he had only seen "rich westerners" and had therefore imagined that life in Australia would be good for him and his wife, too. Even though he would be far away from his relatives and would especially miss his five-year-old daughter, he reasoned that being far away did bring those back home a more comfortable lifestyle, through the money he would remit.

Cross-border relationships thus paved the way for (imagined) socioeconomic advancement not only for migrant men, but also for the couple, as well as men's families. The accounts above illustrate that (some) men considered such a move from the perspective of the couple and felt that migrating would be good for their relationship. This was evident from men taking into consideration the lack of opportunities for their partners in their home countries or in the countries where they were currently living. While most men did not mind the move to Australia, and were in fact excited about the move due to socioeconomic opportunities for them and their families, if it was not for the

---

6   Vigh (2009) describes how the classic notions of push and pull factors for explaining migration patterns are too simplistic. Instead, he argues that migration is related to "regional differences, historical processes, social ties ... and, last but not least, imagined places and spaces" (2009: 93). Vigh proposes a perspective linking the "social imaginary" to the praxis of migration. The social imaginary is related to what he calls a global awareness from below: "an understanding of a world order consisting of societies with different technological capacities and levels of masteries over physical and social environment, as well as the spaces and social options which are open or closed to persons of different social categories within it" (ibid.).

relationships men may not have given migration much thought, or deemed it a possibility.

The examples illustrate that a presumed dichotomy between love and money does not exist. While "Western ideology and common sense often oppose [the idea of links between] emotional attachments and economic interests, much scholarship makes clear that they are entangled at the level of practice" (Thomas & Cole 2009, 21). Research in the United States (Zelizer 2005; Illouz 1997), and elsewhere including Brazil (Rebhun 1999), emphasizes how romance and economics are connected. Further, literature on intimacy on the African continent illustrates how exchange is part and parcel of intimate relationships (see for instance Cole 2009; Hunter 2009). As Christian Groes-Green argues in his study on transactional love in Mozambique, intimate relationships are "part of broader moral economies of exchange and obligations" such as among kin (2014, 238). But, as the literature indicates, socioeconomic changes, globalization and migration, and economic hardships on the African continent often influence the character of such transactions.[7]

But not all men were happy about the move to Australia; instead, some felt it was their only option for continuing the relationship. A few men indicated that they would have preferred to stay in their home country with their Australian partner. Peter, for instance, who I met in a bar one afternoon, explained that he met his wife on one of his excursions when he worked as a tour guide. One of the things he had liked about her was that she wanted them to open their own travel agency together in his hometown. He would be guiding the excursions while she would manage the office work. She had a plan to start up the business while living in Australia together, and then to move back. But Peter was not sure why it had to be like that, and eventually it turned out that his now ex-partner was not interested in the business plan once they settled in Australia together. Even though it had been over a year since they separated, Peter still felt disappointed about this trick. "She just set me up, and now I am stuck in Australia while I could have just stayed home," he explained to me with an angry, somewhat aggressive and bitter tone, before finishing his beer in one gulp. This observation further emphasizes how "intimacy rests on a complex blend of material and affective relations" (Fernandez 2013, 282. See also Groes & Fernandez 2018). Peter had agreed to move to Australia because of his romantic feelings for his partner, as well as his excitement about their future

---

7   See for instance *Africa Today*'s special issue, "Objects, money and meaning in contemporary African marriage" which collates recent ethnographic work on marriage in relation to transnationalism, love and gender (2016, number 62, 3).

plans together. From what he explained to me that day, I wondered whether he would have agreed to emigrate if it was not for their business plans.

William and Matthew, who both met their Australian partners in Europe, also did not see Australia as a particularly interesting place to move to. Both said that while their jobs were not particularly good in Europe, their social networks had been very strong. Indeed, in comparison to Australia, European countries have a much longer history of Africa-origin immigration. Local as well as transnational networks among such immigrants to European countries are for instance described by Saraiva (2008), Krause (2008), and Riccio (2008). In Europe, both William and Matthew lived in neighborhoods heavily populated by African immigrants and had felt very much at home there. While both had lived in Europe as irregular migrants, by the time they met their partners, they had gained residency and had long established their extended network of friends and acquaintances. As such, they felt hesitant about starting a journey that they knew was going to be difficult, all over again. But since both their partners preferred Australia to Europe, Matthew and William eventually relocated to Australia. Such narratives indicate that family life, love and emotion can be stronger motives for a move than economic or mobility factors. Both Matthew and William understood that it is not necessarily easy to earn a lot of money in Anglo-European countries and were therefore not lured by Australia's presumed riches. Nevertheless, both men agreed to undertake the love migration journey.

Daniel's story also illustrates the importance of love and other emotions in deciding to migrate to Australia. It shows how perceptions of African men deceiving Australian women and using them for visas can be far from truthful. I was linked to Daniel by the African Communities Council and met him for the first time at the campus of the university where he studied. We sat outside on a bench where he introduced himself to me and began telling me his story of how he came to Australia three years earlier. Daniel was born in a West African country but had moved to the United Kingdom when he was still young. He was living in London with his parents and siblings when he met his now ex-wife. Daniel was a freelance journalist and often travelled to Asia for his job. Daniel, in fact, talked at length about his previous job and its perks. He provided me with multiple stories of human rights issues he had reported on and that he felt strongly about. Daniel's enthusiasm when talking about his own interests, which he could express through his work, revealed nostalgia, and how he seemed to miss his previous cosmopolitan lifestyle. His elaborative account of his life prior to moving to Adelaide, also seemed to indicate that this part of his life had been better for him than the relationship that brought him to Australia.

Daniel and his former partner had met online. Subsequently, during one of his travels to Asia, she came to visit him. Because they enjoyed each other's company, they kept meeting each time he travelled. She had also stayed with him in London, one time for one and a half years, and another time for six months. "We always tried to be together as much and as long as possible," Daniel recalled. He himself had come to Adelaide for a period of six months. While he loved his partner, he did not particularly like Australia, as he found it "too far away from the rest of the world." While his partner kept on asking him to move, each time he had refused. But things had changed when his partner's mother got sick. "She wanted to take care of her, and for me that was a very good reason. So I agreed to come and live with her in Australia." All in all, the couple had been together for almost nine years before he moved to Australia. They got married soon after his arrival, but the marriage only lasted for seven months before the couple separated.

For Adelaide and Melbourne women, the most important reason for choosing Australia as their home was their perception of a better quality of life. This is where they had their family, friends, jobs, and a general feeling of belonging, as well as an expectation of a comfortable continuation of life. With a few exceptions, it seemed as if women had not given settling in other countries any serious thought. In some cases, it seemed that Australia's high living standards made other options for settling down completely irrelevant. In other cases, however, male partners had not given women the impression their home countries would be an option at all—as men also wanted to move to Australia. Sometimes, their family had made women feel they needed to settle in Australia. For most women, settling in Australia was the only and obvious thing to do, and other options were not worthy of a discussion.

Charlotte was the only female interlocutor who had preferred to live in her husband's home country. As described above, Charlotte and Zachary had been living in his country for a while already and had not thought of moving to Australia until Charlotte's mother in Adelaide had become terminally ill. The couple therefore decided to move to Australia together. While both of them saw their future in his home country, they both agreed that for now, they had to move to Australia to take care of Charlotte's mother. The couple was enjoying life in Adelaide as much as they could, but by their description of "we are making it work" it also seemed that their lives could have been better in his home country. Their ultimate plan was to move back to that country, and only visit Australia for extended holidays. This case, as well as that of Daniel, illustrates Nicola Mai & Russel King's (2009) observation that love as a reason to migrate is not limited to romantic love between partners, but that it can also include love for others such as children, friends, or in this instance, a parent.

For other women, the decision to settle in Australia had much to do with having children. Emma, for instance, at first had moved overseas to be with Matthew, all those years ago. The couple had been living quite comfortably in Europe, when she found out she was pregnant. The pregnancy significantly changed her ideas of how to live life. She recounted that back then she felt she needed stability. While they had a great time together in Europe, she felt that it was not a good environment to raise a child. She explained that "It was a very corrupt country and I felt I could not rely on that government for help. It was hard enough for its own citizens, let alone us migrants." In Australia, Emma knew she was able to get welfare benefits and more importantly, she had her family for support. "So, all of a sudden" Emma knew "Australia was the country [where] I wanted to be." While her partner Matthew had been happy in Europe, he had agreed with his wife that they needed to go "home."

For many, children were named as the most important reason for settling in Australia. While both Eileen and Anne had settled in Melbourne with their partners before becoming pregnant, having children now meant that they would not consider relocating from the place they called home. Before they had children, both had thought that living in Australia might be temporary, and that in the future, Africa could be an option. This was also true for Naomi, who met her second Africa-origin partner Otto in an Asian country. She felt that her having a young child from her previous marriage meant that moving to another country was not an option. Naomi said that staying in Australia offered her child so much more in terms of education and safe surroundings, while in Africa there would be too many dangers: children could get sick easily, health care would be below western standards, and the educational system would not be as good as it would be in Australia. Moreover, Naomi felt she had her own and more trusted social network of family and friends to help and support her here in Australia. Naomi's arguments for living in Australia mirror those of other women with children, with whom I spoke.

The feeling of being at home in Australia seemed to be the most shared reason for women to choose either Adelaide or Melbourne as a place of settlement with their new partner. It also seemed to be the most logical. First, women owned or rented houses and, in this way, already had created a home, whereas men often were on the move and had only temporary accommodation. Secondly, because women had lived in the same city for a long period of time, they had their strong networks of family and friends. Men, in contrast, had often lived in multiple places and as such did not have a similar supportive environment. Often, the men would be the ones that took financial care of their families back home in the village by sending money from new locations. As such, in terms of settling down, women had more to offer than their partners, and in a country able to provide a higher standard of living. This was the also case for Jade and her now ex-partner Desmond. After we scrolled through her wedding album together, she elaborated on how they had decided to settle in Adelaide. Jade described how Desmond had been living in a very tiny apartment in Asia, which he shared with two other Africa-origin men. He was only there to study, and after that Desmond did not have any clear future plans. Jade recalled how happy she had been when he expressed his willingness to move to Adelaide. Her children as well as her parents lived near her in Adelaide, and she preferred to keep it that way. She also felt that she would get homesick if she had to leave, as she was very attached to Adelaide. In addition, as she was living in a three-bedroom house by herself, she thought it would be "good for both of us if he moved in with me. Here we could make a home together, and he would not need to worry anymore."

While Jade explained the reasoning behind her partner moving to Australia instead of her relocating to be with him, other women did not seem to have considered this possibility at all. Sarah, for instance, appeared to feel that her partner moving here was the only and obvious way it was done. Possibly because her partner also preferred to move to Australia, she felt that her home could offer them more than any other place in the world. Sarah seemed to be very much aware of the fact that her home situation would be better than his, making such comments as "he can take better care of his family when he is here" or "at least I had a home for us." Possibly, in Sarah's case, the only option *was* for them to settle in Australia.

The above accounts indicate that couples saw the move of the male partners to Australia as upward socioeconomic mobility, which would help the couples' joint happiness projects to prosper. Even though not all partners stated a preference for living in Australia, love was reason enough to pursue the move. Relocating to men's home countries or other third countries was mostly perceived as downwards mobility or at most stagnancy. Most importantly, couples imagined Australia as the location that would generate and accelerate their happiness and lead to the happy endings they desired. According to Ahmed, "happiness is directed towards certain objects, which point toward that which is not yet present. When we follow things, we aim for happiness, as if happiness is what you get if you reach certain points" (2010, 26). For couples, the promise of happiness was easy to pinpoint, the direction was clear, yet the terminus was far from sight. Happiness was something experienced in the initial stages of their relationships and they expected it to be found in their unfolding romantic togetherness in Australia. Right at this stage, though, the continuation of the desired happiness required work and suffering. In the next section,

I elaborate on couples' experience of long-distance relationships, which many had to bridge before being reunited in Australia.

4.3   *Distance Makes the Heart Grow Fonder*

Before being able to pursue the idea of living happily ever after in Australia, 24 interlocutors first had to face the prospect of a long-distance relationship. It was mainly because of visa regulations that couples were forced to live separately for a period of time, while in a few cases this was also necessary due to a need for time to get to know the other person better. This section illustrates how couples experienced and practiced long-distance love. It appears, from my interlocutors' accounts, that distance did make hearts grow fonder. Through their geographical separation, couples perceived that their relationships became even stronger and more likely to deliver the eventual and longed for happiness. The distance as well as the different time zones made it hard for couples to stay in contact, in part because it was expensive to keep connected. It then also appeared that one way to bridge the long-distance was through the "commodification of intimacy" (Constable 2009). While at first such commodification can be seen as contradictory to romantic love, this section illustrates how relationships became deeper and couples more connected through gift giving and communication through the use of (mobile) phones and social media.

The accounts above indicate the importance of the narrative of romantic love and love at first sight for both sponsoring women and migrant men. Yet for most couples, love could only be experienced temporarily, as return flight tickets were already booked, work commitments had been made and visas would run out. It seems that the volatility of the romantic experiences in fact increased the impact and the grandness of the romantic experience; there was only a short period of time in which couples could be together, could feel this romantic love; a clear end date was always in sight. The limited time available in a particular place seemed to have a significant impact on the directions relationships took, as well as the intensity of love experienced.

For the couples, the following time of separation was experienced in various ways, but all described the time apart as one of suffering and longing. Interlocutors would "count the days" until they would see their loved ones again. Couples and partners who were in the midst of the visa application process, especially, shared their longing with others by posting on social media. Both women and men would express how they were missing their significant other, and how it was "unfair" that they had to be separated for such long periods of time. While some interlocutors explained that the time apart also made them doubt their decision: "What am I thinking, what kind of relationship is this anyway?" and "How can I trust that the other person is as committed as I am?," they also felt that the distance made the relationship more dramatic, more passionate. As Sophie expressed, when I visited her for a morning coffee after her partner Lucas had returned home due to visa conditions, "Now that Lucas is so far away, I realize we really belong together. I miss him so much it hurts."

It thus seemed that even though the distance was a hurdle for couples, it also increased their feelings of being "meant to be," their confidence in the strength of the relationship, and their chance of a promising future together. This corresponds with scholarship demonstrating that partners in long-distance romantic relationships paradoxically show more stability in their relationships than do people who live close to their romantic partners (Stafford & Merolla 2007; Borelli et al. 2014). According to Laura Stafford and Andy Merolla (2007, 37), the idealization of one's partner—which includes the four aspects of "idealistic distortion, romantic love, relational reminiscence [and] perceived agreement"—as well as a greater level of satisfaction partners have with communication, seems to initially indicate that long-distance relationships are more stable than geographically close relationships.

Couples stayed in touch through letters, email, phone and video calls, social media, and messaging. Often, women would make sure to visit their partners in their home country, and some men managed to visit women in Australia. While Naomi was waiting for her partner to join her in Adelaide, they had contact multiple times a day. With their smartphones, they sent each other messages when waking up, wishing each other good night, sending photos or videos of daily activities, and sometimes they had video chats. In this way, Naomi felt they were not that apart, after all. Yet, whenever her partner would not reply or pick up, or was not fast enough to respond, she became worried that he was doing other things, or would not be as committed as she herself was and that he said he was. It seemed that the effort to stay in touch made her sometimes more stressed than happy.

Dylan and Eileen did not have access to modern technology when he was still living back home. Eileen lived in Melbourne where she worked at a university. She had been studying at the same university 18 years ago when she went on a study trip to Africa. It was during this time that she had met Dylan who is now her husband. When they were in a long-distance relationship, the couple had agreed that they would call once a week. This had been a bit difficult because Dylan did not have a phone. Eileen recalled that she would call the post office in his village, and ask for "Auntie Letitia," who would then make sure to get Dylan on the line. Often, Dylan was indeed there, patiently waiting to receive the call. "But sometimes he was not there" Eileen remembered,

"Because something had come in between" Sometimes something—either work or family matters for instance—caused him to not be able to reach the post office in time. Those instances had not worried Eileen at all, because she "understood that he could not be there each and every time."

My data indicates that no matter how recent or how long ago long-distance relationships occurred, migrant men had less means to actively stay in touch than sponsoring women.[8] Eileen's partner Dylan could not make the phone call himself as it was too expensive, and Naomi had given her partner the smartphone to keep in touch. One of the exceptions was Paul, as he was the one sending monthly remittances to his partner when she was pregnant with their child in Australia. For women, although it had often not been easy to come up with the financial means, they eventually were able to initiate contact, as well as (re-)visit their partners in their country. In contrast, most migrant men were financially in no position to purchase a flight ticket; and even if they could, a tourist visa was difficult to obtain. Thus, women often instigated contact, by going to visit, making phone calls and providing men with mobile phones. Another way to show love to their partner was through sending gifts to him and his extended family, as well as supporting him financially when necessary.

Such examples illustrate how money and other material exchanges are an inherent part of intimate relationships. Numerous studies examine the cultural constructions of love and romance in different localities and consider how they are commodified in terms of gift exchanges, mass-mediated modern romance, and marital expectations (Constable 2009, 55; see also Hirsch 2003; Padilla et al. 2007). The "commodification of intimacy" (Constable 2009) has become an important focus within the field of intimate migrations. According to Nicole Constable:

> Recent studies of cross-border marriages, courtships, dating, and sexual partnerships of various sorts have pointed to new patterns of commodification and to rapid growth of profit-oriented and electronically mediated forms of matchmaking or marital introduction that facilitate wider global patterns of cross-border relationships.
>
> CONSTABLE 2009, 53

---

8 As initially my aim was to gain trust among interlocutors, I intentionally did not ask about financial arrangements in the early days of couples' relationships. While it could be assumed that women financed dates and outings when visiting their partners in Africa or Asia, none of my interlocutors mentioned this. Money therefore did not seem to be a source of potential tension or conflict, at this stage in their relationship. Perhaps, interlocutors were reluctant to talk about money. But even after couples separated, none of my interlocutors mentioned an initial financial disproportion to be an issue.

For instance, Constable (2003) and Caren Freeman (2005) describe how international marriage partners are promoted online as if they were commodities. But as Constable (2009, 54) notes, commodification is rarely unambiguous, or complete, and one can ask how far love and intimate relationships are completely separated from monetary value. Thus, instead of considering practices of commodification and, romance and intimacy, as dichotomies, there is a fluidity and interconnectedness between the two (see for instance Faier 2007; Spanger 2013). Constable goes on to argue that:

> Commodification of intimacy is not an analytical end in itself, but instead offers a valuable starting point for analyses of gendered social relations, cultural meanings, social inequalities, and capitalist transformations.
>
> CONSTABLE 2009, 54–55

Transnational intimacy does not necessarily only increase the commodification of intimacy and intimate relations. Rather, new relationships may be defined, and give way to "redefining spaces, meanings and expressions of intimacy that can transform and transgress conventional gendered spaces and norms" (Constable 2009, 58). Dinah Hannaford, for instance, describes remittances as acts of care among Senegalese transnational families. The sending of remittances by husbands, who are working abroad, to their wives become "gestures of care" as the geographical distance implies the absence of other opportunities to show affection (2016, 93).

For my interlocutors, women's gift-giving, the sending of remittances and the purchasing of flight tickets to visit men were means to express love and care that were essential to maintain intimate contact in long-distance relationships. Expenses were thus a direct demonstration of love, and such acts were only performed because of the romantic connection among partners. But while men as such seemed to become the receivers of love and attention, their much smaller gestures often counted as the same or even more. For instance, while Eileen estimated she spent hundreds of dollars on phone calls to Dylan, that he made the effort to be there at the post office waiting for her to call was understood as an exceptionally romantic move. Furthermore, a man sharing an expression of love for his Australian partner on his Facebook page was often considered as more special than her sending a sum of money for a cousin's school fees. This may be due to the popular idea that romantic love should be separated from any economic transactions (Illouz 1997), as well as the gendered idea among interlocutors that men generally are not as good in "doing romance" as women (see, for instance, Thompson & O'Sullivan 2012). Simultaneously, it seemed that there was a general understanding that because men were from African countries, they were assumed to have less means to stay in touch. Anything they did, then, to increase the closeness between the partners, would count as an important gesture.

It became evident through the commodification of intimacy, that gendered, class-based and geo-political power relationships had become discernible for the first time. Women aimed to stay in touch whereas men took on a more passive position, as they generally depended on women to initiate and define the contact. As I indicated in the previous section, Africanist research indicates that intimacy and transactional love are influenced by the continent's economic hardship, socioeconomic changes, globalization and migration. Lynn Thomas and Jennifer Cole argue that in recent years, the monetization of intimacy has become increasingly visible, and that "material exchanges not just ... reflect but ... produce emotionally charged relationships" (2009, 21; see also Cornwall 2002; Helle-Valle 2004). In today's disparate world, love, sex, intimacy, money, gender, and power are inextricably entwined (Groes & Fernandez 2018). For my interlocutors, such newly introduced gendered relationship dynamics were related to socioeconomic positioning on both national and global scales. As will be illustrated in more detail in the chapters to come, with some exceptions, men came from lower socioeconomic strata from their home countries and these countries in turn are not as prosperous as Australia. With a few exceptions, women also mostly came from lower socioeconomic and middle-class backgrounds in Australia. But in a globalized world in general, and in the context of cross-border love, and marriage migration to Australia in particular, women's nationality generated an advantaged position. While such differences between partners had been present from their first encounter, they now became more visible.

As Susan Frohlick (2013), in her study on relationships between Black Costa Rican men and Euro-American women in Costa Rican holiday destinations, describes how for these women, an uncomfortable juxtaposition between "respectability" and financial exchange within intimate relationships became discernible. She explains that for women, western discourses about respectability encourage white women to have intimate relationships with men from similar ethnic and class backgrounds. Such discourses emphasize that either men are supposed to pay for dates, or for both partners to contribute equally for dates and outings. For white women in Costa Rica, the reversal of such ideologies caused some uncomfortable moments (Frohlick 2013, 136). While women in this study never mentioned such discomfort with being the main providers of transactional intimacy, it is worth noticing that such non-normative practices either consciously or subconsciously may have been uncomfortable for women. It could also be possible that the receiving of gifts and remittances did make some men feel uncomfortable, as they did not have the means to reciprocate at a similar level. However, none of the men I asked about this expressed such discomforts but instead underscored their contributions to the relationship. At this stage, interlocutors dismissed or did not seem to recognize the major impact and consequences of socioeconomic inequalities between partners on their happiness projects. Instead, they emphasized the romantic nature of the various acts of gift giving and imagined their happy future together, full of anticipation.

5   Conclusion

This chapter narrated the romantic beginnings of relationships that would eventually lead to marriage migration. It illustrated couples' and partners' experiences, practices and descriptions of romantic love that served as the start of their path to future happiness. Interlocutors described their first encounters as magical and serendipitous, and the initial stages of their relationships as exceptionally romantic.

Simultaneously, couples' decisions to pursue happiness in Australia illustrated how love in fact is not separate from social, economic or political spheres of life. Instead, love, it appears, is embedded in larger social worlds (Fernandez 2013), and various external factors influenced couples' choice for residency in Australia. While it is often assumed that intercultural cross-border marriages are generally engineered for financial gain for the non-Anglo-European spouse (Neveu Kringelbach 2013), the accounts above indicated otherwise. Most migrant men in this study, *as well as* the sponsoring women, preferred to settle in Australia together due to the socioeconomic circumstances that they deemed to be better in Australia. This decision to settle in Australia illustrated that the couples' love was characterized by romance, but was not entirely separated from practical matters.

How intimacy becomes commodified (Constable 2009) was illustrated by the focus on couples' long-distance relationships after their first encounters, but prior to settling in Australia. Long distance changed the course of relationships. Although it was experienced as a period of suffering and longing, it also helped couples to think about the importance and great promise of their happiness projects. It created a longing and even stronger desire to be together. Simultaneously, it became apparent that money and material exchanges mirrored, but also changed intimate relationships (Groes-Green 2014). Love now was expressed through phone calls as well as through gift giving and expensive visits. Almost always, women were financially in a better position to enable such contact and practices of commodification offered the first glimpses of gendered and geo-political dynamics between partners (see Groes & Fernandez 2018). Such inequalities, which would become increasingly more visible as marriage migration journeys evolved, will be discussed more, and in-depth, in the chapters to come.

But while romantic love may be intertwined with the "practical everyday" (Eggebø 2013), for interlocutors, their main focus was on pure romantic love as the foundation on which their happiness projects were built. As described in the introduction to this study, happiness can be both a long-term project, and a specific moment in time (Robbins 2015; see also for instance Lambek 2016). Walter and Kavedžija explain that happiness can be seen as a process, and is future-oriented, when they argue that

> While it can be useful and important to consider what happiness "is," including how it is imagined or (in some cases, perhaps) achieved, we are equally concerned ... with how happiness "works," or what it "does": how it enters into peoples' lives, leading them to choose one path over another—and what it reveals about those people in the process.
>
> WALKER & KAVEDŽIJA 2016, 7

Furthermore:

> Happiness is often aspired to, as it 'provides a sense of orientation; like a horizon it delimits a space of action and understanding, even as it recedes from view. Situational and contingent, it brings some things into focus while occluding others, and adds a sense of depth to the mundane and everyday.
>
> WALKER & KAVEDŽIJA 2016, 16

For the cross-border couples, without romantic love there would be no happiness to pursue. (Heterosexual) romantic love therefore becomes the object that points toward happiness, and to follow its "point would be to find happiness" (Ahmed 2010, 26).

For couples and partners, romantic love legitimized the upheaval that would soon be caused by marriage migration projects. Such obstructions are illustrated in the chapters to come. In the next chapter, I will continue to narrate my interlocutors' journeys of marriage migration towards a happy life in Australia by focusing on the next step: the visa application process. I will illustrate how this process, with its focus on 'genuineness', was understood by interlocutors as both a process causing stress and suffering, and simultaneously as a struggle in which the mutual love between partners gave them the motivation to fight for a shared future.

Couples' Experiences with Visa Procedures

1 Introduction

The Department of Immigration and Border Protection (DIBP) booklet *Partner Migration* states that, "when you apply for a Partner visa, you must provide evidence that supports your claims of a genuine and ongoing relationship with your partner" (2017, 41).[1] Genuineness, which becomes evident through intimacy, companionship and equality, has become the only legitimate means through which partners can live together in Australia. This chapter elaborates on the ways in which the Australian visa application procedure influences the journey of love migration among cross-border couples through an administrative focus on genuine relationships. I demonstrate that, although the visa application is a step towards the couples' imagined happy and romantic futures, it simultaneously is experienced as an obstruction to happiness. The application process uses and impacts on the notion of the genuineness of relationships in various ways. By doing so, it negatively affects couples' everyday lives and the lived experiences of their relationships. Below, I focus on the practicalities of the visa application procedure to explain how meanings and practices of genuine and romantic love change. I clarify how the visa procedure's focus on genuineness and romantic love may actually shift the meaning and feeling of romantic love among couples.

Although anthropological accounts of love migration to Australia are scarce, the data presented below reveals similarities with European countries that apply increasingly strict policies towards marriage migration. The result of this protecting of borders increases the emphasis on romantic love as the only morally correct motivation for marriage migration (Andrikopoulos 2019;

---

1 On 20 December 2017, the DIBP merged with other Departments under the new name Department of Home Affairs. Other federal responsibilities coming under the Home Affairs portfolio are Australia's law enforcement, national and transport security, criminal intelligence, emergency management and multicultural affairs. Throughout this monograph, however, I will keep referring to the DIBP, as the research was conducted just prior to this name change. The DIBP, prior to the organizational and name change, created the booklet *Partner Migration* to help applicants understand the visa procedures. Since the DIBP was integrated into Home Affairs, the booklet is no longer available on the Home Affairs website, but similar information can be accessed.

Pellander 2019; Eggebø 2013; Lavanchy 2014; Fernandez 2013; Cole 2014). In Australia, the visa application procedure is framed within a discourse of romantic love, and couples are required to prove their genuine care and love for each other. This chapter demonstrates that the desire of the Australian Government to control and decide which relationships are genuine, and thus who belongs in Australia, generates different reactions from couples. Through myriad bureaucratic process, the highly romantic period is replaced by a period of strategic filling-in of the application along with experiences of separation, uncertainty, and anxiety. Simultaneously, a tendency becomes noticeable wherein couples start to overemphasize romantic love because they assume that it is the only way for the couple to show the genuineness of their relationship and thus for the foreign spouse to obtain a visa for Australia. Through this process, the notion of romantic love loses some of its meaning as it is made a tool for use in the visa application. This, in turn, may be detrimental for their romantic experience and forms a serious obstacle for their imagined futures together. In sum, this chapter illustrates how genuineness becomes vitally important in the processes through which cross-border couples apply for Partner visas. It will show how the visa application procedure's cultural insensitivity, and its sometimes racist and sexist tone, influence the shape of relationships, and couples' experiences of their romantic togetherness.

To advance these arguments, I begin with excerpts from an informal conversation I had with an employee of the DIBP. This exchange illustrates how couples' encounters with the state are, as Maite Maskens puts it, "saturated with assumptions about intimacy" (2015, 46). As was also the case for this DIBP employee, who had told me about trusting his "gut feeling." Maskens (2015) emphasizes how state agents use their intuition and feelings to establish whether or not a relationship is genuine and by doing so, if couples are eligible for residency. Scheel and Gutekunst (2019) call this the "implementation bias." I continue the chapter by conceptualizing the genuineness of relationships in the context of marriage migration. The next section outlines the Australian application process in more detail. Finally, I turn to the ways in which visa procedures influenced the lived experiences of cross-border couples. These last sections cover how couples dealt with practical visa issues including waiting periods, geographical distance and high visa costs; how couples experienced demonstrating their mutual love and genuine relationship; and lastly, the character of interviews with immigration officers and the influence these had on couples.

2   That Gut Feeling

One Saturday morning, at the very end of my fieldwork, I awoke excited about a final interview. That day, I was finally going to meet an employee of the DIBP. Serendipitously, the meeting came about at the suggestion of a colleague, who knew the DIBP officer as a neighbor and friend and helped to arrange the meeting. This opportunity felt particularly fortuitous for me as I had experienced numerous failed attempts to interview government officers. I had called the DIBP various times, but each time their answer had been that my requests concerned personal information about Australian citizens and residents and that therefore they were unable to be forthcoming. As a result, I had lost all hope of getting any information from the perspective of the Australian Government about how they make decisions about the authenticity of intimate relationships. Despite my excitement, I was also nervous because after speaking to many couples and ex-partners about their experience with their visa applications, I had come to understand the DIBP as something of a source of negativity; after all, this was an institution, which many of my interlocutors said had been obstructive to their happy relationships.

To provide evidence of a genuine relationship was described as a long and elaborate process by cross-border couples I interviewed for this study. To obtain a Partner visa, couples are for instance required to have known each other for an extensive period of time and must know specific details about one another. Couples should also have joint financial responsibilities, pointing to the notion of equality between partners. While all couples had to elaborate on such matters in written form, some couples were also invited for an interview with a migration officer. The two-year period couples needed to stay together before the foreign spouse obtained permanent residency was experienced as a testing period. After having spent many weeks with individuals who were clearly not happy nor in agreement with such policies, I was both curious and a bit skeptical about how my DIBP interviewee—who I will call Steven—would explain the Department's stance on such matters.

Meeting a government official was new to me. I also did not know the extent to which I could interview Steven because, up until that point, my interactions with the DIBP had been short and uninviting. Luckily for me, Steven turned out to be a friendly and interesting man. He had just come from a yoga session opposite the café where we met for a coffee, and he talked about how this newly taken up hobby uplifted his spirit immensely. Our shared passion for yoga and a healthy work/life balance, as well as Steven's interest in my cultural background and studies made me feel comfortable, and I looked forward to spending the coming hour listening to his experiences.

Prior to his current role, Steven had been responsible for assessing visa applications and conducting interviews with marriage migrants and their sponsors to establish the genuineness of their relationships. Steven explained that he had enjoyed his time assessing Partner visa applications greatly. In fact, he stated that this past role might have been the highlight of his career because he liked knowing that he helped truly in-love couples be together. He particularly had enjoyed hearing the love stories that his interviewees, the visa applicants, shared with him. Steven even claimed that, after a while in this role, it was often within an instant, right when the couples walked through the door, that he could see whether or not couples were genuine about their relationship. He would pay attention to the way couples interacted with each other prior to the interview, and during the interview, as well as how the partners would talk about each other. While couples sometimes would prepare for the interview, Steven thought that this should not be necessary for genuine couples. He explained that with genuine relationships, "Couples know about their everyday lives, what worries the other person, what makes them insecure." Knowing such daily intimate details about the other, Steven felt, was evidence that couples had invested in each other and were genuine. "If people do not know such things about each other, you can see they do not care about each other. If couples do not share their daily lives together, I can say it is not a genuine relationship."[2]

Another focus point to find out about the genuineness of couples for Steven was to pay attention to nervous behavior. If couples acted nervously, that would be a good sign: "Couples that are sincere are often very worried, because they realize their whole lives are at stake." He thought that not being nervous would mean that the interview was too rehearsed. Other things that Steven paid attention to were age difference, and how long couples knew one another. It would be a concern if people met during a two-week holiday and a bit later applied for a visa, he thought. Steven explained that it would be easy for couples to fill in the form, to attach some pictures from a holiday and "tick all the boxes." He said that during an interview it would become apparent how connected the couple really was. Steven reiterated that it was a gut feeling of his that would tell if couples were genuinely wanting to spend their lives together. According to him, officers should really be aware of that gut feeling and if they sense that a couple is insincere, they should investigate how they could prove that.

---

2   The quotes are recorded from notes and is a close paraphrasing of the original statements.

On almost all characteristics of what a genuine relationship is constituted, I agreed with Steven. As an ethnic Dutch, middle-class young woman, I expected or at least hoped for my own relationship to be based on good communication and deep knowledge about the other person. And during my fieldwork period, I too had subconsciously used my gut feeling, as well as my own ideas about what constitutes a good relationship, to assess couples' motives for being in an intimate relationship. It was not that I needed or wanted to do that, I just automatically did it. Therefore, everything that Steven said made sense to me. I also understood that if an employee at the DIBP is asked to assess couples' genuine intentions, this becomes a subjective matter. But as friendly and empathetic as Steven appeared to be, I could not help but think about the stories my interlocutors had told me about their often hostile and distrusting encounters with DIBP employees. Whereas for Steven assessing couples' genuineness may have left him with fond memories, for my interlocutors the visa application process had left them with feelings of discomfort and emotional upset.

3   Genuine Relationships and the (Australian) Border

3.1   *Defining Genuineness*

Despite stricter border control, or perhaps because of it, marriage migration to Anglo-European countries is on the rise as a way to gain citizenship (Neveu Kringelbach 2013, 4). As family reunification remains one of the few ways for entry (Kofman 2004; Schmidt 2011; Pellander 2019), strict policies have been instituted regarding this type of migration. As Mikkel Rytter (2012) argues, laws have turned the geographical borders into moral ones, by deciding and guiding how marriages should be contracted and families organized. While these policies are mainly aimed at family reunification of non-autochthone citizens, intercultural couples are also required to show the genuine character of their relationship and their romantic attachment to each other, in order to avoid sham marriages (for example, see Neveu Kringelbach 2013).

Elizabeth Povinelli (2002, 2006) describes the connections between modernity, emotional intimacy, marriage, and the western nation state. She asserts that rather than kinship or rank, it is membership or citizenship that makes one belong, and worthy and qualified people base family formations on intimate romantic love. She links such connections to the Enlightenment project's liberal humanist claims of democracy, capitalism, and individualism. Likewise, Cole (2009) connects the ideas of romantic love, Christian ideals of love and the Christian concept of the autonomous subject. According to the author, "The subject who can generalize his or her attachments and use them for the common good adds, as is presupposed, to the political contract in lib-eral states" (cited by Fernandez 2013, 273). In this way, intimate love becomes "the foundation not merely of true families, but also of true nations; therefore, denying the foundational role of human love in family formation is seen as a threat to the nation" (ibid.).

The romantic, companionate, and love-based marriage has become a sym-bol of Anglo-European countries (Padilla et al. 2007). Love, intimacy, and mar-riage are ways to express oneself as an autonomous person, rather than having relationships related to tradition, reproduction, or kinship (Padilla et al. 2007). Mai and King argue along similar lines as they state that "the currently hege-monic notions of romantic love among 'equal' individuals are consistent with a highly individualized and neoliberal model of society, celebrating the expres-sion of individual autonomy, gender equality and emotional fulfillment as key and fixed criteria of Northcentric 'civility' " (2009, 300). As a result, marriages that are not based on romantic ideals and pure love do not match with the Anglo-European ideal; they are thus seen as immoral, and undermining and threatening to the principles of the nation (Rytter 2012; Block 2019).

Anglo-European countries use the notion of romantic love to further already restrictive migration policies in order to identify those who belong, and those who do not. As Nadine Fernandez (2013; 2018; 2019) mentions in her research on Danes marrying Cubans, it seems that the government finds that "real" Danes can marry for love, but that immigrant-Dane marriage prac-tices are called into question regarding their purity. Such marriages would possibly be forced or arranged, and do not align with modern individual self-determination. Moreover, in several European countries marriages of conve-nience are prohibited, and marriages for personal interest, such as to obtain money or a visa, are seen as inhumane and wrong. The fear of sham marriages, as described by Cole (2014), Neveu Kringelbach (2013), and Lavanchy (2014) makes governments especially wary when a native citizen marries a non-Anglo-European person from a poor non-Anglo-European country. In order "to protect" their (often female) citizens from sham marriages, governments ask the couples for proof of their commitment to each other. As a result, spouse migration turns into a lengthy bureaucratic struggle through which binational couples have to prove the genuineness of their relationship. Requests for fam-ily reunification can be denied by immigration services if it is suspected that a marriage is not contracted for love, but for a visa (Fernandez 2013; Neveu Kringelbach 2013; Maskens 2015; Bonjour & de Hart 2013).

To sum up, genuineness can be defined by describing what relationships should entail. Genuine relationships are based on pure love, romantic ide-als, morality, intimacy, care among equal partners (in terms of gender and sexuality), companionship, and commonalities (such as age and ethnicity, but also shared interests) among partners. Partners enter genuine relationships as free individuals and with self-determination. The opposite of such genuine relationships are unions that are not freely chosen such as marriages of convenience, forced marriages, or marriages for visas or money. Such sham relationships are immoral, impure, and can sometimes be seen as 'traditional' and based on 'collectivist' principles. Marriages that are for reasons other than genuine love can be characterized by structural inequalities among partners, such as religious, ethnic, age and class differences (Neveu Kringelbach 2013; Fernandez 2013; Moret et al. 2019; Maskens 2015; Lavanchy 2014; Bonjour & de Hart 2013; Eggebø 2013).

However, as Andrikopoulos (2019) argues, the 'sham'/'genuine' dichotomy as applied by governments is misleading. The author argues that as love and interest are intertwined, attempting to separate the two is deceiving. As both Eggebø (2013) and Fernandez (2013) point out, it is difficult to operationalize love. The concept of love has numerous meanings. As the previous chapter also demonstrated, the division between money and love, seen as intrinsic to romantic love and the companionate marriage, is questionable, if not unrealistic. As Fernandez (2013, 282) argues, "love is embedded in a broader political economic context and does not exist above the material world" (see also Wardlow & Hirsch 2006; Padilla et al. 2007). Structural factors in a disparate world influence and blur the assessment of the veracity of love (Groes & Fernandez 2018). Thus, categories of 'sham' and 'genuine' relationships may not be particularly helpful in assessing relationships. In the remainder of the chapter, I illustrate how for interlocutors of this study, the visa application process, and its focus on genuineness transformed love from being predominantly romantic to something enmeshed with, and in, structures and procedures.

3.2   *Applying for a Partner Visa in Australia*

Acquiring a Partner visa is not easy. It is a timely and costly affair and the numerous visa categories and requirements can be confusing. When outside Australia, couples can apply for a temporary visa for the foreign spouse that is called "Subclass 300—Prospective Marriage." With this visa foreign spouses can travel to Australia and marry their Australian partner. This visa is valid for nine months and so marriages should be contracted within this timeframe. Then, couples can apply for a temporary visa for the foreign spouse, called the "Subclass 820—Partner" which grants temporary residence to the foreign spouse. If the couple is still together after two years from the application, the foreign partner can obtain a visa called "Subclass 801—Partner" granting permanent residency. Alternatively, couples can apply for a provisional visa that is called "Subclass 309—Partner." Couples are eligible for this visa when legally married prior to migration, when they intend to legally marry in the near future, or, when in a de facto relationship for at least twelve months. Subsequently, two years after applying for this temporary visa, couples can apply for visa "Subclass 100—Partner" which grants permanent residency. From within Australia, foreign spouses can apply for visa 820 when legally married to an Australian partner or Australian permanent resident, or when in a de facto relationship for at least 12 subsequent months, and after two years apply for visa 801. This two-stage process was introduced in 1996 to prevent foreign spouses from marrying an Australian resident purely for visa purposes (Khoo 2001, 112).

There are many eligibility requirements when applying for a visa, although these may vary depending on the particular visa (Subclasses 300, 309 and 820).[3] A sponsor must: be an Australian citizen, Australian resident, or an eligible New Zealand citizen; be aged 18 years or over; be in a relationship with the partner; and have no other partner. Limitations on sponsorship include having previously sponsored a partner or been sponsored as a partner.[4] Sponsors are required to undergo a police check, and when a relationship breaks down, must immediately notify the DIBP and withdraw from sponsorship. The migrant partner must also undergo a police check, and furthermore meet health requirements to be eligible to obtain a Partner visa. A medical examination, chest x-ray, and sometimes specialist and laboratory tests are required.

Partners must provide evidence that their relationship is genuine. Statutory declarations must be written by both partners, as well as by Australian citizens or permanent residents over 18 years-of-age who know the couple. Such declarations should support the existence of the couple's relationship. Partners must also provide individual statements regarding: the history of their relationship, including how, when and where they first met; how the relationship developed; when they decided to marry or commence a de facto relationship;

---

3   This latter part of the section is based on information found in the DIBP booklet *Partner Migration* (2017).

4   Since 1996, a limit has been placed on the number of spouses one can sponsor, following an increase in problems related to "serial sponsorship" (see for instance Iredale 1994). The *Partner Migration* booklet explains that sponsorship is not possible if one has sponsored another spouse within the last five years; been a foreign spouse him/herself in the last five years; or if one has previously sponsored two or more foreign spouses. Compelling circumstances such as the following may allow for waiver provision: the death of a previous spouse; the relationship and/or children to be neglected by the previous spouse; a long-term relationship with the current spouse; and children with the current spouse.

their domestic arrangements; any periods of separation, plus the reasons and length of separation; and future plans.

Furthermore, "Evidence of the relationship" must be provided by both partners. As all relationships are different, the DIBP booklet *Partner Migration* states, it is better to be comprehensive and to provide as much evidence as possible to support the case. Four categories should be elaborated upon. First, financial aspects must be covered. This provides evidence that the couple shares financial responsibilities and commitments, such as evidence of joint ownership of real estate or other major assets (vehicles and appliances), joint liabilities (loans and insurance), and shared household bills, or shared bank accounts. Second, the couple is asked to provide evidence of shared responsibilities within the household. This includes living arrangements, a statement outlining the basis on which responsibility for the housework is distributed, details of joint utilities accounts (gas, water, and electricity), or correspondence addressed to both partners at the same address.

Third, the social aspect of the relationship is considered. This includes evidence of the couple being generally accepted socially through such things as joint invitations to events, going out together, having mutual friends and acquaintances, and evidence of the relationship that the couple has provided to government bodies, commercial/public institutions or authorities. Finally, evidence confirming a mutual commitment between the partners is requested. This could include such things as knowledge of each other's personal circumstances such as background and family situation, evident intentions that the relationship will be long-term (for example through relevant correspondence), and itemized phone accounts to show that contact was maintained during any period of separation. Couples may be asked to attend interviews with migration officers regarding their relationship's character, if more information is required. Such interviews are conducted over the phone or in person.

In 2016, at the time of fieldwork, the application prices varied per visa category, starting from 6,865 AUD, and increasing when additional applicants, such as children, are included in the application.[5] Prices have been steadily going up over the years, with the steepest rise a 50 per cent increase announced in December 2014. The average processing times have also increased, with only estimated processing times for visas given. In 2020, a Partner visa costs 7,715 AUD, with 75 per cent of the applications processed in 21 months, and 90 per cent processed in 28 months. The DIBP differentiates between "low risk" and

---

5   By the end of 2016, the additional applicant charge for persons aged 18 years or more was 3,535 AUD and for an additional applicant under 18 years the cost was 1,720 AUD.

"high risk" passports. All African passport holders fall under the high risk category, making the visa processing times longer. At the time of research, for most of the interlocutors, processing times were estimated by the DIBP to be between eight and 12 months.

4   Couples' Experiences with the Visa Application Process

4.1   *Dealing with Regulations, Time and Money*

Application experiences varied as couples applied both from within Australia as well as offshore. Some couples and partners had applied years—sometimes decades—ago, while other couples and partners applied within the last two years or were still in the process of applying. It became clear that the longer ago the application had been made, the less complex it was to apply for a visa. This corresponds with a global trend towards stricter border control and stricter marriage migration policies, as described by Maskens (2018), Neveu Kringelbach (2013), and Martin Jørgensen (2012) amongst others.[6] As explained earlier, two groups are especially distrusted: those entering arranged marriages and couples that are being considered as too different from each other (specifically in terms of background and age) (Maskens 2018; Neveu Kringelbach 2013).

Some of my interlocutors, who had experienced the visa application process many years back, agreed that it was not that strict then; they also mentioned that immigration officers had hardly ever asked difficult questions. I was often told that if one obtained a student visa, it was easy to "just marry an Australian to gain residency." Lucia, as I illustrated in the previous chapter, explained how about thirty years ago, she married a friend of hers who wanted to stay in Australia. When I asked her why she had agreed to marry her friend, she explained that since they got along well, she figured she might as well marry him. In retrospect she explained that it was "a visa thing" and she was "just helping him out" as they separated soon after he gained residency.

Many foreign students who came on scholarships provided by the Australian Government were required to go back home after graduation, with a minimum period of two years before they could re-enter Australia. This policy, my older

---

6   Yet, Charsley (2012) and Wray (2012) remind us that there always have been groups of marriage migrants who had difficulties crossing the borders of Anglo-European countries (for instance Japanese wives married to American men during and after World War II). Any such restrictions are based in part on processes influenced by gender, race, class, and sexuality (Eggebø 2013: 774).

participants told me, broke up many African-Australian relationships. Among the exceptions were Robert and Jo who have been married for over thirty years. As described in the previous chapter, Jo and Robert met in a café where Jo worked and instantly fell in love. I met Jo at an event for migrant women's empowerment where she was a guest of honor. I soon learned that she was the wife of Robert, who was a retired university lecturer and a prominent member of a large and influential African community organization in Adelaide. She agreed to an interview and invited me over for lunch the following week. On the agreed day, I was about to catch the bus up to their home on another side of Adelaide from where I lived, when I got a phone call from Robert. He asked me if I would be able to find their place. When I got out of the bus, he was there to pick me up and walk me to their home. Once inside, I found Jo sitting at the table, in a large kitchen full of ornaments and family photos hanging on the walls. While Robert was making us tea, she got up and introduced me to all the relatives in the photos. Over lunch, Robert and Jo told me that Robert was an international student when he met Jo. They had met in a shop where she was working and they started dating. Eventually, they became pregnant and got married. Yet, even though Jo was expecting their baby, Robert had to return home for two years after his studies before he was reunited with his family in Australia. The couple stayed in touch through letters, and a one-time visit from Jo and their child to her husband's home country. As soon as possible, Robert moved back to Australia. Back then, after those two years, it was just a matter of applying and one would get the visa, according to both Robert and Jo.

Nowadays, couples spend thousands of dollars on the visa application and in the case of offshore applications, thousands more on maintaining intimate contact through visits, phone calls and gifts. One couple that had recently received the good news that their visa application was approved were Naomi, a care worker in her mid-thirties, and her husband Otto. I met Naomi for the first time at her sister Sarah's home, which she rented in a suburb about an hour away from Adelaide's city center. Naomi and her daughter had come to meet me for afternoon tea. Naomi directed her daughter to go and play by herself, so she could talk to me about her experiences with her visa application. As she was rounding up a text conversation on her smartphone with her husband who was still in his West African home country and had just woken up, Naomi explained that they had applied for the visa right before the fees had been increased. For them, in 2014, the fee had been 3,000 AUD. Naomi continued by naming all the costs of her relationship. Since the visa application, she had visited him twice in his home country, which she estimated cost her over 6,000 AUD in total. And there, even though she considered it a "cheap country" they still spent money on travelling around and staying in hotels. And, she added, the first time she was there the couple married, which also cost her "lots of money." Then, she continued, "My husband had to go to Pretoria [South Africa] for the interview with a migration officer, and for his health checks and all." To help stay in intimate contact, the couple called and texted each other as often as possible, generally a couple of times per day "just to wish each other a good night, or a good morning, you know."

Naomi sighed and shook her head, when thinking about how much money the relationship had cost her. "To be honest, I have no clue how much I spent on our relationship like this, and to be honest, I do not know if I want to know." Naomi estimated that the total sum she spent was over 15,000 AUD. But she then added that she had not included the bill she would get from her lawyer who guided her through the visa application process. Like Naomi, all couples and ex-partners felt the application fee was absurdly expensive, and none of them really understood why it had to be that expensive, as the service deteriorated, and the waiting time lengthened as the fees increased. Interlocutors argued that the government charged these fees, "just because they can" and "to avoid fake marriages" and because "couples wanting to be together will pay anyway."

Another issue for couples was that the time taken by the DIBP could not be accurately predicted. While the DIBP indicated that the average waiting period for an offshore application is approximately 12 months, it sometimes takes much longer. For instance, one couple had to wait for 28 months to obtain their Partner visa. In this case, the Australian spouse had sponsored a foreign husband from the same country in the past, which may have resulted in increased scrutiny from the DIBP. Another couple, however, only had to wait 12 months for their visa to arrive, even though both had been married previously (but to partners from their own cultural background). Lucas and Sophie, who had just had their visa approved after the fieldwork period was completed, had only waited 10 months to get their visa approved, even though Sophie had sponsored a husband previously, which could possibly have been a red flag for the DIBP.

Men and women reacted differently to such long waiting times. Women would openly complain about visa costs and processing times, and almost all women admitted that they called the department time and again to ask about the status of their application. But while women were frustrated with the waiting periods, men, except for one, made comments such as "one needs to be patient" and "it will come." It became clear that the men, as newcomers to Australia, did not feel they had a right to complain about Australian procedures. The first time I met Paul, he provided me with a summarized overview of his marriage migration journey, now five years ago. While sitting on a sunny terrace of a trendy Adelaide bar for an afternoon drink, Paul explained his feelings about the application process in a matter-of-fact way. He stated that indeed it had been expensive, and it also took a long time to get the visa, "especially since they had forgotten about us." But, he wondered out loud, "what could I do?" Paul felt that they had applied, followed the procedure, and now could "only pray" that Australia would accept him as a resident.

While women had their frustrations with Australian regulations, men were annoyed by corruption and other difficulties in their home countries. According to all eighteen men with whom I spoke, it was not easy to collect documents such as birth certificates and police checks in African countries. All of them laughed when thinking back about collecting all the official statements, as none of them were able to get them the "right" way; while most of them did try the formal way first, in the end they all had to bribe someone to get their forms and information. Peter, who had been in Adelaide for four years now and who was particularly outspoken and skeptical about visa-related policies, explained that he did not even try to get his documents in the official way. He felt that it would only take more time and it would all be in vain eventually. "No." he continued, "I just called someone I knew in the right position, paid some 'chai' (meaning bribe in his native language), and the same week I got all the documents signed."[7]

Moreover, sometimes it was very hard for applicants to adhere to application requirements. Naomi's partner Otto, for instance, experienced many difficulties when trying to obtain his police clearance. Otto had lived in an Asian country (where he met Naomi), and so he needed a clearance from that particular country, even though he was applying for the visa from his birth country. It was difficult to request a clearance from this Asian country since in the meantime he had moved back to his home country due to the visa application requirements. Unfortunately, it turned out that since he had been undocumented in Asia, he was not in a position to obtain a police clearance from there. This put his application in serious jeopardy as it provided a reason for the DIBP to deny him his visa. Eventually, Naomi and her lawyer managed to have this requirement waived by the DIBP.

But for most men, apart from the financial costs, the biggest hurdle was the cost in time of having to deal with health checks and interviews. As

---

7　Migration agents also criticized the DIBP for being too static and inflexible in not taking into account that different countries may not be as functional and highly regulated as Australia. They emphasised that the DIBP should consider individual cases and be more accommodating as documents that are easy to obtain in Australia may be (almost) impossible to get in African countries, due to the high levels of corruption in government offices.

Australian embassies and consulates are sparse in Africa, much travelling was involved. While for some men this meant travelling to the capital city of their home country—which would take them from a few hours up to more than a day—others had to travel abroad to undergo health checks or to be interviewed. Patrick, for instance, had spent four days on his health check, and it had been a struggle to get leave from work. Some men from West African countries had to travel to Pretoria, South Africa, to have an interview with an Australian Government official. Moreover, according to a migration agent, the 2013–16 Ebola crisis in West Africa delayed many visa applications from the region, as people were not able to obtain visas from South Africa to travel out of their home countries to attend their scheduled interviews in Pretoria. From Australia's perspective, the agent argued, these individuals then would appear to not be interested in their planned migration, which would influence visa decisions.

Yet when I asked men how they experienced the application process, men all responded in a calm way. Generally, men replied that it was "all fine" that they were "not worried at all" and that "everything went smooth."[8] None of the men seemed scared or worried that their visa would not come through, or at least none of them expressed being worried about this. All men felt that since they were genuine about their relationship and had "ticked all the boxes" required for obtaining a visa, they were confident about the results. Men did state they had been excited, impatient and a bit nervous about their future and their new life as husbands in Australia. One day, I went over to see Sophie for a morning coffee and chat. Not only did I find her sitting at the kitchen table, but to my pleasant surprise, also an exceptionally excited Lucas, who normally had a gentle and quiet demeanor. A few weeks back, Lucas and Sophie had received the happy news that their visa application had been approved, and so as soon as he could, Lucas had flown back to Adelaide to be with his wife. This was good timing for me to be able to ask Lucas to reflect on his experiences with the application process. Lucas explained that "those days I had to wait to be reunited with Sophie were the slowest days of my life." He felt that it was "taking forever." But even though he missed her, he also said that he had felt good, because he knew that "one day we would be united." He had not felt nervous, or "maybe only a little," because he "just knew it would all be all right one day."

---

8   That men expressed they had not been worried or anxious about the visa application outcome may partly have to do with them not wanting to publicly express fear, especially to a white, young female interviewer.

From my conversations with migrant men and their sponsoring partners, frustration about the visa application's lengthy and costly procedure turned out to be key to their experiences. They saw the procedure as harassment to couples that could not wait to be reunited. Partners argued that since they were set on living together in Australia, they would make sure to meet any requirement necessary, wait as long as needed, and pay whatever sum needed for the visa to come through. Particularly, the Australian spouses felt their government was unsupportive, and actually showing distrust instead of support. They thought that visa requirements, processing times or costs would not stop romantic couples anyway and felt that therefore it was unfair of the DIBP to charge such high costs whilst not providing them with appropriate services.

Australia's strict policies are not exceptional and can even be seen as relatively flexible in their determination of genuine relationships, compared to other countries. In Denmark, for instance, Jørgensen (2012) explains, a strict age criterion applies. For spouses to be eligible for a visa, they must be at least 24 years of age. This criterion is backed up by the argument that Danish people culturally would not marry younger than this age. Amongst others, Denmark also excludes citizens from sponsoring a spouse if they received social benefits within the last three years, and couples are required to have a "greater mutual attachment to Denmark than to any other country (in terms of education, relatives, social networks, employment and language)" (Jørgensen 2012, 61). In the Netherlands, sponsors of a foreign spouse are required to have a permanent job and to earn above the country's minimum wage (Dragojlovic 2008). Also, other European countries such as Norway and the United Kingdom have income requirements as part of the partner visa procedure (Pellander 2019). Lastly, in France, it can take up to ten years and multiple temporary visas before foreign spouses are granted residency or citizenship (Neveu Kringelbach 2013). But while such policies are certainly stricter than Australia's visa conditions, the latter's visa application procedures are still difficult for couples.

For the romantic partners taking part in this study, intimate relationships were imagined to be the key to living a good life. While couples were looking forward to beginning their new and happy lives together in Australia, such dreams and prospects were challenged by the lengthy and costly visa application process. This procedure not only caused frustration among partners, it often also caused suffering. In the next section, I turn to ways in which romantic love was (and needed to be) overemphasized time and again during the visa application procedure. While couples used a narrative of romantic love strategically to receive the much-desired visa, the formal focus on love as the basis of genuine relationships caused many partners great anxiety as they feared heartbreaking outcomes.

4.2   Accumulating Evidence and Anxiety

According to my interlocutors, the largest part of the application consisted of providing evidence of the genuineness of their relationship. Practically, this resulted in the obsessive collecting of evidence, including: letters, emails, post-cards, copies of texts and *WhatsApp* conversations, phone bills, receipts for dinners and hotel stays, and flight tickets. Also, they would be sure to have joint activities, love statements and photos on Facebook. Lillian had been par-ticularly thorough when collecting their "kilos of proof." Lillian had invited me to come and talk to her during her work hours in a restaurant. She was very busy, she always emphasized, but at the same time she was happy to share her story with me as she deemed it important to share her experiences with marriage migration. We sat down in the small courtyard at the back of the restaurant; she had thirty minutes before she had to start preparing for lunch. Lillian laughed aloud as she thought back to that hectic period of gathering information. She remembered how she used to keep "every-single-thing" that proved they were in a close relationship—"restaurant receipts, movie tickets, photographs, letters and emails we sent each other when I was in Australia, phone bills ... especially the phone bills added lots of extra centimeters to the pile of proof." She explained that the phone bills were particularly important as they showed a record of their daily contact through telephone conversa-tions and text messages. Lillian held her hand about a meter above the ground to illustrate how extensive her collection of proof was. She did not find it hard to provide the evidence, as she said, "We were sincere. We had plenty to show how much we wanted to spend time together."

Eileen, also, remembers that it was easy to collect the evidence, as she and her partner had been together for long enough to gather ample material. Eileen had a part-time management job and was able to meet me on one of her days off, and while her children were at school. Over an extensive lunch at a popular café in a Melbourne suburb, we went through her complete love story from the beginning to the present. Their correspondence by post, copies of phone bills and a pile of photographs is what they handed over as evidence to the DIBP. Furthermore, as they had met each other's families by then, they made sure that parents and siblings wrote the statutory declarations that were part of the required evidence. Eileen thought that such interpersonal contact would be the best proof of "a genuine relationship that is accepted within society." It was only last year, 16 years after their application, that Eileen and her husband burned all their proof in the fireplace: "He has had his citizenship for years now, and so it was about time to just leave that period of time behind." She explained that they kept the documentation for years, "just in order to be sure because you just never know, but now we felt we needed to get rid of that pile of unrest." The stories of both Lillian and Eileen demonstrate that even though couples may have had faith in their case, as they felt they were sincere, they still assembled their evidence carefully.

That feelings of anxiety can come up when providing evidence of a genuine relationship became particularly clear each time I met Charlotte for a catch-up. As Charlotte and I often met each other at social events, and my office at the university was close to her workplace, it was easy to find out the latest on her visa developments. One day Charlotte and I met for lunch during our break in a café in between her workplace and mine. She had just sent in her visa application to the DIBP the week before and was extremely nervous about it. Even though Charlotte felt that although it was clear that they were sincere ("We [have] know[n] each other for years and have really no trouble whatsoever to collect the right material to prove our relationship is real"), she was still very stressed about the visa. "What if we will not get the visa? What are we going to do then?" she thought out loud. To mainly reassure herself, she explained that they had ticked all the boxes. Her mother had met Zachary multiple times, she had met his family and they were married. She continued to explain that they also had many photos of them as a couple, and that because he has an income, he does not need to worry about getting a job in Adelaide. Also, she emphasized, he had been to Adelaide already and had also left in time. Nevertheless, Charlotte felt that "they [the DIBP] can just decide against us. If we made one mistake they will deny us a visa. I am so scared of that."

It was interesting to be able to follow Charlotte and Zachary's visa application process closely. Each time they received news from the department, Charlotte would update me, partially to ask me what I thought about the situation. That Charlotte was this anxious about the application process indicates the importance of the visa decision for the future happiness of couples and partners. The process can be seen as a major hurdle for couples wanting to live a happy life together. If the visa is not granted, their futures will take drastically different turns. Charlotte's nervousness only increased after reading a book written by an Australian woman who waited years and had a number of denials before her Nigerian husband was finally granted a visa, and this made Charlotte very upset.

Often, sponsoring women felt it was their responsibility to be in charge of completing the application, a part of their role as the Australian partner. Women explained that since it was for their government, they had a better understanding of what evidence was needed. Also, they argued that their written English would be better than that of their partners. Women spent many hours on completing and perfecting their responses. Many regarded it as a part-time job, to collect all the relevant information and fill in the forms.

Samantha, married to Thomas with a young baby girl, recalls the many hours, nights, and weekends she worked on perfecting their application, spending more time on this than her actual job as a care worker. It had to be perfect, as so much was depending on it. Samantha did not like to talk about their application, as she felt it was a "ridiculous procedure" that had kept her and her partner from living their normal lives. Samantha was always a bit secretive about the fact that they had applied for a Partner visa for her partner. She often started conversation on the topic by stating "just between you and me" indicating that I should make sure not to tell anyone in our overlapping social circle. I felt as if she was ashamed of having to go through the procedure, more than finding it ridiculous.

Emma never felt more pressured, responsible, and tested than when applying for the visa, she explained over a home-cooked meal for her daughters, husband, a family friend, and me. She explained how she thought carefully about whom to ask to write the statutory declarations, and decided to ask people with highly regarded jobs, so as to put "more weight on the scales." She also made sure to emphasize that her husband would not be of any burden to the state, as she and her family could provide him with a place to live and a job. She recalls how scared she was, as she was pregnant during the application process and when awaiting the decision. She feared that if he was not granted a visa, she would be alone in Adelaide, with his baby. Luckily, her partner was granted the visa and Emma had to wait only six months before her husband could join her in Australia.

Such narratives show how nerve-wracking and anxiety-causing applications sometimes were for couples.[9] Prior to applying for the visa, couples had focused on romance and intimacy. The visa application emphasized the other side of what it means to be in a cross-border relationship, the legal and formal consequences. The visa application was a "wake-up call" making couples realize their journeys to togetherness—and consequently to happiness—were also complicated and procedural, not merely romantic and self-evident. Such stories indicate that relationships, even though they may be based on romantic love, have a practical character, too. Illouz (1998) describes two narratives of love: a realistic and a romantic perspective, which, according to Eggebø (2013, 783), underscores how questionable it is to try to have a purely romantic

---

9   Due to privacy reasons, the DIBP was not forthcoming with information regarding the success rate of applications. Although I do not know of any applications being denied, couples and partners themselves may have heard of such instances that could explain their anxiety. But moreover, it seemed that the potential risk of having to give up on the dream of living happily ever after in Australia that made couples—in particular women—very anxious.

relationship. Both Eggebø's research as well as the narratives above demonstrate that not only are relationships romantic, they too consist of practicalities and other unromantic matters that are simply a part of daily life. Certainly, at the time of applying for the visa, the practical may have significantly exceeded the romantic side of the relationship. Ironically, having to focus on the genuineness of relationships turned them into rather unromantic entities.

It seemed that in fact visa procedures influenced courtships, and that relationships were adjusted to evolve in accordance with visa conditions. This applied particularly in the eight cases where couples met in Australia and/or applied onshore, where the focus appeared to be not so much on providing evidence of keeping in contact and visiting each other regularly, but more on living a daily life together as visa conditions encouraged. For example, over the course of my fieldwork, two couples started cohabiting early on, and were engaged to marry as early as possible. By doing so, they speeded up their courting phase in order to make their "official time" together as long as possible.

Lucas, for instance, moved in with Sophie only a few months after the two had met, even though the circumstances were not ideal for this move to happen. Whereas Sophie's youngest child adored Lucas, her adult children questioned their mother's relationship with Lucas, and did not feel like sharing the house with him. It took many talks within the family to make the situation livable, and for a period of time Lucas lived elsewhere until Sophie's children were comfortable with their mother's relationship. While Lucas and Sophie's love for each other would have been a factor in them wanting to live together so quickly, it is also true that the couple knew that their time could be running out, as visa extensions remained uncertain. Since the visa requirement of having been together for over twelve months could be proved by evidence of cohabitation, it may very well be that both Sophie and Lucas knew they had no time to waste, despite her children's opinions. Possibly without any pressure of visa requirements, they might have taken longer to move in together, particularly as children's opinions did seem very important to both Lucas and Sophie.

Furthermore, when Lucas was anonymously reported for working in Australia while he was not permitted to, and subsequently had to leave the country as soon as possible, Lucas and Sophie quickly arranged to marry. They decided not to tell many people about their spontaneous marriage. Sophie told me this when I came over to her house for a coffee—something I did at least once a month. That time, Lucas had just left Australia to go back to his home country, as the DIBP requested of him. While we were enjoying some rays of sunshine in her lush garden, she explained that they had not told many people because it would have come as a shock to them. She did not even tell her parents, nor did she tell her children. She felt that "they were not ready for this step" but, "we were, and we knew we did not want to wait." For Sophie and Lucas their marriage added an extra layer of commitment: whilst now physically apart, their marriage united them more strongly than distance separated them. Simultaneously, marriage meant avoiding the requirement of length of cohabitation for de facto partners. According to visa regulations, if a couple is married it does not matter how long they have been together. De facto partners, though, need to have been together—meaning cohabiting—for at least twelve months. Since Sophie and Lucas knew each other for less than a year when he had to return to his home country, marriage was the only option available to them to be able to apply for a visa.

Sophie and Lucas were not the only couple that seemingly had to adjust their lives in accordance with visa conditions. Katherine and Emmanuel also had a short and intense period of courtship, quickly followed by marriage. This, according to some friends and acquaintances, only made sense, but others saw it as remarkable. The couple met in early 2015 when a mutual friend introduced them to each other. Both had been single yet looking for a partner for a while. To others they did not seem to be a good match, appearing to have no mutual interests at all: Emmanuel was the spiritual hippie type while Katherine loved jewelry, make-up, and shopping. They became engaged about five months later and married nine months after having met for the first time. Emmanuel was in Australia on a temporary visa and had to leave the country soon. Through the marriage, however, Emmanuel and Katherine were able to apply for a Partner visa onshore, which gave Emmanuel the opportunity to stay in Australia while awaiting the outcome of their application.

Katherine and Emmanuel's relatively quick decision to marry and their lack of commonalities may provide grounds to question the genuineness of their relationship. At the same time, however, it seemed that Katherine and Emmanuel enjoyed spending time together and formed a good family, which included Katherine's children from a previous relationship. Emmanuel and the young children got along well. Since he was not allowed to work, according to visa regulations, the children soon became his main concern. As was shown by the many photos posted on social media, Emmanuel took them to school and picked them up, played with them and took them to the park each day. As the children had an Africa-origin father, outsiders may have assumed that Emmanuel was their biological parent, and which could have made him, the children and Katherine even more comfortable with the new situation.

Other posts on social media made it clear that either Katherine and Emmanuel were definitely in love, or they were performing the romantic love sought after by the DIBP, perfectly. Possibly they did both. With or without children present, they spent a lot of time together on both social and romantic outings. That their connection was genuinely romantic became clear from the many photos in which the couple was depicted in a loving way: kissing, hugging, or looking deeply at each other's eyes. Moreover, photos would be accompanied by texts expressing the deep love between one another and the gratefulness of being in each other's lives.

Both the stories of Sophie and Lucas, and Emmanuel and Katherine make it clear that love and visa strategies are in fact very much intertwined. Neither relationship seemed to have been embarked upon just for the sake of a visa, although both couples did marry to help fulfil visa regulations. I want to emphasize, however, that romance did play a major role in their stories of courtship—regardless of how suspect the couples may have looked to others. Fernandez (2013, 2019) describes similar cases, arguing that Cuban-Danish couples often had no other choice than marriage, even after short periods of being together, if they wanted to continue their relationship. As migration to Cuba was difficult to realize, Danish regulations made marriage the only option for staying together and living in Denmark. Ironically, couples felt that the Danish Government forced marriage upon them, while it simultaneously preached the importance of choice in regard to love (Fernandez 2013). In both the cases of Emmanuel and Katherine, and Lucas and Sophie, marriages also seemed to have been rushed for the purpose of the visa application. Both accounts make it clear how couples use romantic love both for visa purposes as well as a means of staying together.

4.3   *And Finally, the Interview*

After having submitted all the required documents and evidence of genuine togetherness, couples then had to wait for months before the DIBP processed their application. All the couples I interviewed were successful in their application.[10] However, the likelihood for success did not stop them from worrying about the application. The period of waiting for a possible interview, and eventually the processing of the visa was the time when individuals would reflect on such issues. Lillian described how she had "nightmares every night for weeks" until her husband's visa came through. Even though she felt it would have been "impossible" for their application to be denied as she had provided the DIBP with a strong and extensive case, "only the thought of it caused me panic attacks." Also, Emma remembered vividly that after she submitted all the

---

10   This study has an implicit bias: couples denied a visa would have been hard to locate as the male would no longer be living in Australia, and the woman would not be as visible as other women who had longer-term relationships that included courtship, visa application, cohabitation, and either a successful marriage or a divorce.

requested documents, she first felt relief, but that feeling was soon replaced by fear: "I was so scared that [the DIBP] would find something wrong with our application and that Matthew and I, and our little one, would never be reunited again. I have never been more scared about anything than this."

Couples, and especially Australian women, experienced this period of waiting as having their lives put on hold by the government. For Lucas and Sophie, the time Lucas had to spend back home, on his own, was experienced as "useless." When Sophie came to visit Lucas in his hometown, not only did they celebrate a second, and this time more festive, wedding ceremony, they were also lucky to fall pregnant. Throughout the pregnancy Sophie could not rely on support from her husband, either emotionally or financially, because he was back home and without a steady income whilst Sophie was in Australia. Lucas in turn felt as if he failed as a man, a husband, because he did not take care of his wife during the pregnancy. Luckily for Lucas and Sophie, nine months after applying for the visa they were invited for an interview. The visa approval came through right before she was due (ten months after they had applied) and he was present when Sophie gave birth.

All couples debated the difference that important and life-changing events would make in visa processing speed and outcome. Some believed that a pregnancy, proposal for marriage or marriage itself would positively influence processing times and outcomes, while others were certain that the DIBP would not care at all about such events. While some couples believed that pregnancies, especially, were a reason for the DIBP to approve a visa request, according to Charlotte, the government would not care about such things. She had called to inquire about this and had received the information that pregnancy was considered a conscious choice and therefore it would not influence the department's decision-making. Charlotte reasoned that "what they argue is that couples should not make big decisions like that when awaiting a visa outcome." She was informed that, "they just look at the evidence handed to them for being a genuine couple." Seemingly, children are not regarded as evidence of genuine relationships, but Charlotte speculated, are possibly viewed as indicators of sham relationships, as strategies to obtain visas.

Eventually, some couples were invited to take part in an interview with a government official either at an office in Australia or overseas, or via phone. Couples were generally very excited about the interview as it meant their case was being processed and it would now not be long before a decision would be made. The end of the long period of waiting was in sight. Interlocutors often shared the good news of the invitation for an interview on social media where friends and family responded with congratulations and encouraging words.

At the same time, however, interlocutors felt that the interview was the ultimate sign that they, as a cross-border couple, had to prove their love for each other, showing that ultimately Australia did not trust foreigners. Couples and partners felt that the government's fear of sham marriages constructed their relationships as bad in essence, whereas they felt Australian relationships were seen as inherently positive from the start. This is consistent with Lucy Williams' observation that cross-border couples are by definition falling short when their relationships are being measured against the "pure" relationship, which idealizes equality among partners; cross-border relationships are often "even less likely than marriages between citizens to be truly equal" (2010, cited by Eggebø 2013, 782). Female interlocutors felt that it was unacceptable for their government to be making judgements about them having foreign husbands, as it betrayed their faith in them as citizens and their ability to make good decisions. "I wish they would just leave us alone," "Do they think I am stupid or something," "They are just racist and bullies," and "They just do not want foreigners to come in" were common responses when I asked women about their general opinion on the visa procedure.

Couples were interviewed separately in order to cross-check their answers and thus determine how well they knew their significant other. Couples prepared for the interviews, but at the same time, appeared to have faith in knowing their partner well enough. Sometimes, couples who were about to be interviewed obtained advice about what to say and do from couples that had gone through the interview process in the past; sometimes they looked for advice on the Internet. In these ways, couples learned about potential questions immigration officers could ask, such as: How many siblings does your partner have? What are their names? On what side of the bed does your spouse sleep? What sports team does he support? How many good friends does she have and what do they do when they meet?

The two migration agents I interviewed felt that interview questions were often culturally biased. For instance, they explained that Africa-origin applicants would often fail to correctly answer questions due to a different understanding of concepts such as marriage, family or children.[11] A question such as, "How many children do you have?" could be confusing, as the applicant may have biological children and/or children they took care of and/or there could be other children living under the same roof.

---

11   For instance, traditional marriages are often unregistered in African countries and therefore not recognized by the Australian Government. None of the couples had any difficulties proving their Australian marriage as they were legally contracted.

The interview Lucas had with a migration officer reveals confusion concerning children, as well as marriage. When sitting around the kitchen table, after Sophie and Lucas had been reunited again, I asked Lucas how the interview went. He explained to me that it all went very well, that he was able to answer all the questions easily and that he had taken photos to the interview to emphasize how authentic their relationship was. However, at one point they had asked him a trick question, which he still seemed confused about. They had asked about his wife and children, and how he could be married to two women and what he would do with his children back home. Lucas thought he had not understood the question and had asked for the question to be repeated. He then realized they were serious in the inquiry about his "other family." Lucas asked them where they got the information from that he was already married. Apparently, he had told immigration officers this the first time he was interviewed, when he had come to Australia on a temporary visa about two years before this interview. At that time, he had stayed in Australia for approximately nine months. He told me that he explained to the immigration officers that they must have misunderstood him back then. "I told them I took care of children, yes, but they are my brother's two children." Those children had lived with Lucas because "that is how we do it back home: my siblings' children are like my own to me." And about a presumed wife, "I never said anything about having a wife because I never married in my home country." Lucas felt that they were testing him. But, he added, he may very well have made up that he was married at the first interview, but he could not remember this.

Lucas and Sophie agreed that it would have made sense to pretend to have a family. Sophie explained to me that, "Many Africans pretend they have a family in Africa because that makes them look better." I also heard this from other interlocutors. Apparently having a family in Africa would appear to an immigration officer to reduce the chance of overstaying a visa. As Lucas explained, "Western governments are scared that when Africans enter their countries, they will never leave again. So, Africans tell the government: I have children and a wife, so do not worry, I will go home again." While both Lucas and Sophie felt a bit uneasy with this particular question, they otherwise felt good about each of their interviews. And they did not have to worry for long, as only two weeks after the interview they received the good news that the visa was approved, and that Lucas was welcome in Australia.

Some interlocutors who had to go for interviews found them to be uncomfortable where questions concerned personal topics. Naomi, for instance, updated me on how her interview went when I met her again at her sister's home. Naomi, who was newly wed to her second husband from an African country, became really upset when the officer kept asking her about her ex-husband, and why they broke up. She felt as if the official was judging her, and her marriage skills, instead of focusing on her current relationship: "As if I am proud of the fact that I married another African before. Yes, I made that mistake, but also, not all Africans are the same, and now they treated me as if I am a stupid woman making the same mistake twice." It made her nervous about the outcome because she felt the interviewers did not like her because of her life choices. That this was her second marriage, and that it was her second time applying for a Partner visa with an Africa-origin partner made Naomi worried. That Naomi might be fearful of a government official making inappropriate judgements about a relationship with an African man is supported by the literature. According to Lavanchy (2014), government officials see Africa-origin men in particular as "deceiving others" who would take advantage of Swiss women. Also, in France, Africa-origin spouses specifically would be suspected of fraud (Neveu Kringelbach 2013).

However, not all interview experiences were only bad. Lillian explained that her interview actually went really well, and was in fact not scary at all, because she and the officer shared a Lebanese heritage; immediately it felt more like a friendly conversation than an interrogation about the genuineness of her relationship. By the end of the interview, however, the officer asked her whether she was aware that she was marrying an African man who could very well be doing it for the visa. She answered that she was aware of that, but that this was a risk she was willing to take. Although she found this an unnecessary and meddlesome question, she also understood that there is a risk involved, and took this question or warning as a friendly gesture from the immigration officer.

Many of my female interlocutors recalled being warned about the potential danger of marrying a foreigner. Such experiences are similar to those of Dutch women marrying Balinese men in the Netherlands. According to Anna Dragojlovic (2008), immigration officers in the Netherlands would warn women that these "other men" might be seeking to obtain their money. This illustrates the patronizing attitude that suggests that women would be in need of protection, as they were blinded by love. She argues that such warnings depict "a patriarchal environment in which a man has to be, if not higher, then equal in social status with his wife" (2008, 337). A general notion that these Dutch women may be used by foreign men to enter the country could be part of the reason immigration officers felt the need to warn women (Bonjour & de Hart 2013; Andrikopoulos 2019; Moret et al. 2019). The well-meaning statements and warnings about migrant men, their husbands and partners, which my female interlocutors received from immigration officers, signal a patriarchal and racialized protectionism.

Australian immigration officers' methods for Partner visa granting were not exceptional compared to those in similar studies, conducted for instance in Switzerland (Lavanchy 2014), France (Neveu Kringelbach 2013), Norway (Eggebø 2013), Belgium (Maskens 2018), and the Netherlands (Bonjour & de Hart 2013). In all countries, immigration officers, embassy and consulate employees, as well as civil servants, are asked to look out for "conspicuous strangeness" and "unlikely combinations" of couples (Bonjour & de Hart 2013, 69), and "atypical" or "unorthodox" relationships may be rejected (Eggebø 2013, 784). Government employees who are assigned to such gatekeeping often do not have the means or framework to be able to professionally assess the genuineness of relationships. As Maskens observes, "there is no clear equivalence between intimate events, the intensity and quality of a relationship, and their formulation in words and sentences. Moreover, cultural settings also shape intimacy and the way we talk about it" (2015, 52). Officials who determine the genuineness of marriage migration couples in Switzerland, according to Lavanchy, tend to rely on their personal and subjective impression of the couples, which is mainly influenced by mainstream ideas of romantic love and compatibility: couples too different from one another would be "discrepant" or "problematic" (2014, 13). As readers will recall, this practice was echoed by Steven, the above-mentioned Australian immigration officer who spoke of his gut feelings when assessing whether couples were truly in love.

5   Conclusion

This chapter has illustrated the ways in which genuineness is a focus point for couples practicing marriage migration. I elaborated on the various and significant effects the Australian Government's focus on genuine relationships, and resultantly, the visa application procedure, had on cross-border couples' lived experiences of their intimate relationships. I showed how the Australian Partner visa model does not take into account the different contexts in which the desired documentation can be hard if not impossible to obtain. The entire process causes applicants stress as visa outcomes are extremely important for their future lives. The application process is long and expensive and therefore caused much inconvenience for couples, as they have to put their lives on hold. As such, the visa procedure draws a clear line between the here and now filled with fear and bureaucratic hassle, and the imagined beautiful yet uncertain future, in which couples can *finally* start living their lives together. Such findings about the Australian visa application process, correspond with Eggebø's observation that "Even though most applications for marriage migration are accepted and the majority of relationships are recognized as real, the application process places people in a frustrating situation of indeterminacy" (2013, 785).

Couples regarded the Australian Government as a force that is purposely obstructing their envisioned happy and romantic futures. Having to prove their genuineness created feelings of anxiety and fear among couples that a happy future may not be as realistic as imagined. The bureaucratic procedure also projected such happily ever afters much farther into the future than couples initially expected, thus shifting couples' orientations of when and where happiness is to be found (Walker & Kavedžija 2016; Ahmed 2010). Simultaneously, visa regulations, with their emphasis on the importance of romantic love, turned couples away from their first so romantic experience in their relationship, to an everyday harshness of mainly having to deal with the practical (Eggebø 2013). Furthermore, relationships were sometimes rushed, and couples forced into more static or formal unions, as visa regulations did not offer space for them to let things unfold. Thus, in several ways, the Australian Government's impact on relationships changed the character of those relationships, as was also described by Fernandez (2013).

As mentioned in the Introduction to this study, nationality, in the context of marriage migration, can develop as an acceptable euphemism for racialization (Lavanchy 2014, 9). As others have found, this chapter illustrated how the long and often anxiously awaited interviews with migration officers demonstrated a racialized and patriarchal desire to "protect our women' from 'other men" (Dragojlovic 2008; see also Bonjour & de Hart 2013). It also indicated a cultural bias disadvantaging people from the continent of Africa, as is also described by Lavanchy (2014) and Neveu Kringelbach (2013). While all interlocutors in this study eventually were issued with a visa, they often seemed to come with a warning attached. Sponsoring women would be cautioned about the dangers of bringing a migrant man to Australia, as he could be seeking things other than love. Such apparently well-meaning advice reflects underlying bias and racism. The visa application procedure reflects institutional racism; it appears to assume that women are naïve or innocent victims of predatory men and implies that migrant men may be engaging in sham practices and therefore undeserving of Australian residency. But not only did couples and partners encounter institutional racism. As the next chapter illustrates, cross-border couples also experienced numerous instances of everyday racism after settling in Australia. Such racism can be seen as yet another obstruction to couples hoping for happy endings.

CHAPTER 5

Cross-border Couples and Everyday Racism

1   Introduction

This chapter focuses on cross-border couples' encounters with everyday racism and everyday prejudice. I demonstrate how various encounters influenced couples' romantic lived experiences and feelings of comfort and belonging. While there were some positive moments, there were also negative experiences that were counter to the expectations that partners had of an easy life after marriage migration. These negative experiences can be seen as another obstruction to their imagined happy marriages and happy futures together.

It appears that couples were often viewed with suspicion in workplaces, social circles and among family. It also appears, regardless of whether the context was predominantly African or non-African in demographic, that both partners experienced various acts of everyday racism and prejudice when navigating different sociocultural settings. Sometimes this turmoil arose because of having an "other" partner; sometimes it arose from being the "other" partner. It is for these reasons that I argue that alongside good experiences—moments of comfort and belonging—in most spheres of their lives, couples and partners also experienced racism, and hence, feelings of not being welcomed as a couple. While the existing literature, discussed in what follows, often deals with non-white migrant experiences of everyday racism in societies where whiteness in the norm, in this chapter I will also describe sponsoring women's experiences with bias and racism, and couples' experiences of everyday racism and non-belonging among African familial and community groups.

I start this chapter with a personal vignette illustrating the blurry lines between everyday racism and prejudice. Then, I elaborate on the latter two concepts. In what follows, I share examples of the ways in which romantic couples experienced marginalization. After showing how migrant men and sponsoring women each experienced racism in their daily lives, I then focus on couples in relation to their families, both in Australia as well as in Africa. Lastly, I turn to the ways in which partners and couples relate to African community organizations in Australia.

2   "Be Careful with African Men"

My first home in Adelaide was a room in my landlady Dawn's house. Located in the suburbs but a bicycle ride away from the city, the university, and the beach, this detached house with a large backyard felt like a perfect welcome to Australia. Dawn lived in the "granny flat" at the back of the garden, while I shared the three-bedroom house with international students. I arrived in February, in a blistering heat wave, which Dawn decided we could only survive with a glass of wine after work. This habit developed into a household ritual with Dawn and I sitting in the garden together, a couple of times a week, sipping from our glasses of cold Chardonnay wine, chatting away while observing the chickens clucking around the yard. Sometimes, we would even go out socializing. She would take me to the beach or to salsa nights in the city. Dawn really liked dancing, especially to Latin music. I felt lucky to have come across such a nice and generous landlady.

But our good relationship was short-lived. Changes in our friendship started to occur when I met my partner Kassim, about eight months after I moved in with Dawn. Possibly typical for anthropologists, I had met my partner during fieldwork. Kassim had come to Australia in 2006 from his home country Tanzania. When one day he came to pick me up to go to the beach for a swim, Dawn apparently had noticed his van in the driveway, a Mercedes Vito. When I got back that evening, Dawn grinningly commented that such cars would be so typical for *them*, that *they* would always want to have the fancy brands, that it would all be about status with *them*. I had noticed the car brand, but I had been more stunned by the mess of this tradesman car's interior, and the one window that could not be opened.

Over the following weeks, Kassim came over several times to enjoy a ginger beer with me in the garden. The temperatures were still high, and we felt lucky we had access to such a beautiful and shady garden—something that Kassim's apartment close to the city lacked. However, after three of Kassim's visits, Dawn took me aside with a warning. She told me that while it was fine to have him over every now and then, I should not make this a daily occurrence. She had furthermore noticed, she told me, that my flatmate had locked her door, each time Kassim came over. My first reaction was that it was sensible for her to have rules regarding male visitors. My second reaction was a mixed feeling of sadness and consternation that my flatmate had felt unsafe. Later, however, the motivations behind her comment weighed upon me. Since Dawn had not always been in the house when Kassim visited, I wondered how she knew about the locked door? My flatmate also seemed to get along well with Kassim, I thought, as she had insisted he should try her cooking each time he came by.

While these occurrences had certainly hinted that Dawn was judging Kassim based on the color of his skin, at that moment in time I did not feel I could or should comment on her racist-tinged comments, which had always been subtle. As our wine sessions continued as normal, Dawn elaborated on the Latin scene in Adelaide, and how men from Latin American backgrounds, but also African men, were very different from Australian men. According to her, even though such men would be much more charming and smoother than Australian men, women had to be careful in entertaining such advances. Dawn could name a few men she had heard about who were unfaithful to their wives and/or had used their Australian partners in order to obtain residency. Personally, Dawn said she would be unable to trust any man with a Latin American or African background.

While Kassim had always been wary of Dawn, the penny for me only dropped when I heard Dawn's reaction when I told her about his daughter from a previous relationship. In a loud and clear manner, Dawn warned me and asked me to reconsider my decision to start a relationship with him. She told me to be careful because, according to her, African men would want to have as many children as possible, but would not care about them, nor the mothers. She explained that Kassim already having a child was an indicator that he was a risky choice. She urged me to use protection and also warned me that he could very well be still together with his wife. Dawn said that she knew about African men and their habits of using their friends' apartments for sexual extramarital relationships. Australian men, on the other hand, would never do this, she said. It was after a couple of such tirades, that I decided it was time to move out.

Tellingly, Dawn had not been the only one with such prejudged notions and racist attitudes towards men from African countries. When I told people about my research, I often received curious and excited reactions. As one person said, "Well I know this Nigerian ... ," staring off a narrative of a man who married a woman under false pretenses, and by doing so had come to live in Australia. Another person commented, "Women are too desperate and need to fly all the way to Africa to get themselves a husband." Several Australian women even confided that they would "love" to have a "black lover," or at least have sex with an African man—just to "see what it is like." Some even mentioned that they would love to have "brown babies." For the cross-border couples and ex-partners I studied, encounters such as these with racism, prejudice and exoticism had become a normal part of their everyday lives, significantly affecting their wellbeing. The result was a further shattering of previously held imaginaries that once in Australia, they would be happy.

3   Everyday Racism and Everyday Prejudice

Everyday racism, a term first coined by Philomena Essed in her book *Understanding Everyday Racism* (1991) refers to experiences of routine marginalization based on notions of race. In her study, Essed focused on the banal and blatant racism experienced by African-American women in the United States. She describes racism as "a process … routinely created and reinforced through everyday practices" (1991, 2). Everyday racism reflects on both the micro-sociological level of the everyday, as well as the macro-sociological structures such as the economy, the media and political institutions, and their role in producing racism (Hill Collins 1992, 790). Such acts of racism, Essed argues, are not incidental, arbitrary or random, but are specific instances that "acquire meaning only in relation to the sum total of other experiences of everyday racism" (1991, 288). As other scholars also explain, the reason that everyday and interpersonal instances of racism are connected to institutional racism is because they reflect racialized power relations evident in society (Noble & Poynting 2010, 493). Institutional racism:

> refers to the institutional policies and practices that are put in place to protect and legitimate the advantages and power one group has over another. Institutional racism can be overt or covert, intentional or unintentional. Either way, racist outcomes are achieved and reproduced.
>
> AUGOUSTINOS & REYNOLDS 2001, 4

As Robert Miles and Stephen Small (1999) state,

> Racialized structures are the institutional pillars of society, they are the routine, recurrent and organised features of contemporary life. The idea of "racialized" structures has two key components. First, it refers to the distribution of valuable resources such as political power, employment, education and housing. Primarily this aspect involves who owns what, works and lives where, and has good health. Secondly, it refers to the normal, recurrent and routinized procedures of institutions that shape and constrain our daily lives, from politics (voting and political representatives), economics (business, employment), education (universities, schools), health (hospitals) and other spheres of social life (family, media, music, sport). These behaviours and actions sustain the distribution of resources'.
>
> cited by MADISON 2005, 72

Racial categories become produced and reproduced in everyday life, by practices of inclusion and exclusion (Madison 2005, 72). Racism, both on the
institutional level and as an everyday experience, "maintains and reproduces
the *power* differentials between groups in the social system" (Augoustinos &
Reynolds 2001, 4).

This presence of power is what, according to psychological studies, differentiates prejudice from racism. Prejudice was first defined by psychologist
Gordon Allport (1954) as "thinking ill of others without sufficient warrant"
(cited by Valentine et al. 2015, 569). Since then, a plethora of terms have been
used to describe prejudice, such as discrimination, ethnocentrism, ingroup bias,
and stereotyping (Augoustinos & Reynolds 2001). As Martha Augoustinos and
Katherine Reynolds state, "while prejudice is usually regarded as an individual
phenomenon, racism is a broader construct that links individual beliefs and
practices to wider social and institutional practices" (2001, 3). The difference
between racism and prejudice, then, is enactment: a person may display race
prejudice, but if there is no power exercised and it remains an attitude, this does
not constitute racism (Augoustinos & Reynolds 2001, 4). But while it is important to differentiate between prejudices (biases) and racism, I argue that they
both are examples of racialization that are often entangled and interrelated
in everyday life. Such instances of racialization are detrimental to individuals'
wellbeing and happiness, in this case that of cross-border couples in Australia.

4 Cross-border Couples' Experiences with Everyday Racism

4.1 *Men's Experiences with Everyday Racism*
In this section, I focus on the racism encountered by fifteen migrant men in
Adelaide, with additional observations of the racism experienced by three men
living in Melbourne. I chose to also narrate the experiences of seven migrants
who did not practice marriage migration. It is my aim to illustrate how a general discomfort with male migrants (as perceived by my Africa-origin interlocutors) generates feelings of non-belonging among the migrant men in general,
and male marriage migrants in particular. It is through the exploration of such
feelings and experiences that I demonstrate how everyday racism affects the
imagined happy marriages and futures of male migrants.

The experience of racialization among migrants and minority groups in
Australia is an everyday reality. For example, a study by Greg Noble and Scott
Poynting (2010) conceptualizes racialized experiences of social marginal-
ization among Arab and Muslim Australians. The authors describe how the

global vilification of Muslims and Arabs underlies instances of everyday racism, of "everyday incivilities" (2010, 493). Noble and Poynting illustrate how Arab and Muslim Australians encounter subtle and not so subtle acts of racism daily, such as swearing, police harassment, certain glances and sexual threats. Furthermore, Noble (2005) illustrates how interviewees experienced what he calls "social incivility": "the everyday behaviors of others, mainly Anglo-Celtic Australians, that (Muslim) respondents often found rude and insulting, even as they dismissed their significance" (2005, 110). The sense of discomfort, of non-belonging, was often experienced through the senses: how people looked at Muslim migrants and how others treated them as nuisances (see also Sayad 1999).

Noble relates the idea of comfort, of recognition, to what Giddens (1990) calls ontological security, or "the confidence or trust we have in the world around us, both in terms of the things and the people with which we share our lives, and hence which provide stability and continuity to our identity" (Noble 2005, 113). Ontological security relates closely to being able to fit, the ability to be recognized, and as such to be recognized as belonging (Noble 2005, 114). As with the migrant men that were part of this study, Muslim migrants in Australia experienced the opposite of recognition, namely an inadequate existence, which challenged their status as social participants within society (Noble 2005, 115). Comfort, thus, seems to be essential for feeling belonging to a place, but it may not be easy to experience due to other people's performances.

According to Udah and Singh (2019, 844), Black African immigrants in Australia face significant stereotyping and exclusion in their everyday lives, as they argue that the "white nation fantasy still rejuvenates in contemporary Australian social landscape." Such othering influences feelings of belonging for the authors' interlocutors in a similar vein as my interlocutors reported. Being visually different, being Black in a predominantly and ideologically white Australia is what Udah and Singh describe as making their interlocutors feel like they are being "categorised and positioned as different" (2019, 850; see also Khan & Pedersen 2010). Such observations of othering and exclusion are also observed by Udah et al. (2019) in their study on Black African immigrants and job opportunities in Australia, as they describe that discrimination affects opportunities for meaningful employment, and therefore also negatively influences immigrants' sense of self, their ontological security.

Also, in the Australian media, as explained by Chivaura (2020), are Black African immigrants negatively portrayed, as reporting often focuses on the particular topics of crime, "refugee trouble," and disease. Such negative portrayals in the media relate to the public discourse on "deserving migrants" and the continuing debate on who or what migrant groups, are worthy of migrating to Australia. As Black African immigrants are generally thought of as refugees, they become subjects that are perceived as to be pitied, and simultaneously are expected to be grateful, to integrate, and to become invisible. However, media reports on crime and refugee issues are often not supportive of them. For instance, in the mid-2010s, a moral panic about so-called "African gangs" terrorizing the city center of Melbourne was introduced and invigorated by media, reporting on "African thugs" and "out of control African youth" (Gaffey 2019). Thus, although Black African immigrants only arrived relatively recently in Australia, their arrival has not been welcomed particularly warmly. It is this context in which migrant men (and their partners) had to try to settle and live their happily ever after.

Essed explains that those who are subject to everyday racism become experts in recognizing the cumulative patterning of everyday racism over time (1991, cited by Smith 2016, 8). Indeed, male migrant interlocutors reported suffering from stereotypes and racism—both subtle as well as openly expressed racism—on a daily basis. Men named numerous examples including: the avoidance of eye contact, not being offered a seat in public transport, job discrimination and being refused entry into clubs and bars. Furthermore, all men I spoke to had experiences with being identified as a refugee—something they all loathed. This was because, as one man stated, "Just because I am Black, Australian people think I am a refugee." Being assumed to be a refugee made men feel insulted, as they felt stereotyped and categorized. They became positioned in a narrative of vulnerability, with not much power ascribed. In this context, men's skin color made them into someone people feel sorry for.

From a conversation with five men and three women from African countries about work relationships, it became clear that background and skin color could cause uncomfortable workplace social relations. The men and women, all of them friends, were at the home of one of the men's parents in an Adelaide suburb. They had invited my partner Kassim and I was allowed to tag along. When I heard one of them joking about something "typically African," I became curious and asked the group in general about their experiences with prejudice and racism. One of the men, who worked at a mining site, said it was especially tough sometimes, as white colleagues kept on calling him "Crazy Monkey." He explained that while they all got along, and that his colleagues probably thought about it as "being just buddies—mates." to him it mattered, and he wished they would not say such things. But he did not want to say anything about it, as that would have turned the otherwise positive work environment sour.

Ramsay (2017) describes the practice of nicknaming based on racial thoughts as "mis-interpellation" a term coined by Ghassan Hage (2010), "in which contesting ideological forms of recognition and rejection are experienced as a basis of identity formation" (2017, 175). The man who was called Crazy Monkey was first recognized as "being one of the guys" and therefore given a nickname. Being granted a nickname indicates his belonging in the group, but the racist nature of the nickname turns the man into an other again, a racialized subject. According to Ramsay, Australia's multicultural policy conceals such everyday occurrences of racialization:

> Although whiteness is a primary basis from which exclusion and inclusion is mediated in Australia, hegemonic whiteness is often only implicitly reproduced and concealed through the contrary state-sponsored claim to multicultural cosmopolitanism that seeks to recognise and promote racial and cultural diversity.
>
> RAMSAY 2017, 175

Australia's claims of embracing multiculturalism, diversity and cosmopolitanism thus obscure everyday racism, while simultaneously "implicitly reinforcing colonial racialisations" (Ramsay 2017, 175).

In another instance, Geoffrey, a man in his early thirties, explained to me how he started dressing up in a smart manner in order for him to feel respected. One afternoon, we were sitting in the garden of his city rental apartment, where I had come to collect him and accompany him to his friends' theatre performance. Over a pre-event cup of coffee, we touched upon the topic of fashion. Geoffrey actually asked me to write the following down, as he insisted it was necessary to emphasize the subtlety of racialization. Geoffrey explained that he started to wear nice shirts when he realized that, "white people would not take me serious otherwise." He said this happened often to him, for instance, when he would be walking down the street, together with his girlfriend, in a T-shirt. When people approached them, or when they asked others for something, people would reply to her, and ignore Geoffrey. He felt that this happened

> because she is white, and I am Black. And with my Tee, I would just look like an imbecilic or something to them, not capable of anything. So, at one point I realized that if I wanted to be taken serious[ly], I should start dressing similar to them, or even more sophisticated.

He found this particularly disappointing and upsetting. As he lamented, it was only by "matching" Anglo-Europeans—and even by "actually overruling them" with even better attire—that "white people come to tolerate and accept you."

Through his comments, Geoffrey touched on an issue that many Africa-origin migrants brought up during my research. The issue was how migrant men were often compared with white men while simultaneously appearing as different and on another level compared to them. The mediation of this required, at times, an approach of visual assimilation that could often include efforts to flag refinement via a well-planned choice in clothing. Migrant men in Australia thus may strategize for them to be seen not just as African men, with a negative connotation, but as sophisticated men—by dressing even better than white men.

Jacob, on the other hand, said that he sometimes gets so tired of prejudices that he actually performs negative stereotypes, to "strike back," to keep control over the situation. He explained that when he would be walking on the street in the dark, he could see women cross the street to walk on the other side "so that they do not have to pass me and run the risk of getting harassed or their bags stolen." Jacob said that "to give them what they want, I sometimes scream and yell funny words, or make strange sounds, just to scare them."

African male bodies, in fact, were often seen as sites of pleasurable danger, instigating both arousal and fear. Throughout Anglo-European history, Black men have long been presented as inferior to white men, as uncivilized, highly sexualized and lustful, as objects, in order to underscore a narrative of white-supremacist patriarchy (Saint-Aubin 2005; Arnfred 2004; Hoch 1979). According to Frantz Fanon (1986, 177), people in Africa became Black when Europeans colonialized them, and not only did they get their color, but also their sexuality. Fanon explains that while we all know the sexual superiority of Black people is untrue, fear makes people believe it anyway. As such, race becomes, or has become, fetishized (see Ratele 2004). Also, in Australia, such colonial imaginaries inform racialization (Ramsay 2017, 177).

In Adelaide, and to a lesser extend Melbourne, Africa-origin males were objects to be kept at a distance while also serving as objects of intense interest and attraction. The dual elements of repulsion and attraction were apparent, for instance, in the ways in which white women showed interest in men in bars and nightclubs. "Hens nights"—also known as bachelorette parties—were particularly interesting events in this sense. At any Hens night that I have witnessed, migrant men were always a focus of attention by the women. One night, I went for drinks with friends, including two men from East African countries. At another table in the room a group of women were celebrating with the bride-to-be. I heard them whisper, "We have not yet got a photo with a sexy dark man." We were not even seated before they approached us and asked for a photograph with the men in our group. In another instance, a migrant

man was approached by a bride-to-be who asked him for a condom while he
was on a date with his partner.

It depended on the men in question whether this behavior was seen as
offensive. While some men argued that women treat all men like this and
would want a photo with all sorts of men during a Hens night, other men felt
offended as they believed they would not have been approached if they had
been white. And while some men experienced events like this as highly disturbing, other men used them as a way of being able to interact with a whole
group of women. Such instances indicate that migrant men were seen as exotic
others, as attractive objects. That men are only approached on a Hens night
may indicate the relative unease women would have on a normal night out. In
this way, a Hens night can be a liminal space in which one can behave alternatively to the normative cultural script.

It was not always overly visible to me, as a white woman, when instances
of racialization occurred. When going out with male interlocutors or friends,
for instance, I was often surprised by the amount of attention they received
from white women. However, men pointed out that white women would only
be interested in them because they were sitting with me, a white woman. If it
was just them by themselves, or with their Africa-origin friends, women would
show no interest. According to the men, the fact that I was sitting there showed
that "this particular African man is actually proper" as he would be capable
of having normal interaction with a white woman. My interlocutors felt this
would not be the case for a white man, who would not need to prove that he
is a good man.

The depicting of African men as hypersexual and unfaithful also became
clear from a conversation I had with Sarah. While having a cup of tea with
her at her home, she shared her recent dating experiences with me. She was
active in using a popular online dating app after her relationship had ended.[1]
She explained that she met "heaps of African men here, and I only swipe them
to the right, not the Aussie men." Sarah was in contact with two of them and
confided in me that one had come over last night. "But," she said, "They all have
wives or girlfriends, of course" and rolled her eyes. "This other guy ... we spent a
couple of nights together. All of a sudden, I get a call from this woman ... 'what

---

1   This dating app for smartphones works like this: a person interested in dating scrolls through
    profiles—containing photos of people, plus an optional short "about" text—and can swipe
    left or right. To swipe a person left means "not interested," to swipe right means "yes, inter-
    ested." If two persons swiped each other to the right, they have a "match" and can now start
    chatting. Although relationships do stem from apps of this type, they are better known for
    arranging "one-night stands."

I am doing with her man'? she asks me." "Of course," Sarah said, "I suspected he was with someone, because they always are!" Sarah's story indicates the perceived naturalness of African men's infidelity.

When I asked migrant men how they felt about being depicted as hypersexual, initial reactions were multiple, ranging from agreeing to seeing it as a compliment, to the rolling of eyes, clear annoyance and feeling aghast. Abid, a man in his early forties and married to an Adelaide woman for over ten years whom he met during his university years, elaborated on his experiences with everyday racism. While he came to Adelaide as a refugee, his experiences are also telling for male marriage migrants. Abid worked at a government-funded organization established to improve multiculturalism in South Australia. I met him at his office, where he invited me to talk about the experiences of African migrants in Australia, as well as his experiences of being in an intercultural relationship himself. He sat me down in the small kitchen of his workplace and made us a cup of tea. He explained that he used to go out a lot, when he was still a student. Back in those days, he said, there were fewer Africa-origin migrants and there used to be a "good spirit; people liked us." Then, with the coming of more migrants from the African continent, Abid felt things changed. He described how some men embraced the image of the hypersexual African man by "using that image, living that image!" while being very active in pursuing Australian women. Even though Abid was shaking his head and was clearly disapproving of such behavior, he grinningly admitted that he also had enjoyed the attention he and his friends received from women. However, the other men he referred to above were more aggressive. He felt that the actions of those men were part of the reason why African men were seen as "rude, that they are just there to chase girls." As an example, Abid told me about a recent experience, which occurred when he went to a bar with colleagues. One of his female co-workers had seen him chatting to a girl standing next to him while ordering drinks. She had assumed he was flirting with the girl. Abid wondered if she would have come to a similar conclusion if he were white, which he clearly doubted.

Some men explained that it was good that people imagined African men to be highly sexual and highly successful when it comes to love and sex. This was because it gave them a feeling of being on top, of winning a sexuality battle with white men. But like Abid, other men explained how they got tired of this stereotype, and that they often felt that women wanted to be with them or sleep with them just because they are African, without looking at them as a person. During the same conversation, Abid eloquently elaborated on stereotypes of African masculinities, and the way he felt they affected African men living in Australia, and African-Australian romantic relationships. Abid explained, with a serious tone of voice, that he was very aware of the stereo-types, and felt it was harmful for men to enjoy such stereotypes. He felt that "stereotypes and myths were created by white people and for very bad rea-sons." He could see how stereotypes could be useful when trying to impress women, but also how they could backfire. "On a larger level," he explained that "this stereotype makes ... some people avoid being with African men. A girl may be interested in a guy, but she may not want to act on this because of what society may think." As Abid further elaborated, migrant men may use the stereotypes, sometimes re-enact them, and by doing so negatively affect other men and intimate relationships. Indeed, while some female participants were clear about their preferences for African men, other women were very clear that they had no interest whatsoever in African men, exactly because of such stereotypes and behaviors.

To conclude, it became evident that instances of subtle and not-so-subtle acts of racialization were part of the everyday lives of migrant men. Such perceptions about African men and African male bodies negatively affected cross-border romantic connections. While couples had imagined or hoped for "smooth sailing" once in Australia, instances of racism and prejudice made their everyday lived realities not as positive, and countered their expectations. In the next section, I elaborate on how sponsoring women experienced life as a cross-border couple, and the accompanying racialization that took place. Such narratives emphasize how because of their relationships, women's social positioning shifted from rel-atively invisible, to highly visible; in a sense, they became an other themselves.

4.2   *Women's Experiences with Everyday Racism*

Through their relationships, sponsoring women's positioning within society changed from being included and accepted in Australia, where "assumptions of white sovereignty continue to be accepted and normalised" (Ramsay 2017, 172), to suddenly acquiring a mixed social status due to the otherness of their partners. Women in my study emphasized the racially based comments they received regarding their relationships from family, friends, acquaintances, and people encountered in everyday life. In Sophie's opinion, most of the ques-tions about her Africa-origin partner amounted to an inquiry about whether she could trust him or not. Other questions, most often posed by white women, included: "Is he faithful?"; "How is the sex?"; and "Does he have a huge penis?" White Australian men, by contrast, were apt to ask: "Is he a good man?" This lat-ter question sought to determine if the Africa-origin partner had a respectable job and/or if he was open about his finances and whereabouts. Both Australian men and women might also ask, with a thinly veiled meaning: "What visa is he on?" which implied that Africa-origin men may be primarily interested in getting married to obtain a more permanent visa.

Female interlocutors described the way that stereotypes about African men and presumptions about marriage migration made it difficult for them to trust their partners fully. When meeting for an after-work drink in the city, Charlotte told me that she always had negative voices in the back of her mind: "Maybe he is just using me for the visa; maybe he has lots of girlfriends back home; maybe I am too naïve to trust him." Even though she had known her husband for years, and they have lived together in his home country, she described how the stories about African men and the frequent separations of couples, post-marriage migration, made her doubt her ability to judge his character.

Comments and warnings about women's partners could thus plant doubts about their partners' sincerity in women's minds. In this way, women like Charlotte started to question how realistic their imagined happy futures together were. Also, Lillian, who had been married to her Africa-origin partner for over a decade, described how people had warned her about her partner. This affected her, especially in the early stages of their relationship, she told me, while imitating the rolling of eyes as expressions of concern and pity, which she had seen in the eyes of others, all those years ago. But while she knew "he was not like what people were thinking," she did test him, in a way. Her husband was a devout Catholic, and he insisted that their wedding would take place in a church. Even though Lillian was not Catholic herself, and had converted for him, for her, a Catholic church wedding was the ultimate sign of his seriousness about their relationship. As she explained, "If he would have wanted a quick wedding at the Town Hall, that would have shown that he would have other interests than being with me."

Women's relationships with "racial others" generated a shift in their visibility, observable through such everyday encounters as described above. That women felt they were suddenly visible, as well as held accountable, for their cross-border relationships illustrates that they had previously been fitting in with a hegemonic whiteness that had made them go unnoticed. Whiteness, according to Harrison:

> is a structural location that confers exclusive privilege, a standpoint from which to view and assess Self and Other, and a set of cultural practices that is usually unmarked, unnamed, and normatively given. This relative invisibility both enhances and is an effect of its dominance.
>
> HARRISON 1995, 63

Whiteness in itself is not a static category but instead "differentially shaped by and co-constructed with class, ethnicity, age, gender, and sexuality" (Frankenberg 1993, 233). Racial hierarchies and paradigms are fluid and ever shifting (Silverstein 2005). Groups that were previously seen as others can later be included in the white category, due to either the passing of time or as a way to further marginalize other minorities (Silverstein 2005; Palumbo-Liu 1999).[2] Ironically, for instance, Lillian, a second-generation Lebanese woman, similarly experienced the judgment of other people for being in a cross-border relationship and practicing marriage migration. She explained that when with her partner William, she was often treated as "white" while without him; she was "back to being a Leb." Emma also observed that while her family—and in particular her grandmother and her parents when they were younger—were perceived as outsiders because of their Mediterranean background, Emma felt she was being judged "as an Aussie for being with an African."

While there is a lack of studies on racism as experienced by white women in relationships with Black partners in Australia, there is some literature on the experiences of white mothers of mixed-parentage children (Britton 2013; Harman 2010; Rauktis et al. 2016; Twine 1997, 2010), although most studies are from a North American or British context with very few from an Australian perspective (Childs 2019). While these sources not necessarily focus specifically on the way that white women experience structures of whiteness because of their *intimate relationship* with a Black man, intimate relationships are covered to some extent. For instance, my observation that women's relationships made them feel *different* and made them navigate public spaces slightly more uncomfortably as they felt they experienced social disapproval, corresponds with Harman's work on lone white mothers of mixed-parentage children in the United Kingdom. As Harman (2010, 187) notes, "feeling different" is "an interesting juxtaposition to mainstream theories of whiteness where whiteness is equated with sameness (to a perceived invisible and privileged norm)." As is described by Frankenberg (1993) and Twine and Steinbugler (2006), through their intimate relationships with Black men, white women get to experience and develop "an acute awareness of the symbolic and material dimensions of racism" and "experience 'rebound racism' through encounters that are second-hand and diffuse, but still painful" (Twine and Steinbugler 2006, p. 343).

As the observations earlier in this section illustrate, women were perceived to be vulnerable, lonely, desperate for love, and craving attention. While

---

2   Within an Australian context, one can think of the position and shifting status of Greek, Italian, German, Yugoslavian and Vietnamese populations over time, as they have become more accepted, relative to newer immigrant populations.

women generally were described as naïve, there seemed to be a difference between younger women, who would choose an African partner to get attention from the outside world, especially with their "cappuccino babies" while the older women were seen as having African partners just to have some company. What both groups of women shared, however, was often a perceived desperation, and a need to rely on "the last resort" of choosing—or having to be with—an African man. Such observations are comparable to the questioning of cross-border couples in the Netherlands (Dragojlovic 2008) and Switzerland (Lavanchy 2014). In both countries, local women in such relationships were imagined to be naïve and in need of protection from other men (Dragojlovic 2008). Moreover, such treatment of women in cross-border relationships can be linked to the idea of "protecting the nation." In other words, because of "unfit women" potentially threatening men are entering the country (Lavanchy 2014, 15).

Such "rebound racism" (Twine and Steinbugler 2006) was also visible for women when in public spaces with their African-Australian children. Historically, white women have been considered "as guardians of the 'purity' of the population" and therefore "have faced criticism and censure when involved in relationships with men from minority ethnic backgrounds" (Barn & Harman 2013, 1268). Indeed, sometimes, other people's imaginaries made women feel as if their intimate relationships, and their children, were undesired, or unwelcome. To initiate a discussion, I decided to share my questions and thoughts about the general acceptability of women's relationships on a Facebook page for mothers of African-Australian children.[3] I wondered, I wrote, what reactions Australian women, with migrant partners, get regarding their relationships and children, and how it makes them feel. All thirteen women who responded said that most of the reactions they get from strangers are about their children and based on their children's dual heritage. Most women found that generally, comments were positive, or simply ignorant and therefore not necessarily harmful. Simultaneously however, all women did have experiences with openly racist encounters. While some women took such experiences personally, and sometimes got extremely upset about them, other women said they did not care about such experiences, but figured they were just part of life.

---

3   The purpose of the group was for mothers to share tips and advice on how to handle the curly hair of their children, what products to use, to share African recipes, etc. However, that there is a special group on Facebook used by Australian (and a few Africa-origin) women with African-Australian children, may actually reveal their uniqueness, or standing out of their normative surroundings.

In general, women in this discussion group felt that most people react because they see something different and need some explanations for it to make sense.

It seemed to depend on the individual whether questions about where their child comes from were experienced as offensive. Some women in the Facebook discussion group remembered they had laughed about the question, "where did you get your baby from?," which would have implied an assumption of adoption, whereas other women felt this was a highly inappropriate question. But almost all women had experienced strangers referring to their babies as "it": "where did you get *it* from?," which made all of the women furious. While all of the women had developed their own boundaries of accepted behavior and questions, referring to their child as *it* was generally too much to bear. There is a fine line between racism, and curiosity and ignorance, it seemed, and this line was sometimes an obvious one. While some women would respond to negative comments by ignoring such rude strangers, others gave examples of how they would retort with sharp and insulting comments.

The perceived otherness of African-Australian babies was remarkable. On the one hand, women indicated that they experienced clear disgust from strangers when noticing their babies. On the other hand, however, babies were perceived as extremely cute, much cuter than other babies. One day, as I was having lunch with a friend from an East African country, I was holding her two-month-old son for a cuddle. Seated next to us were two white women in their mid-sixties who could not hide their joy at the sight of the child in my arms. One of them stood up and came to me, explaining she thought this baby was so cute and asked if she could take a photo for her daughter, who had worked in a nursery in Africa and wanted a "cappuccino baby" herself. When I answered that actually my friend was the proud mother, the woman acted as though she was surprised, and went to ask her. From her facial expression, I could tell that it was either less scary to ask me—a fellow white woman—than an African woman or, that she was a bit disappointed that it was not a white mother with a brown baby. I had a strong sense that both of my feelings were right. And while my response to the woman was terse, my friend reacted kindly and said she did not have any problems with her taking a photo. Later, my friend told me she did not know what to say; she wanted to say no, but she also did not want to be unfriendly or give the women a "bad feeling." She wondered, however, how white people would react when strangers wanted to take photos of their babies.

In another instance, one of the interlocutors who had a child with her Africa-origin partner was asked if her son could be in a photo for an advertisement for the local swimming school where she and her husband took their son each week. But, they did not want her, the mother, to be in the photo; they explicitly asked for the boy's dad to be in the pool with their son, with the other children and parents. While she was fine with it, and so was her partner, she did laugh about the occurrence, suggesting that who knows, maybe they just wanted "an African baby and daddy" in the photo shoot. While the intention may have been to be inclusive, it is interesting to see how uncomfortable situations can become when multiple races or cultures are part of a scene. The swimming pool manager may have wanted a dad in between all the mothers present, or they may have wanted to reflect Australia's multicultural society in their advertisement. But simultaneously, the first question that came to her mind was, "Why them? Because they are Black?"

Navigating instances of racialization—whether relatively subtle or innocent as in the swimming pool case or blatantly harmful as in the sometimes outright disapproval of children—had become part of the daily routine for women in cross-border relationships. Women (except for Lillian and Emma, with Middle Eastern and Mediterranean backgrounds respectively) had never felt this visible; they identified a clear difference between being with their partners and/or children and being without them. The visibility of couples and their children, the constant "being in the spotlight" had both surprised and affected women negatively. While women had hoped for a mundane yet happy and romantic family life, they now felt their relationships were exposed, scrutinized and questioned. But not only in public spheres were women and couples the subject of scrutiny. As the next section illustrates, the female partners' Australian families also influenced the happiness of couples' migration journeys.

4.3   *Couples and Australian Relatives*
From what my interlocutors said, amidst a general distrust, stemming from institutional as well as everyday racism, their Australian families sometimes had difficulties navigating cross-border relationships. Family members had mixed feelings about their intimate relationships. This in turn influenced partners' sense of togetherness and belonging, and as a result negatively affected the experience of their relationships. While partners had hoped for happy relationships once in Australia, relatives could obstruct such romantic imaginings.

While in all cases there was at least one family member opposing the relationship, in general, both partners described their Australian family as welcoming. Simultaneously, couples felt that an awkwardness was often palpable. Some sponsoring women recalled how their mothers "simply adored" their partner, and "treated him as her son from the moment she first met him." Often, women would underscore this after break-ups occurred, seemingly to emphasize how awful and painful the break-up was—not only for women themselves, but also for their families. It seemed that generally the women's parents were accepting of their migrant sons-in-laws, although in the beginning it may have been difficult to get used to them, being "so different". One parent explained to me that it was hard for her sometimes, to speak openly when her new African son-in-law was around, as she was overly concerned about what to say and what kind of jokes would be appropriate. She did not feel she was racist, did not want to come across as such, and thus sometimes overthought what she should or should not say. For other parents, however, that their daughter's partner came from an African county was not an issue. Some of them showed their interest by contributing financially to the education of nephews and nieces back home. A select number of parents even joined their daughters and in-laws for holidays in Africa.

Almost all the women in my study explained that their intimate relationships made them lose at least one friend or relationship with a family member, either for a period of time or for good. Women were surprised to see that sometimes people who were closest to them turned out to be the least accepting of their relationships. Sometimes their partners were simply not welcome in women's social circles. Lillian, for instance, was on bad terms with a cousin who only invited her, and not her husband William, to her wedding. Kevin and Natalie were on particularly bad terms with her parents. Natalie had contacted me through the Facebook page for African-Australian children's mothers, showing her interest in an interview. She also lived in Adelaide and invited me for lunch one Sunday. Kevin and Natalie had met each other—now over twenty years ago—at a mutual friend's house-warming party. He was an international student at that time, and they were inseparable from that moment on. Eventually, they applied for a Partner visa onshore. But her parents never accepted him as part of the family, and after many years of trying to make things work between the parents and the couple, Natalie and Kevin gave up. Even now, Kevin felt very sorry for Natalie, especially around holiday periods, as he says it is because of him that she cannot spend Christmas with her parents.

But more often, family members had expressed concerns about intimate relationships that were sometimes well meant, but simultaneously borderline racist. Sophie and Naomi, who at the time of my research were both in the midst of the visa application process, explained to me that their parents had had difficulties trusting their new partners because of what had happened in the past. Both Sophie and Naomi had sponsored men from the African continent before, and both ex-husbands had turned out to be less loving and trustworthy than they appeared to be in the beginning. Back then, their parents had welcomed the husbands with open arms, and treated them like sons. That they turned out to be bad husbands, who both women suspect married them only for the visa, was a devastating experience not only for them, but for their parents too. Now, their daughters had fallen in love with yet another African man. The parents could not understand why their daughters would want to go through the same hardship again. How could they give away their hearts to another African man? Did they not learn anything? Both women explained that their ex-husbands had ruined their parents' trust in African men. As such, they had great difficulties accepting their daughters' new relationships, and opening up to get to know the new men in their lives.

It may be that the families' experiences had shown that particular migrant ex-partners were not to be trusted. At the same time, it seemed that parents were anxious about their daughters marrying a foreigner as it inherently meant starting a new visa procedure, arranging the migration and having to set everything up for this person. International love is a huge project, financially as well as emotionally, and I suspect that parents preferred to keep things easy and running smoothly for their daughters. Furthermore, both women recalled the disarray they were in when they separated from their first husbands; it had taken them years to get over the feelings of pain and betrayal. Parents had seen clearly how devastated their daughters had been and as a result, it seemed very hard for them to trust a new African man. For the parents of one of these women, it took months, but they eventually did accept the new husband. For the other parents, they were still not ready to open their arms to their daughter's new husband.

The Australian family's opinion about the relationship mattered to both partners. When talking with migrant men, especially, the in-laws were a much-discussed topic. Contact with the Australian family was regular, as all of them lived in Australia, almost always in the same city, and everyone spoke English. Almost all men cared about their relationship with their new family, especially since the journey of marriage migration meant they were far removed from their own families. Many men recalled how welcoming their partner's parents were or had been, especially in the beginning when they first arrived and did not know many people. Fathers would take them on fishing trips or teach them about the *barbie*,[4] and as families they would go for a hike or on a camping trip. For those men who got along well with their in-laws, break-ups caused additional sadness as it also meant not being part of that family anymore. Daniel recalled how he had not seen is ex-partner's mother again since the separation,

---

4   *The barbie* is Australian slang for barbecue. Amongst other things such as the tool shed and the surfboard, the barbecue is a tool inherently related to Australian masculinity (see further in Hibbins & Pease 2009).

which was causing him pain and guilt. He had felt that her mother had been "like a mother to me." He would visit her at least once a week to help her with errands around the house, do shopping for her, or just for a cup of coffee. He felt that "she had to get used to me first, because she was not used to Black people, but soon we were like best friends."

Like Daniel, some men felt apologetic towards their in-laws about their break-up. However, in three cases, men stated that the in-laws were the very reason for their divorce. Elijah, for instance, had nothing positive to say about his in-laws. He explained to me that his ex-partner's parents would always disparage him, telling her that he was no good, not good enough for her, and eventually making their daughter think the same about him. Similarly, Jacob had bad experiences with his previous in-laws. According to him, his now ex-wife had been too attached to her parents and the three of them never made space for him. This made him feel even more of an outsider, him alone against her and her family. He also told me about an incident where he said that his father-in-law invaded his privacy. Apparently, one day while his wife had been at work, Jacob was bored and decided to smoke some marijuana in the back-yard. He emphasized that, because he was sitting at home every day, all by himself, he felt like smoking, which he claimed he would not do if he had a job. On that particular day, whilst sitting outside, he saw the female neighbors in the adjacent yard and he invited them over. Suddenly, he went on to tell me, his father-in-law arrived. Jacob was now using wild arm gestures to indicate the scope of the situation. "He caught me by surprise!," Jacob exclaimed. "I did not hear him coming!" What bothered Jacob is that while his father-in-law had promised not to tell other members of the family, without Jacob asking him to do this, his father-in-law told his wife, who then told their daughter. Jacob said that this incident had disappointed him. From that moment, he said he "never really wanted to see her parents anymore; so my wife had to go by herself," if she wanted to visit them.

It appears that cross-border relationships often produced tensions within family dynamics, albeit to various extents. While most family members were not opposed to cross-border relationships, and most in fact were supportive, interactions could be tense and uncomfortable. Such instances are compara-ble to "hopeful intercultural encounters" as discussed by Amanda Wise (2005). She describes the complicated nature of actually "doing" everyday multicultur-alism on a micro level in a Sydney suburb. While exploring the complexity of multiculturalism as "place-sharing, of cross-cultural interaction, or multicul-turalism of inhabitance," Wise vividly illustrates the struggles and disjunctures that inhabitants of the suburb navigate (2005, 171). It is these navigations she calls "hopeful intercultural encounters" (Wise 2005, 171).

Wise illustrates how changes in the multicultural composition of a location can cause a sense of unfamiliarity with the specific social field, a "rupture in the locality and forms of sociality" that were once familiar to residents (2005, 176).[5] Inhabitants feel that because of "invading others," they are lost in a place that was once comfortable to them and they no longer possess the "bodily habitual knowledge to reproduce [the neighborhood] as a locality for themselves" (ibid.). Still, Wise calls encounters "hopeful," as her ethnography reveals that even though inhabitants of the suburb struggle with difference—the "everyday togetherness-in-difference" (Ang 2001), or the "multicultural *real*" (Hage 1998)—they nevertheless possess a shared sense of hopefulness for belonging within the difference. In a similar vein, my data suggests that on the micro level of the family, the "Africanness" (difference) of the migrant partner was a reason for discomfort and tensions in an otherwise familiar locality. Because of this Africanness, the welcoming of the partner was either grander or minimal, the betrayal of the break-up became more scandalous, and Australian women had become more conscious about their parents' attitude towards their partners. In turn, such instances of racialization negatively affected couples' wellbeing. But it was not only Australian families that were uncomfortable with cross-border couples; African relatives, also, expressed concerns and uneasiness.

4.4 *Couples and their African Relatives*

When I asked migrant men what their relatives thought of their relationship with their sponsoring partners or ex-partners, men's initial responses were that they absolutely did not have any problems whatsoever with their cross-border relationships.[6] When I asked the men to elaborate, however, prejudices became palpable. Some men explained that at the beginning of their relationships, relatives raised concerns. "White women" would be "too controlling," would emasculate men by forcing them to do household tasks, and would be "crazy and wild." Moreover, it was feared that women would limit contact, and would not know anything about their culture. I also heard that some men had been called traitors for being with a white woman, that white women would have a "cold vagina" meaning that they would be cold-hearted, strict and impassionate. Lastly, men would be warned that the high level of divorce rates

---

5   Inhabitants for instance feel they are not welcome in the new Chinese supermarkets, as the shops are darker than they are used to, use Mandarin advertisements, and do not know how to interact with new neighbors from a different ethnic background.

6   None of the couples' African relatives lived in Australia. While contact with them was not necessarily less frequent or intense, it was certainly different to that with the Australian family due to the geographical distance.

in Anglo-European countries meant that such relationships were of high risk, and that "western people marry for [temporary] contracts." Yet none of the men reported having lost friends or connections with relatives because of their cross-border relationships.

According to Ethan, an East African friend living in Melbourne, and with a passion for my research topic, African families were more strongly affected by the journeys of marriage migration than were the Australian families. One evening, over a glass of red wine at his house he explained that marrying a white woman may not necessarily be a bad thing, but it does imply a break with traditions and family structuring. He emphasized how in many places in Africa, marriage concerns families instead of individuals, and requires dowries and other negotiations between the two families involved. Ethan explained that "intercultural marriages do not fit in this traditional framework," as families would be unfamiliar with each other and with their respective traditions. He went on to say (and other male interlocutors generally agreed) that though exogamous marriages may be disappointing to some relatives, there seems to be a general understanding and acceptance that traditions are impossible to keep in place when marrying a foreigner. Thus, while African families had to part with not only their sons and brothers, but also with certain marriage traditions, Australian families did not share such experiences of loss.

It seemed that bending or departing from marriage traditions had much to do with class positions as well as geo-political circumstances and power relations. Indeed, while marrying an Anglo-European woman meant there was the disappointment due to his relocation to Australia, but it often also meant upward social mobility for the men and their families. In 2011, I conducted fieldwork on cross-border relationships among European women and Zanzibari men from lower socioeconomic backgrounds in Zanzibar. There, it became clear that members of the society first scolded men who chose to marry European women, who chose to "marry out." Their ways of meeting up with foreign women on the tourist beaches of the otherwise deeply religious Zanzibar often involved drinking alcohol, using drugs, and pre- and extra-marital sex. However, the moment they "succeeded" and married a European woman, their status changed from being an outlaw to an established man. Maybe their families still did not agree with how they had obtained a partner, but now the men had become the main providers for their families and were suddenly wealthier than other men. This wealth came with power and status, and family members had no other choice than to respect these men for making possible things that otherwise would not have been dreamt of, like sending siblings, nieces and nephews to private schools and being able to afford better medical care for family members who got sick.

None of the migrant men who were or had been in relationships with Australian women would apply this to their own situation and this seemed to at least partly stem from a fear of being labelled as insincere and a bad husband— one who would marry for money and status instead of love. However, more generally, many agreed that power relations had shifted. As will be described in the next chapter, which focuses specifically on migrant men's experiences with marriage migration, all but one of the men came from lower socioeconomic backgrounds and all of them kept sending home as many remittances as they could, to meet the ever-increasing pressure of demands. It was not their relationship per se that increased their power, but the fact that through their relationship men migrated and were granted permanent residency in Australia, which increased their (socioeconomic) position of power within their families. Such observations, however, assumedly would not completely mirror experiences of migrant men from middle or upper-class backgrounds.

Older and conservative Africa-origin migrants who did not practice marriage migration, and with whom I had informal conversations about marriage, elaborated at length on the many deeply rooted cultural traditions surrounding their marriage practices.[7] But while it would be expected that marriage migration and cross-border relationships turn family structures and traditions upside down, migrant men married to sponsoring women did not necessarily give me this impression. Male marriage migrants as well as other migrants, acknowledged that upholding traditions may be the ideal situation, but it was often not very realistic.[8] For instance, participants told me that while ideally a dowry was organized when a couple were married, this often did not happen, due to the families' inability to afford such practices. Furthermore, as I pointed out in Chapter 3, literature on intimacy in African localities shows how younger generations (but also throughout history) choose to marry for love rather than family obligations (for example, see Cole & Thomas 2009; Spronk 2006). Young Africans would be looking for partnership, compatibility, and passion, rather than for marriages arranged by their family members and for reasons other than love. And this is what all the migrant men I interviewed did: they chose their partners themselves and the main reason, they argued, was a desire for love and intimacy.

---

7   Literature on marriage on the continent of Africa emphasizes the lively traditions of arranged marriages, negotiations, dowries, and formal festivities on multiple wedding days (see for instance Hunter 2016; Solivetti 1994; Stiles 2005).

8   Tradition, of course, is not something static but rather, is a dynamic construct influenced in diverse ways. For instance, see Bochow and van Dijk (2012) on the influence of Pentecostalism on traditional marriage systems in African contexts.

While some families may have preferred a local marriage, there seemed to be a general understanding that the power of globalization changes marriage patterns. Gerald, an older man who came to Australia as a student and obtained residency through a relationship with a sponsoring partner claimed that "before, in the old days, people only married within their region. But later people started marrying people from other parts of the country, and that is an intercultural marriage, too!" Gerald enthusiastically summed up examples from his home country where people from different ethnic groups intermarried. In his tiny kitchen, he was busy cooking, and used a loud voice to make himself heard over the sizzling pans of meat, rice, and vegetables that he later presented to me as his local food. Gerald continued to explain that, "if you are from the south and you marry a girl from the north, you do not know her language, her religion, her staple [foods] and her customs." Gerald felt that cross-border marriages, whether inter-ethnic or international, are a "normal and unstoppable development" resulting from improved infrastructure and globalization.

Cross-border relationships transformed families into transnational families. From the perspective of back home, men told me that this was often regretted. Migrants started families in Australia and children were raised as Australians. Even though all couples focused on and celebrated their children's African heritage, the Australian context made them as Australian as their school classmates. While some parents sometimes took children on holidays to their father's country of origin, read them African stories and children's books, let them taste region specific food and took them to African-themed events, children often did not speak their father's language, and had little understanding of specific norms and customs. The regret for the family back home was that they were increasingly unable to connect with new members of the family, and ties with their son's Australian family were becoming less tangible.

As I described in Chapter 3, women generally preferred Australia for its comfortable living, safety and schooling system, and because of closeness to their Australian families. While many women had either lived in or travelled to their partner's home country, and had met his family, all but one of the women did not see relocating there as a good or realistic option. Migrant partners agreed that Australia was the best option for living, even though they might still hold dreams of building a house back home and perhaps even retiring there. For women, perceived cultural differences installed a sense of fear of feeling isolated. One woman, a mother of two who had visited her partner's home a few times, explained to me that she did not feel at ease when she visited his parents, as she did not speak the language, and thus could not communicate with anyone. When I asked her why she did not learn the language, she explained that it was too difficult. Also, the "practical stuff" was difficult for her. For instance, she was unfamiliar with the ways of cooking and cleaning, which made her feel reluctant and too uncomfortable to attempt to participate. Many women shared such feelings of unease towards their partner's or ex-partner's family and home country.[9] Simultaneously, however, most women underscored the importance of regular contact, and most agreed that they as a couple should help to support the family financially.

The discomfort women experienced when visiting the home countries of their partners helps to explain women's hesitation with moving there permanently. The language, culture, customs—almost everything—were considered different and therefore uncomfortable. It was a place that women generally did not prefer to be in and therefore did not want to visit often. In a similar vein, encounters with African community organizations in Australia also caused a sense of ill ease among women. While African community organizations were mostly happy and pleasurable places for most migrant men, they often caused strains on cross-border relationships. I will turn to such experiences in the next section.

4.5   African Communities in Australia and Everyday Racism

There are many different African community organizations in Australia, most of them country specific, and ethnicity specific for larger and/or more pluralist African countries. Such organizations provide various kinds of support for migrants, and can function as a surrogate family, as a "home away from home." The committees of such organizations make sure to organize social events on country-specific public holidays, or at least occasionally, to keep communities connected. While relatively many men attended community events as often as possible to experience a sense of belonging, a few men were not that interested as they felt that such communities acted as agents of unnecessary social control, were "narrow minded." or simply uninteresting. Nevertheless, most couples crossed paths with their country-specific African community regularly.

One of the main reasons that African community organizations caused discomfort among sponsoring women was because they directly challenged the authority and taken-for-granted-ness of whiteness in Australia. It seemed that in a generally white Australian context, with their partner's family far away on the other side of the world, their migrant partner would act in similar ways to them, and women would feel comfortable in the setting. However, at an African

---

9   Other reasons given for this unease were: the food would be bad, the country would be too poor and too busy, and it would be boring since women did not speak the language.

community function, the presence and influence of fellow migrants from the same home country seemed to remind women of the otherness of their partner. Eileen, over our long lunch in a café in a Melbourne suburb, explained this to me. In the community setting, her partner would wander off with other men, chatting and joking in an unfamiliar language, while she would be left with women she barely knew and whom she could not understand. She experienced these events as "hard work," where she had to keep on smiling while getting grumpier by the minute as she became more and more self-conscious and feeling more and more out of place. She recalled how especially during the first years of their relationship, she had to get used to the fact that in this setting, her partner felt most at ease while she was very tense and felt that it was difficult for her to be understood.

Women often perceived these community events as places where they were not readily accepted, and where they were judged as not being good enough. Women said they initially felt that they had achieved a great milestone to be invited to events, as they thought it meant they were being considered as good partners in serious relationships. However, once they began taking part, the women experienced problems with group dynamics, with language, gossip and judgements, and a general feeling of being out of place. When one day I went grocery shopping at the Adelaide markets, I met Emma. She asked me how my research was going, and I told her I was writing about African community organizations. She sighed and elaborated on her experiences. While Emma had been married to her partner for over 15 years, she told me that in the first years of their marriage, she felt that women in his community made things particularly difficult for her. She recounted that she felt they were judging her for not being involved enough, for not knowing the language and for not cooking food in the correct ways. She felt that the women were "harsher because I am Australian." After a few years Emma said that things got easier, but that she still "does not really look forward to community events."

It seemed to the women, that the various community organizations acted as gatekeepers and set the boundaries of group belonging. It was clear to the women that they would perhaps never be able to fully cross those boundaries. Interestingly, none of the migrant men viewed their communities as scrutinizing their relationship choices. Like Emma, Charlotte felt she was only accepted by the community eventually, after she had shown herself to be a good partner by remaining with him for a number of years. Both Charlotte and Emma felt that women who persist in their relationship, who show their good intensions and efforts and who can demonstrate they are good women and wives will eventually be accepted as members of the community. However, women whose relationships had ended often felt they were not welcome in the community without their partner, indicating to them that they never really belonged in this African sphere in the first place.

Sponsoring women felt that it was less likely for them to be considered a good partner, than it would be for women with an African background, and often felt more judged by African women than men. Alice, who had met her ex-partner in Adelaide where he was studying to become a nurse, had found it difficult to get along with women in her now ex-partner's community organization. They had been together for just over a year and had been preparing for their application for a Partner visa, as his student visa was due to expire. Unfortunately, their plans did not eventuate as they had drifted apart as romantic partners. At the time, Alice said that she had felt that she had nothing in common with women in the community. She felt that she was "not as submissive as they are; I do not like all that women's stuff." While she emphasized she did do "lots of housework" and cooked, she also liked to "hang out and drink beer, instead of just being in the kitchen the whole day."

From such accounts, it became apparent that some female partners had the sense of being judged based on their own presumptions about African gender scripts.[10] Women felt insecure, as they could not meet what they thought were the conditions of being a good partner, that they felt were being imposed upon them by the partners of other migrant men. It is unclear to me whether these other female partners may have had such intentions. But the visible joy migrant men experienced during social events with others from their home country clearly indicated that men were at ease with other Africa-origin migrants. Not only did men seem to have their closest friends there, they could also enjoy such things as their "own" food and their "own" music. Sponsoring partners sometimes read this enjoyment as their partners being more comfortable with people, including women, from their home country, than with them in their own household. African communities, and in particular their female members, seemed to have the ability to form a threat to Australian women, and as a result, to couples' wellbeing.

That sponsoring women felt threatened by female members of African community organizations, along with the difficulties they had in participating in these groups made the women feel uncomfortable; in these community contexts the women's otherwise unquestionable white hegemonic position had now disappeared. African community organizations turned the women's hegemonic position upside down; they had become the minority, which also

---

10   That sponsoring women mainly complained about other women may also be due to the gendered scripts of such community-led events where men mainly mingled with other men, and women shared most interaction with other women.

made them feel uncomfortable. As a response to such a distressing position, women, like Alice above, started to categorize and stereotype. Harrison (1995, 63) argues that the "cultural dominance of whiteness" cannot be challenged and quotes from Ruth Frankenburg (1993): "In times of perceived threat, the normative group may well attempt to reassert its normativity by asserting elements of its cultural practice more explicitly and exclusively." Women such as Alice and Emma, when questioning or commenting on gender roles, seemed to try to emphasize the legitimacy of their own cultural gendered practices.

Cross-border relationships were not always welcomed with open arms. When talking to other Africa-origin migrants about cross-border relationships, I sometimes noticed distrust and feelings of ambivalence related to moral perceptions of intimate relationships. Often, when talking about my research, the topic of sham marriages came up. It seemed to be common knowledge that international students, for instance, use marriage to an Australian as a way of gaining permanent residency.[11] Furthermore, it appeared to be a well-known fact that "desperate Australian women" would go to Africa and bring back a husband, or find their Africa-origin partner on dating sites. According to this perception, these migrant partners would be separated as soon as they gained their permanent residency. This stereotype of Anglo-European women in insincere relationships may be the backdrop against which sponsoring women in relationships with migrant men were measured. However, it seemed that although women, as outsiders, felt judged by members of African community organizations, it might have actually been the cross-border relationships that were being scrutinized. Such interactions with African community organizations, like everyday encounters with strangers and relatives in Adelaide and Melbourne, indicated a general questioning of the genuineness of cross-border couples practicing marriage migration.

5   Conclusion

This chapter focused on the ways in which everyday racism and prejudice obstructed couples' wish to live a happy life after marriage migration to Australia. Instances of racialization were entrenched in everyday lives and were encountered in many ordinary situations. The discomfort that couples, family members and strangers experienced because of the interracial

---

11   During fieldwork, photos and videos were being shared on social media, depicting much older and/or obese white women with exceptionally handsome young black men, with captions like "it's visa time again."

character of the relationships led to feelings of non-belonging among partners. Interlocutors were particularly confronted with whiteness and the effects of their defiance from this norm. The consequences of whiteness and racialization among migrants are well-documented (Noble 2005; Wise 2005; Noble and Poynting 2010; Ramsay 2017). Such studies reinforce the experiences of my male interlocutors. This chapter demonstrated that because of their cross-border relationships, sponsoring women encountered an unexpected and uncomfortable visibility, as well as acts of racialization. Such observations concur with Allen's observation that "as white women's public identities and affiliations may change, negative assumptions about their character, morality, sexuality and mental health status are made by family, friends and strangers" (2019, 132). And as couples, both partners felt non-belonging and judgements in numerous contexts in which they were involved, including family life and social groups.

The data presented above demonstrates a blurry line between everyday racism and everyday prejudice. Generally speaking, "prejudice or related terms refer to negative attitudes or behaviors towards a person because of his or her membership to a particular group" (Augoustinos & Reynolds 2001, 2). Traditionally, the term prejudice had a value dimension, describing it as bad, unjustified, or irrational. More recently, however, scholars use more neutral terms to define prejudice as bias, or ingroup favoritism (Augoustinos & Reynolds 2001). It is this sense of ingroup favoritism that we see in both the Australian women's experiences of otherness when they are seen in public with their migrant partner *as well as* their experiences of feeling like outsiders when they struggle to fit into the normative sociality of African community organizations.

The notion of everyday prejudice is also significant because, as described, there is a sense of protectionism at work among the family and community members who are associated with the intimate couples. This protectionism results from concerns for wellbeing that stem from fears stoked by stories heard and prejudices displayed elsewhere. At the same time, these well-meaning concerns and prejudices are also fueled by everyday racism. This became evident for instance when women were warned for being with African men, both to protect the women, as well as to "protect the nation" (Lavanchy 2014) from "other men" (Dragojlovic 2008). Such narratives highlight that while prejudices, regarded as bias and stereotypes, need to be differentiated from racism as the latter involves power dynamics, in people's everyday lives; the two terms are not easily distinguishable and often interrelated. Cognitive processes that underlie prejudice can partly derive from sociohistorical ideas and ideologies about race and culture.

For cross-border couples, marginalization in everyday life was yet another unanticipated obstruction that made couples' lives together less happy than they had previously imagined. Not only did couples experience institutional racism when applying for a Partner visa (as described in the previous chapter), everyday racism and prejudices experienced in their everyday lives also negatively influenced couples. There is the potential for such social obstacles to affect the interpersonal and intimate connection between partners. This is considered further in the two chapters to come, which describe the ways in which the journey of marriage migration has an insidious effect on romantic imaginaries of happy relationships. Both men and women experienced their intimate relationships as disappointing, rather than the optimistic happily ever after they had anticipated. Such disappointments were often related to ideas surrounding masculinity and femininity—constructs severely affected by migration journeys. Sponsoring women's disappointing realities will be illustrated in Chapter 7. But first, the next chapter describes how migrant men were affected by the migration journey, which influenced their ability to be good and happy husbands.

Migrant Men and Intimate Relationships

1   Introduction

This chapter describes how while migrant men had expected their lives in Australia and with their partner to be good, comfortable, and happy, life in Australia turned out to be unexpectedly hard. The chapter is specifically concerned with the ways in which male marriage migrants tried to make sense of their extremely complex and unstable position of conjugality in a not yet established context. The everyday lived experiences in Australia turned out to be very different from what they expected and had imagined, and undermined their sense of what it means to be a man and a husband. Intercultural relationships magnified the hardships faced within the already difficult context of migration. Gender roles and power balances changed and became unequal through the process of marriage migration, which bestowed unforeseen power on Australian spouses.

In what follows, I elaborate on various themes to draw a common narrative among the male migrant interlocutors. First, I turn my attention to the gendered expectations men had of the relationship with their Australian partners. Then, I turn to the experiences of male marriage migrants regarding sociality, work and finances, and class in relation to marriage migration. Finally, I elaborate on the ways men experienced their Australian partners as too controlling, and the strategies they used to counter such perceived emasculation. Before I turn to the empirical part of the chapter, I provide a model of masculinities that frames my discussion on men's sense of self. Of specific importance is the work of Esther Gallo (2006) on marriage and masculinity among Malayali male migrants in Italy, and that of Katherine Charsley (2005) on "unhappy husbands" a term she coined to describe Pakistani marriage migrants in the United Kingdom. Both authors describe how men perceive marriage migration as an ambiguous practice, severely affecting their sense of self.

The model of unhappy husbands serves as a blueprint for this chapter. Like Charsley's participants, male marriage migrants were often not prepared for the difficulties they faced in Australia, which were often related to cultural, social and economic factors. Below, I illustrate the ways in which marriage migration to Australia turned men into unhappy husbands/partners. This is important since often migrant men are seen as marrying for visa purposes instead of romantic reasons, and often men's experiences with marriage migration are overlooked as a possible factor in explaining relationship breakdown.

I begin by drawing on Liam's narrative after being in Adelaide for almost one year. Liam encountered particularly hard times about halfway through my research. We met each other every week for a few months, and each time he poured his heart out. He was happy he could finally share his worries and problems with someone, as he otherwise felt extremely isolated in Adelaide. This fragment comprises our conversations over a few weeks' time. Liam's situation—common for the men I interviewed—sums up the many ways in which the journey of marriage migration is experienced as unexpectedly difficult, not as happy as imagined.

2   Looking for Happiness, Finding Sadness

For Liam, the move to Australia has been rather unsettling. In fact, the move has been highly disturbing in so many ways, and quite unexpectedly. Prior to migration, the prospect of moving to Australia seemed to be exciting and with the opportunity to improve his lifestyle significantly (after all, "anything is possible in the West! The things you can do! The house you will be living in! The places you can go!"). But being there, it seemed like a rather depressing place: it is quiet, there are few people on the street, especially in the evening when people are supposed to come outside. And while he wants to explore the city center, nightlife, shops and the whole area, his wife suddenly is not interested in going for a dance or going out much at all.

He does not have a job and so not only are the days very long, but also, he does not make any money. Not having money is very worrying, as he wanted to keep on providing for his family back home: people are depending on him, and he feels the pressure getting more intense as the weeks pass. It has now been almost a year without a job; how can he justify this to his family back home? Also, he does not particularly feel like a good husband. He cannot surprise his wife with a gift, help her pay a bill or get the groceries. Basically, he does nothing, for anyone. It is a stressful situation, and with days that long, he just cannot help but want to drink a beer and smoke a cigarette to ease his mind.

Liam feels that since he is not adding anything to their marriage, he must listen to his wife and do what she is telling him, as otherwise he looks ungrateful. But it is not that he is ungrateful; he just does not feel very well lately. Getting out of bed in the morning has been really difficult. After all, there is no job to go to, and what is the point of waking up early when there is yet another day of nothing ahead? The longer he feels he is this useless, the more he worries, it seems. Some marijuana will make him feel more relaxed.

He did meet some other Africa-origin men the other day. He was walking on the street to go to the shop when someone shouted something to him. It turned out that they were from the same region as him! They will be going to the city this weekend and they asked him to join them. He was very excited about it: finally, he made some friends of his own! But when he got home and told the happy news to his wife, she responded in a cold way, saying that he did not even know them, and he did not have any money to buy beer, and apparently, they were to go to a dinner with her family anyway on the day concerned. He will tell the men that he cannot come with them. What a silly thing to do: to set up a plan for the weekend himself, to even think he was capable of planning something. He should have thought about the fact that there is no money for him to go out, and he was so inconsiderate to not think about the possibility of other plans already made. He now feels ashamed: he thinks that he cannot do anything in a proper way. His wife is always complaining, and she is right; what can he do right, these days? Nothing! Whatever he does is never good enough.

Sometimes, before opening his eyes, he wishes he is waking up in his hometown, and that the Australia-adventure had turned out to be just a dream. If he knew how hard it would be to move here, he would really have given it a lot of thought before doing so. But he cannot go back now. Not only does he pray to God that the relationship will get better, leaving now would also mean that he leaves behind his child. If he left Australia, it would be almost impossible to come back to visit his child, as visas are very hard to obtain. He made this commitment, and he needs to stick to it. But sometimes, when he goes for a walk on the beach and looks at the jetty, he fantasizes about jumping off and drowning. Liam knows he will not do that, but that this thought keeps coming to his mind scares him a lot.

3   Male Marriage Migrants

Liam's unsettling story reveals the emotionally highly disturbing realities male marriage migrants face post migration. Narratives like this emphasize the importance of researching men's experiences with marriage migration. From the 1990s onwards, scholars such as Sylvia Chant and Sarah Radcliffe (1992) and Patricia Pessar and Sarah Mahler (2001) urged researchers to place gender at the heart of migration studies. As Williams notes:

> Gender shapes the degree of choice people have over how and whether
> to migrate; it shapes the social meaning migration has for the individual
> as a member of their specific social group and it shapes the perceptions
> of the migrant by outsiders.[1]
>
> WILLIAMS 2010, 21

Currently, gender has become recognized as an important factor and focus
point in migration studies. However, when attention shifted, it mainly turned
to studying women's migratory experiences (Williams 2010; Fernandez 2018).
While important insights have arisen from this work, it seems that, yet again,
studies are ignoring men's experiences with migration (Donaldson et al. 2009;
but see for instance, Gallo & Scrinzi 2016). As Pierrette Hondagneu-Sotelo
remarks, the "preoccupation with writing women into migration research
and theory has stifled theorizing about the ways in which constructions of
masculinities and femininities organize migration and migration outcomes"
(1999, 566).

The chapters in the edited volume *Migrant Men: Critical Studies of
Masculinities and the Migration Experience* (Donaldson et al. 2009) see gender, and specifically masculinity, as the main analytical concepts for studying
migration. By focusing on Australia as the particular locale, authors describe
the ways in which gender is interrelated with concepts such as class, race, ethnicity, and religion (see also Pessar 1999). In this volume, Raymond Hibbins
and Bob Pease underscore how a focus on men, masculinities and migration is
an emerging and important field. Their efforts aim to document:

> how men negotiate, react and respond to male and female gender iden-
> tities that they encounter throughout the migratory process. With pres-
> sures on men to be the main breadwinner in the societies in which they
> are settled, and to continue their authority in the family, they face a range
> of personal, cultural, educational and systemic barriers that hinder their
> ability to realise their expected role as "men".
>
> HIBBINS & PEASE 2009, 5

---

1   The work of Mahler and Pessar (2006) is especially important, as it emphasizes how using
    gender as an analytical tool for theory building can help to understand migration-related
    decisions and outcomes. Studies using this gender approach focus on how men and women
    experience migration differently, as well as how migration influences gendered norms, rela-
    tions of power, and ideologies (Pessar 1999).

While the number of male marriage migrants is significant and increasing, research-based evidence is scarce (Williams 2010, 29; but see for instance Hannaford 2020; Fernandez 2018; Rodrígues-García 2006; De Hart 2007). The little research on men marrying and migrating across borders "emphasizes how men struggle to adapt to changes in social settings and to their enforced dependence on their wives" and furthermore, it "may be assumed that women marriage migrants share the same feelings but may be culturally programmed and equipped to accept these struggles and may possess gendered strategies to deal with the problems they face" (Williams 2010, 30).

Both the works of Gallo (2006) and Charsley (2005) provide interesting insights into men's experience with migration. Gallo's work explores the construction of masculine identities among Malayali migrants from India, who moved to Italy through their marriages with Malayali women living, and working as domestic workers, in Rome. She illustrates how men struggle with moving to their wives' locales in another country. This non-patrilocal residence, as well as women's presence outside the domestic sphere can be seen as redefinitions of family relations and modern forms of patriarchy. While both men and women actively engage with such transformations, men felt that Italy was not a good place for them as husbands. Often, migration was viewed as an ambiguous process with various impacts on masculinities. The inability to find employment and having to adjust to reverse gender norms and practices, while at the same time legal migration was seen as reinforcing masculinity (being "deserving" of residency as opposed to residing in Italy undocumented), made men feel ambivalent towards their conjugal situation.

Charsley describes the ways in which marriage migration influences the lives and experience of masculinities among Pakistani husbands to Pakistani wives in the United Kingdom. Her work illustrates the "social, cultural, and economic difficulties faced by migrant husbands" (2005, 85). Being far away from their own kin and the proximity to their wives' family are among the factors that "restructure gendered household relations of power" (ibid.). The model of unhappy husbands, Charsley argues, helps to grasp the experiences of migrant men who practice marriage migration more generally. Often, she emphasizes, migrant husbands are viewed as bad men or insincere partners who use their marriage as an entryway into an Anglo-European country. However, her research points out that the post-migration context is experienced as particularly difficult for migrant men, which helps to explain situations of marriage breakdown, violence and the practice of acquiring a second wife.

Although Charsley focuses on husbands and wives with the same cultural background, whereas I describe intercultural relationships, male marriage migrants to Australia face similar social, cultural and economic difficulties through their journey of marriage migration. Reversed gender roles, romantic mismatches, isolation, class and racism issues as well as economic struggles adversely impact on men's experience. Consequently, migrant men describe Australia as a distressing place, as opposed to what they had imagined: the happily ever after.

4   Experiences of Marriage Migration among Migrant Men

4.1   *Expectations of the Relationship*

After months or years of waiting to be united, couples may initially think their happily ever after has arrived when the temporary visa is granted. However, a new difficult period is likely to have just begun. From the date of the submitted visa application a couple is required to be together for a minimum of two years before the foreign spouse can obtain permanent residency in Australia. During these two years, the foreign spouse is dependent on his sponsoring partner. And while such legal dependency can be interpreted as only a formality, in practice, men's social and economic existence was now fully in the hands of—or at least highly influenced by—their Australian partners.[2] Such everyday dependency as Williams (2010) calls it, often contrasted sharply with the gendering of relationships previously familiar to them, whether that was in Africa, online, or elsewhere in the world.

Prior to migration, cross-border relationships enabled men to display a style of masculinity that closely resembled a hegemonic model of masculinity. While different masculinities coexist within a society, and the term "masculinity" itself functions as an umbrella, comprising multiple, flexible, diverse, and ambiguous masculinities, a hegemonic masculinity is ever present, albeit fluid and unstable (Morrell 1998).[3] Characteristics of a normative or hegemonic

---

2   Throughout journeys of marriage migration, the difference in residential status is important as it brings about structural (or at least long-term) political, social and economic inequalities between partners. The migrant spouses, the *dependents*, face restrictions on their rights in the new country of settlement, and indeed depend on their *sponsoring* partner, and on their relationship; if a marriage or relationship breaks down before obtaining residency, the dependent partner's rights in the country of settlement also end (Williams 2010, 5–6).

3   The study of men and masculinity became a popular part of gender studies in the 1980s (but see Tolson 1977). In the next decade, through the publication, amongst others, of Connell's book *Masculinities* (1995), a general rejection arose of the idea that all men are, or need to be, the same. Kimmel studies men and masculinities extensively and defines masculinity as a collection of meanings constructed in relationship with the self and in relation to others, the larger world. Manhood is socially constructed; its meanings change over time and differ per individual. What it means to be a man is often opposed to the other: women, racial- and

masculinity are, amongst others: aggression, competition, independence, strength, being in control, as well as being heterosexual and anti-feminine (Kimmel 2005, 29–31). The hegemonic standard of masculinity is more of an ideal for men to measure up to or to strive for, than it is a realistically achievable model for manhood (Kimmel 2005).[4] During the courtship period when couples first met, men could actively take up the role as leader and women seemed to particularly enjoy following their partners. In a sense, thus, back then, men could be the "real men" they aspired to be, particularly because of their foreign partners. Paul, for instance, described how his now ex-wife would always wait for him to finish work, ready with a plate of food. Since she was visiting him in the country he was living, and had little to do, she would make sure to "pamper her hard-working husband" after which he would sometimes take her dancing or for a drive. Other men, too, described how they would take their partners out for a meal, for a dance, on trips around their country, and to meet family and friends.

While such extreme gendered roles may have worked for their short period together in Africa or in other foreign countries, this dynamic changed drastically in Australia. Many couples quickly seemed to realize they actually did not know their significant other as well as they thought. Many migrant men expected their partners to remain the same, and their lives in Australia to be based on a continuation of the gendered practices they were used to. It seemed that some women held altogether distinct attitudes, mind-sets, and lifestyles while in Australia that were not evident or relevant when visiting their future husbands in Africa.[5]

In the African country, women may have been open to new experiences, ready and trusting to take their partner's lead. In this context in which women were unfamiliar with customs and language, women often relied on their partners to show them around. However, back in Australia their humdrum lives continued much as they did before their marriage, and so did their worries about jobs, money, and mortgages. These worries became magnified as they found that they now also, were responsible for their newly arrived partner.

---

sexual others (2005, 25). In particular, Kimmel suggests, men often compare themselves to other men, and strive to be as opposed to the feminine as possible, to be strong instead of weak, and independent instead of dependent, in order to not be identified as feminine, homosexual or inferior (2005).

4   The term "hegemonic masculinity" although crucial in understanding masculinities, has also been the subject of debate. See for instance Beasley (2008) and Howson (2005).

5   See for instance work on expatriates (Fechter 2007), and sex and romance tourism (Brennan 2004; McEwen 2009; Selänniemi 2003).

Women did not have such responsibilities in Africa. Moreover, these women had come to Africa on holidays and had saved money beforehand to make their trip worthwhile. This may have confused men, who may have expected that their lifestyle would be similar in Australia. From the men's perspective, in this new country the familiar face for them, their happy, obliging and easy-going wife, had disappeared. Their partners had turned from fun-loving and reliant women into serious, responsible and sometimes demanding women.

Men and women often perceived the move to Australia as a committed couple differently. Women anticipated the completion of their happiness project: to finally settle down happily with their partners and possibly have children. All but one of the men, on the contrary, experienced the move as highly unsettling due to experiences of racism, as well as difficulties finding work and fulfilling their obligations to both their wife and their families back home. Men needed space to re-establish themselves, or as Melbourne based Zubair described "to figure out what the hell I was going to do in Australia." Many men felt that their partners were unsupportive or did not understand the hardships they experienced while trying to settle in Australia. The dynamics of the relationship before migration dramatically changed once in Australia and it did not seem easy, if possible at all, to relive them again.

Men were dependent on their spouses for the practicalities of settling, including such things as: finding a job, making friends, understanding the public transport system, learning to cook with different ingredients, and buying a car. As Saleem put it, when he was driving me, without a license, to the supermarket in his flatmate's small car, "I had to ask her advice and help for everything, literally everything." Saleem immigrated to Melbourne three years ago. He had met his now ex-partner in his hometown where she lived as an expatriate. They had been together for many years. When she moved back to Melbourne, Saleem had come to visit her for a few months. Because it was summer, he had enjoyed it a lot. "It felt like a long holiday." Once he got home, the couple found that his partner had become pregnant during his stay in Melbourne. This made them apply for a Partner visa for him to move to Australia permanently. But when he arrived, it was winter, cold and wet. They moved in with his mother-in-law, which was not a good place for Saleem. He did not get along with his wife's mother, and his overall experience in Melbourne had been very disappointing.

Saleem continued by providing an example: "I could not even wash my clothes by myself, and that shit just made me feel like a big loser." In his case, the issue seemed to be that Saleem was dependent on his partner and felt inadequate as a man. It was not so much that he did not know how to wash his clothes, but that he did not know how to do it in the way that his wife was used to and approving of. Being completely dependent on one's spouse is the complete reverse of what men experienced in their home country. The reality of not being able to implement their idealized vision of what a man is supposed to be like often seemed to be accentuated by their partners' visible disappointment in them as men.[6]

4.2   Isolation and Homesickness

Feelings of dependency were also exacerbated by a lack of social relations and cultural knowledge. Most men I interviewed said how they suffered from great loneliness in their first years in Australia. While none would use the term depression, in conversations with men it became apparent that in fact many of them had been particularly downhearted in their first years in Australia. As Farida Tilbury (2007) argues, the Anglo-European and biomedical notion of depression does not cover the negative emotions felt by migrants. In her study among East Africans in Western Australia, interlocutors described feelings of "frustration, uncertainty, hopelessness, shame and embarrassment, loneliness, disempowerment, shock, anger, loss of control, [and] betrayal" (2007, 451). Such feelings of sadness are a result of the migration journey to a new and unfamiliar country.

For my interlocutors, emotional distress often made them reminisce about back home. Saleem recalled how he would call family and friends back home, almost daily, to get some comfort, while Jacob went for long drives to reminisce about home and to "really feel" his sorrows and homesickness (his wife had installed "home" on the GPS for him to be able to find his way back to his new home in the still unfamiliar city). The seemingly peaceful streets of Australia's suburbs turned out not to be as perfect as previously imagined. Rather, the quietness of the suburbs men resided in, often located far away from the city center, made them feel lonely and isolated.

Such feelings of isolation and loneliness often seemed to be strongly related to homesickness (see van Tilburg & Vingerhoets 2005). Men recalled the more collectivist context back home, which was in stark contrast to the more individualistic Australian society.[7] Men expressed how they were used to a certain

---

6   As the next chapter illustrates, for women, too, the dependency of their partners came as an unwelcome surprise. Both men and women had enjoyed the style of masculinity that was previously performed by men, prior to settling in Australia. Even though men would not explain this to me directly, it seemed that both their own as well as their partners' disappointment with this new gendered reality crystallized their inadequacy.

7   Categories of collectivist and 'individualistic' societies are complicated, complex and often dangerous to use without elaboration. I want to emphasize that these are feelings and words

hustle and bustle after work hours, as everyone was outside—going home from work, having some food with friends from the food stall around the corner, or women doing the cooking outside; there would always be people around, and the noises of people talking and laughing and of traffic and other movement. They lamented that "even without knowing anyone, in Africa you would just feel as if you belonged," because "people talk to you anyway, share whatever they have with you anyway."[8]

In Australia, by contrast, men felt that people never make eye contact with strangers, do not talk to anyone on the street, and avoid any form of social contact by going straight home after work and shutting the door behind them. As Peter exclaimed, when we were driving through Adelaide's dark deserted streets around eight o'clock in the evening, "Look around you! There is no one here!" We were on our way to one of Peter's friends who had organized a birthday party, when I asked him if he ever compared Adelaide to his home country. He explained that back home, this would be the time to be out, to visit neighbors, family, or friends and have some food together. The streets would be filled with people and everywhere you would be able to see the lights of the candles and gaslights from the little food stalls that sell beef skewers. "I can still smell that air, filled with the smell of beef and charcoal," he reminisced. In Adelaide, in contrast, he felt that people were generally hiding inside, "behind the closed curtains, having dinner, probably even by themselves." While men like Peter had come to Australia to find a greater happiness, in such instances the temporal dimension of happiness was found in in the past, in memories and lived experiences (Lambek 2016).

Furthermore, all but two men recalled that back home the door would be always open for friends and family to come for a visit. Whatever the time was, my male interlocutors told me, guests could never be refused. People would be much more willing to share with others, and welcome others. That is at least what I was told. In Australia, men argued, people just lived for themselves, not their families. They felt that their sponsoring partners were not as welcoming as they should be and could not appreciate the men's desire to socialize or have friends over frequently.

Interestingly, it seemed that the two Australian women with Middle Eastern and Mediterranean heritage were more understanding of their partners' cultural expectations of greater sociality. Such observations accord with literature on values among ethnic minorities such as Italians and Greeks in Australia. For

---

that are part of the narratives of the male marriage migrants I interviewed and worked with, and thus provide an emic perspective.

8　I realize this is likely an idealization of what it is like in their remembered hometowns.

instance, Doreen Rosenthal et al. (1989) and Jerzy Smolicz et al. (2001) state that for these Australians, a collectivist family orientation was a key marker supporting their minority group identity as opposed to a more individualistic orientation held by Anglo-Australians.

Both couples argued that partly, their heritage and cultural ways were a reason for their successful and loving marriages. William explained this to me when I met him and his wife Lillian at the restaurant where they both worked. As they were preparing for lunch, William was occupied cutting what it looked like were a thousand onions. According to William, while people would complain that "Africans are loud." he argued that "my wife ... she is the loudest person I know!" She would be shouting on the phone, or yelling at him from the kitchen, and he felt he could not "beat" that and then he laughed exuberantly. He felt that he and his wife Lillian were very similar as they both liked to have people at their house. Her family would stay for longer periods of time, as now for example her sister was staying with them for about a month. Lillian, he felt, also understood when he needed time with his friends. When William would have people visiting, she would make sure to go and do something else. Because of her background, William reasoned, Lillian knew that in situations like that "she should be more humble." William expressed his gratefulness for their shared values and understandings. He felt that Lillian knows how to "treat a man" and would never be jealous. Because of this, William wanted "to be a good man to her." All this time, Lillian had been listening to William and nodding approvingly at his words. Then, she clearly thought it was time to get to work again, and started yelling orders at William, which he answered by yelling back, while laughing and shaking his head. A co-worker commented that indeed, the couple seemed to express their love by shouting at each other, with both orders and compliments.

William and his wife Lillian seemed to be an exception to the rule, as apparently other women would not be that understanding of their partner's ways of socializing. Some men recalled how they were not allowed to go out and socialize, but instead had to stay in all day. Liam, for example, when he visited me at home to help me with a garden project, explained how he usually spends all his days at home because his partner did not like him to go out. She would complain that he was not making money and instead relied on her, but at the same time she discouraged his efforts to find work. She also made it hard for him to visit people, or those people he hoped to establish a friendship with. She would always find a reason for him not to go, Liam explained. Sometimes it would be a family visit, other times grocery shopping, or it would already be too late in the evening. Or, Liam repeated the question he was frequently asked, "how can you go out without money?" One time, when he did go out to drink beer with a friend, his wife was beside herself when he got back. She had yelled at him that he was drunk (he insisted he was not) and that he would be a "lousy father." "She just does not want me to go outside. She wants me to sit inside, by myself," Liam concluded. This example illustrates how men sometimes perceived their partners to be controlling, but it also indicates an inability of men to negotiate with their partners. And even though men like Liam would not describe it as such, control and abuse—whether physical, verbal or emotional—in some cases did appear to occur.

Ten men expressed the view that the visa requirement of staying together for two years put Australian spouses in a powerful position, something they thought their partners at the time were surely using to their advantage. While literature indicates that female marriage migrants are often vulnerable to domestic violence and abuse,[9] men also sometimes suffered from abusive situations. Such occurrences often seem to derive from the legal dependence of men on their Australian spouses, which turned into everyday dependency (Williams 2010) and sometimes, as a result, abuse. Daniel for instance, described how his ex-wife would take his full salary, only giving him money to buy the petrol needed to drive to work and back. She did not allow him to go outside for any other reason than work, and when he actually decided to end the relationship and return home, she hid his passport. Furthermore, she forbade him from talking to his family on the phone. His wife would become particularly upset if he called his sister, as she alleged that the woman on the phone was in fact his African wife or girlfriend. It made Daniel feel even lonelier, not being able to talk to his family, as well as ashamed because he was unable to explain his unavailability to them. Daniel felt vulnerable and isolated as he did not know anyone else but his wife and her family in Australia and was not in a position to make friends of his own. He could not argue with his wife for fear of being deported. Daniel describes the first two years in Australia as "an isolated hell."

While Daniel's situation of isolation was an exceptional case, most men, like Liam, felt that their partners always found reasons for them not to associate with other men originating from different parts of continental Africa. Others, like Jacob, felt his partner did not find it necessary for him to spend time with other migrant men. She did not directly forbid him to socialize with other men, but Jacob was under the impression that each time he had an opportunity to go out and mingle with them, she came up with a reason for him not to go. Jacob explained that he thought it was because she had her own established social

---

9   See Williams (2010) for an overview of such literature.

life already and did not deem it necessary to look for new friends and acquain-tances. She did not seem to understand that he felt more comfortable with other Africa-origin men. Because he wanted to maintain the relationship with his wife, he did not want to make a "big deal" out of it. It was only after their relationship ended that he got in touch with other migrant men. In the apart-ment building he moved to, he met an Africa-origin student, who invited him over to spend time together. It was through this other man that Jacob came to make friends of his own, who helped him feel at home in Australia, two years after his arrival. Sometimes I visited Jacob in his apartment after he finished work, and he was always happy to have me or other people at his place. Often when I visited him, there were other men there, some for a short-time or some staying for a few nights or weeks until they had found a permanent address. Jacob did not mind, as he enjoyed their company and felt he knew that "life in Australia is hard for us."

In a couple of cases, sponsoring partners had contacted the relevant African communities in Australia before the migrant spouse migrated, to create a "home away from home." For instance, Matthew's wife made sure they partic-ipated in anything related to his home country from the moment he arrived. He explained that the community circulated his phone number, so that some-times he would get calls from people he did not even know, inviting him and his wife for social activities, or just for a chat. Such moments were very import-ant for him; he would be "waiting for his phone to ring, to be surrounded by similar people and feel alive again." But while Matthew was eager for such con-tact, he also made it very clear that these people, even though they shared a home country and were friendly, he had no intimate connection with them, as their personalities and lifestyles were just very different. He found it very hard to make good friends in this new context.

Such accounts illustrate that men's new status as migrants affected their sense of masculine self significantly. Men often felt lonely, isolated and home-sick. Such feelings and emotions do not reflect normative masculinity, which emphasizes qualities such as being in control, strength, and independence (Kimmel 2005). Yet, within society, different constructions of masculinity exist, and it is important to recognize them, as well as their relationships and the inequalities and power struggles involved (Connell 1995). While currently the scholarship on African masculinities is blooming (see for instance Morrell & Swart 2005; Ouzgane & Morrell 2005; Ratele 2013; Smith 2017; Uchendu 2008), for a long time men in Africa have been overlooked.[10] In African contexts,

---

10   The study of men and masculinities has been criticized for mainly focusing on men in Anglo-European contexts, excluding the work of scholars from the 'global South' and ignoring men and masculinities in non-Anglo-European contexts (Connell 2014).

studies on gender and development often only focused on women, and merely described men as those in power, subordinating women. Men being disempowered did not seem to be an option. Thus, men in Africa have been ignored, overlooked, taken for granted, and seen as a hegemonic category. This has created a notion of African men as powerful "winners," while in fact, evidence shows that men have suffered greatly from various political and socioeconomic changes, including colonialism, post-colonial economic crises and institutionally imposed structural adjustment programs (Silberschmidt 2001, 2005; see also Ferguson 2006).

Naturally, there is no such thing as *the* African masculinity. Numerous masculinities are acted out in Africa, as it is a hugely diverse continent, with many different countries, cultures, ethnicities, classes, families, and individuals (see for instance Smith 2010; Morrell 2001). Moreover, Africans are spread across the globe as migrants, moving for various reasons and experiencing diverse living environments (Hannaford 2020; Morrell 1998; Morrell & Ouzgane 2005).[11] My data supports the findings of Charsley (2005) and Gallo (2006) that male marriage migrants are forced to find new ways to be masculine and that often this process is disempowering and difficult for them. For migrant men, this process is compounded by isolation, which made them feel particularly unhappy and significantly affected their feelings of self-worth. One important part of adjusting to life in Australia was being able to have meaningful contacts with other Africa-origin men. While some Australian partners understood the importance of men establishing their own social connections, my data shows that more often, men felt their partners—albeit to various extents—were not supportive of them creating their own networks. These difficulties made it harder for men to settle in Australia and became part of the reason life in Australia was not as good or happy for them as previously imagined. While feelings of isolation made men feel uncomfortable, as will be illustrated in the next section, men's socioeconomic positioning in Australia further decreased their sense of self-worth.

4.3   *Moving Up and Down the Socioeconomic Ladder*

In a sense, marriage migration to Australia is nothing extraordinary. Africans have always been on the move (van Dijk et al. 2001; Amin 1995; Akokpari 1999;

---

11   Colonialism, Christianity, schools, and urbanization are among many factors influencing African masculinities. But that is not to say that pre-colonial notions and practices of masculinity have been swept away. Other factors such as class, capitalism, and changes in the family continue to influence masculinities, indicating the fluidity and changing characteristics of masculinities (Arnfred 2004; Morrell 1998).

Akin Aina 1995) and for African households, fathers, husbands and sons migrating for employment or other ways of supporting the family is nothing new.[12] Most men expected their journey of marriage migration to lead to socioeconomic betterment. Except for one man, migrant men came from lower socioeconomic backgrounds in their home countries. While all men were employed prior to coming to Australia, except for one, none of them had completed any tertiary education, and very often men had not finished secondary school. Life back home had often not been easy for them, and almost all men had to look for creative ways of earning sufficient income.

Generally, men had moved from their hometown to other towns, cities or countries in search of "greener pastures." For instance, Peter and Zubair moved to a bigger regional town for work, Jacob and Paul to another African country, Daniel, William and Matthew had relocated to Europe, while three other men had moved to Asian countries. All of them found relatively well-paid work and had climbed the socioeconomic ladder relative to their prospects back home, although this did not necessarily mean they saw their daily circumstances as significantly improved. Other men had been artists in their home country. They would perform nationally and sometimes internationally, and had worked with international tourists eager to learn about African dance and/or musical instruments. Even though the work was rewarding, they all described how being an artist would not provide any guarantees. Sometimes, these men felt that life had been hard, a constant struggle to survive.

Prior to their move to Australia, however, men had always found ways of surviving and taking care of themselves. Most men described themselves as "street smart": always able to find a way to survive. They knew how to "hustle"

12　For a long time, migration in Africa has been male dominated, and/or at least has been documented by researchers as such (but see for instance Vaa *et al.* 1989; Cordell et al. 1996; van Dijk et al. 2001 and Gugler & Ludwar-Ene 1995 on female migrants). During colonial times, employers such as colonial governments, missions, mining companies and commercial firms only recruited men (Adepoju 1995). Men were required to work away from home, and the colonial governments often did not allow women and children to join them. This policy was, amongst others, set in place to discourage African families from settling permanently in urban centers (Gugler & Ludwar-Ene 1995; Spronk 2006). Also, in the post-colonial period, "young men, both single and married, tend to migrate alone to the cities, to more easily avail of urban jobs and accommodation and to save enough money to pay for the transport and maintenance of wives, children, and relations who might subsequently join them" (Adepoju 1995, 92). The continent's increased economic hardship, political instability and ecological crises also make intercontinental migration a more popular choice. Over the last decades, migration out of Africa (mostly to Europe) increased dramatically after a period of mostly intra- and international migration, within Africa (Adepoju 1995).

as Jacob called it. Men explained that although life was sometimes hard back home, it was also good, because they knew the right people in the right places. These connections meant that they would always be guaranteed work, or at least have a place to stay and food to eat. In Europe, for instance, Matthew lived in an area with a large African presence, and people would help each other find work and would always share their meals with others. He described his life there as "living in a close-knit community. Even though we all came from different places, we all took care of each other, like family."

Initially, men imagined that their relationships would enable them to improve their socioeconomic position back home, as now they had the prospect, and reality, of moving to an Anglo-European country where opportunities, they imagined, abounded. Men, as well as their friends and family, anticipated great successes stemming from the move. As Saleem described: "I really thought this move to Australia would make my life easy and good. I thought I would be rich in an instant." Possibly surprisingly then, men who presented themselves as "hustlers and go-getters" would later, after arriving in Australia, lose their pugnacity and self-confidence. While at first this move to an Anglo-European country was anticipated as "exciting" and "a new adventure" and "a way forward," relatively soon after arrival men became disappointed with the reality of much fewer opportunities for socioeconomic advancement than anticipated. This resonates with Charsley's findings among Pakistani men as she describes that while financial opportunities were anticipated, "the conditions in which these financial gains are to be made can come as a shock to newly arrived husbands" (2005, 90).

While from the perspective of their African home men enjoyed upward socioeconomic mobility, within their new context, marriage migration involved downward mobility. Men soon realized that their socioeconomic positioning may in fact have been better back home. Men claimed that instead of moving "up the ladder" as they had anticipated, in their everyday lived reality in Australia they experienced a sharp decrease in status. That men's dreams and unrealistic expectations (that partly stemmed from their own imaginings of what life in the west would look like, and partly because of the way that their partners had presented themselves and life in Australia when couples first met) turned out to be far from realistic, discouraged men strongly. This, in turn, influenced their feelings of being a man and their self-worth significantly.

Difficulties adjusting to life in Australia—often related to education, skills, racism and language barriers—made men realize they may "not be prepared for this life in the west." Peter, when we were having a hotel meal together that he insisted on paying for, explained that there were not many opportunities for men like him. Especially in the first months after arrival in Australia, "the system" seemed too complicated and to be working against him. He described how he felt "stuck" and "paralyzed" because of his inability to find, for instance, employment or education opportunities. Also, other men confessed that they thought life was going to be easy, but instead they found a world that seemed impossible to understand without the help of their partners.

From a socioeconomic perspective, men lacked capital to confidently move ahead. Men often had no idea about services available to them, and how to get access to such services. For instance, while applying for a driver's license may seem the easiest thing for the sponsoring spouse, for the migrant partner this meant finding out such things as: where to find the forms, how to fill in the forms, what office to go to, at what times, and how to get there. In this way, the lack of cultural knowledge was a disadvantage in men's quest for accessing a good life in Australia. As described earlier, the cultural knowledge of the Australian partner added a significant layer to the dependency of the migrant partner, affecting his already diminished and vulnerable masculinity. Sometimes long after the couple separated, men still needed to ask their ex-partners for help with issues such as their superannuation, their insurance or Centrelink matters. Accessing Australian bureaucracy, thus, was often a structural obstacle for men's goals of wanting to live a comfortable and happy life.

While most men experienced similar hardships after arrival, they all seemed to have suffered alone as they were not aware of any support systems available to them. A caseworker at the African Communities Council of South Australia explained that whereas refugees and humanitarian entrants would have support arranged by both government and other institutions, migrant spouses do not have any support. "They can come to us, but they do not know about us because Australians [the sponsoring partners] do not know we exist!," the caseworker explained indignantly. She also explained that migrant spouses are different from those who come to Australia on student visas or as skilled migrants, "because these [latter two groups of] people," she reasoned, "they know what they will be doing here, they have the confidence many [African] spouses are missing."

Furthermore, I sometimes got the sense from the men that the relatively small number of people with African backgrounds in Adelaide resulted in an erasure of class differences, as everyone now belonged to a new category of migrant or African. Men compared themselves to other Africa-origin migrants who came to Australia as students, and who had managed to get good jobs and permanent residency seemingly without difficulties. The socioeconomic differences which were apparent in their home country were now ignored and direct comparisons were made between themselves and better educated migrant men. Men would worry about "not having achieved anything in these years in Australia," "lagging behind," and "having nothing to be proud of, no savings, no house, not even money to visit home." It seemed that men were not prepared for the reality that it usually took years for migrant men to get comfortable in Australia. Prior to the move, it seemed to have been impossible for men to picture daily life in Australia. Seemingly, men focused solely on their relationship, and did not think about possible hardship or strategies to create a purposeful day-to-day life in Australia. Without a solid background or back-up plan, and often without any direction, men ended up feeling disappointed and dependent on their spouses for social and, as illustrated in the next section, for financial support.

4.4   *Work and Finances*

According to Robert Morrell and Lahoucine Ouzgane, among the various and significant differences between men in Africa, there are also some similarities, or communalities between them. First, they argue, "all men have access to the patriarchal dividend, the power that being a man gives them to choose to exercise power over women." Furthermore, men are often seen as the "ultimate other." Lastly, they argue that men share the legacy of colonialism and the current influence of globalization (2005, 7–8). Sociohistorical processes and socioeconomic trends have affected African men's positioning in the world, which becomes visible when looking at marriage migration in relation to work and economic positioning. As has been outlined above, the men imagined Australia to be a place full of opportunities, including a much higher income than they currently had, and thus the ability to send home remittances as well as investing in building homes or setting up a business for their family back home.

Ambiguities regarding income and providing for family back home resonate with Gallo's work in Italy (2006). She states that for Malayali migrant men, while any source of income was much appreciated and often significantly better than their earnings back home, often their inability to be the sole provider and underemployment made them feel uncomfortable. Such difficulties influenced their conjugal life considerably. For male marriage migrants in this study, too, finding a rewarding job in Australia was not easy for them for various reasons and influenced their perception of being good men.

In two cases, visa policies hindered men from seeking employment. Zachary could not work for as long as he held a bridging visa, which would be up until he was granted a temporary Partner visa. Although he always preferred to work illegally, his wife firmly discouraged him, as she did not want to run the risk of him getting caught, being deported and subsequently never being allowed in Australia again. For the first six months in Australia, Zachary sat home becoming increasingly bored and frustrated. He felt he was a "burden for everyone, including myself" and felt he was "going crazy." Being alone with his thoughts, dependent on his wife, and with his family back home eagerly awaiting his contributions, made him want to take the risk. He preferred to take care of his "mental health and have a daily purpose."

Racism, as described in the previous chapter, was another important factor men named as reasons for their un/under-employment. Men expressed their frustrations with finding work, as they had not expected it to be so difficult to find a job. Daniel, for instance, described how his perception of racism affected his job search; having worked as a journalist in Europe for years, he had applied for a job at a newspaper, only to find that they had chosen a young newly graduated woman without previous work experience, over him. Frustrated, he said that it was the color of his skin, and her being Australian that made them make this decision. "Yes, I did not have the diploma, but I had years of experience and an impressive resume." The young woman, on the other hand, had no work experience as she just finished university. Daniel told me about this experience, that he persistently described as racist, when we were having lunch in between our respective study sessions—Daniel had decided to attend university after countless unsuccessful attempts to find a job to match his experience. At this stage he had obtained permanent residency, which meant that enrolment costs for university were considerably lower than for temporary residents. Speaking about racism seemed confronting, as I could see the pain he experienced reflected in his eyes. Other men also remarked that racism affected their chances, as employers "just preferred Australians." The men rationalized that "Australians would prefer to give the jobs to their 'own' people." especially as the Australian economy was not currently thriving.

As I mentioned previously, apart from one, all the men came to Australia without certificates or diplomas, which significantly reduced their chances of finding a job. While prior to migrating, some men had well regarded jobs at for instance NGO s, in trades, in tourism, in security or were private business owners, most were not formally qualified. As a result, men were not able to provide the prerequisite diplomas or certificates the Australian employers would ask for. Often, obtaining diplomas in Australia was not possible for men as university or other institutions' enrolment costs for international students were very high. As a result, men generally had low paid and low skilled jobs, often without any prospect of getting promoted or having further learning opportunities. Jacob, who back home worked in hospitality and had enjoyed the trust of his employer in practicing his bar skills and entertaining guests, now worked in a supermarket filling shelves. Peter, who used to be a professional tour guide, training inexperienced tourists for mountain climbing and other outdoor sports, now worked in a factory. And Paul, who worked as a security guard for a private company, responsible for the security of various suburbs in the city he had lived in, eventually found unskilled work at a construction site.

While men who were employed generally were not happy with the work they did, as they often considered it a downgrade, they did emphasize how beneficial work was for their wellbeing. Men highly valued and were even proud of their work ethos, and their ability to provide for their families both in Australia and back home. This became apparent as many men used words such as "respectful," "responsible," "being able to provide," "setting an example," and "doing what a man is supposed to do" when describing their feelings about working. Jobs, even though men may have loathed them or considered them a disappointment, did improve men's self-esteem and wellbeing, as they helped men make their new lives in Australia more purposeful.

The importance of having a job and an income became even clearer when looking at cases where Australian partners made it hard for the men to work, or where Australian spouses controlled the ways in which the men's income was spent. In four cases, migrant partners felt that their spouses were either not in favor of them working or wanted to make sure that they were not able to determine how they spent their money, particularly when it came to socializing. After Liam was granted permission from the DIBP to work, his wife did not encourage this. While complaining about spending all their savings, she simultaneously made it clear to him that he could not work. Liam summed up the many reasons she provided that made it impossible for him to go to work: he could not use the car (except for when he had to transport their child) and hence could not drive to work; he was needed to be at home to be with their child; he would need to help her mother shop for groceries; he did not have work experience; and the job hours would likely not fit her work schedule. According to Liam, his partner was very anxious about him finding work because he reasoned that she feared he would meet other women. Liam felt torn, and did not know what to do, "I really need a job, but I do not want to make her unhappy."

Although Liam's situation was exceptional, men often complained about their sponsoring spouses having control over the finances. In eight instances, women requested their partners' full salaries in order to decide what they as a couple would do with the sum of their combined income. While many men in hindsight could understand the purpose of this practice, and how it benefitted them as a family, at the time it made men feel "small" and controlled. As the case of Daniel above illustrates, sometimes men would only receive a little pocket money from their spouse. Daniel felt that his wife was trying to control him in this way. Zubair also only received pocket money from his wife, even after a full week of work. He said that he did not understand it at that time and wondered what she did with the rest of the income they both earned. Now, since he has gained experience with bookkeeping himself, he understands that she took care of the rent, bills and insurances for instance. At that time, however, he felt "so controlled." Still, Zubair believed that it was mainly that he did not have "any say in anything" which made him feel bad. He was accustomed to "making my own money and my own decisions." Now, he felt he did not have that power.

There are some parallels between the way these men explained shifts in gender roles due to the impact of migration on masculinities, families, and relationships and the findings of Ndungi wa Mungai and Bob Pease (2009). The authors consider gender crises faced by mainly refugee men in Australia from what has become South Sudan. These migrants experienced difficulties adapting to a "modern" context in Australia, as their "traditional" gender relationships did not make sense anymore (wa Mungai & Pease 2009). Men felt that their commitment to responsibility, religion and tradition, which previously underscored their masculinity, were hard, if not impossible, to maintain and therefore did not longer seem valid in Australia with its own different, and to the men, new cultural and religious traditions. According to wa Mungai and Pease (2009) men were uncomfortable with their South Sudanese wives now taking on men's responsibilities, as for instance women sometimes became the main providers, with men having to take on roles they previously ascribed to women, such as domestic chores and childcare. While in some cases men learnt to cope with such challenges successfully, in other instances it has led to family breakdown (wa Mungai & Pease 2009, 112).

Many studies on African migrants in Australia focus on refugees, and the cultural differences arising from their long-held traditions—in particular related to gender—that would be contrary to "modern" Australian customs (for example, see Abuyi 2014; Muchoki 2014). While such studies are of great value in that they offer us insights into the impacts of migration and resettlement on men and the impact on their masculinities, simultaneously, they run the risk of generating a view that all Africans in Australia are refugees, that all African men are traditional, and that Australia is supposedly modern, whatever that might mean. Obviously not all migrant men settle in Australia as refugees, and often I found that male migrants came from larger and more cosmopolitan cities and urban areas than Adelaide. As I described in Chapter 3, men expressed their frustrations with being identified as refugees by strangers. The men in my study differed from South Sudanese men as studied by wa Mungai and Pease (2009), as they did not perceive themselves to be traditional, or particularly felt the need to adhere to all the traditions from home. Yet, men did share the discomfort of women being the main providers and not being able to control or have any say in the household finances. Men were disappointed by their spouses' behavior and control over the finances, regardless of the fairness or perceived need for such practices. Due to the difficulties of getting good jobs, the unexpectedly high costs of living, and (sometimes) controlling partners, men did not find their financial situation to be as comfortable as they hoped. As well, back home, even though it may have been difficult to earn sufficient income, all of these men did work, and did control and understand their financial situation.

By moving to an Anglo-European country, many men felt they were expected to support their families back home to a greater extent than they had done previously. That migration for people from the continent of Africa is fundamentally a family affair instead of an individual journey becomes evident from the sending of remittances.[13] The literature has emphasized that migration is seen as a strategy to enhance family livelihoods, through the benefits of remittances (either from abroad or from an urban center), but also illustrates the effects of pressures from families on migrants (see for instance van Dijk et al. 2001; Hannaford 2016).[14] While some men seemed to ignore requests from back home, for most men it was a major worry and a further cause of anxiety. Sarah's ex-partner, she told me, would send as much money home as possible, even before thinking of paying their rent, which caused many arguments between them. But Jacob told me that while he had been stressed about this for a long time, at one point he had to tell his family that they should stop asking, saying: "I send them everything I have, and if I do not have anything, I am not sending anything. They should stop expecting the world from me."

Because men were not in control of the finances, they felt they were not able to send much money home. This lack of control did not directly stem from wives forbidding or preventing them from supporting family back home—or at least none of the men mentioned that their partners refused to send any remittances. All sponsoring women I spoke to were quite dedicated to helping

---

13   Studies emphasize that while remittances are an important source of income for those who stay home, this is balanced via a form of reciprocity, which includes prayer sessions, taking care of children, supervising building projects, performing traditional ceremonies, and of course through emotional support. Studies on transnationalism and African migratory networks illustrate such practices of mutual support (Riccio 2008; Krause 2008; Saraiva 2008).

14   However, increasingly, and often as a result of the International Monetary Fund's structural adjustment programs, "urban dwellers become, at least partly, dependent on rural sources of food and/or income, causing a reverse flow of goods and perhaps even money from rural to urban areas" (van Dijk et al. 2001: 17).

families overseas, especially if they had been to Africa themselves and had got to know their relatives. I sometimes found that men did not dare to ask for more money to be sent to their families as they felt it would be onerous and they were uncomfortable being in the position of requester. Men felt that the women were already doing so much for them, and they could not ask for more.

It seemed that the exact amount of money that could be sent home required negotiation among couples. Whereas often for women the main priority was their household in Australia, after which "extras" could be sent to his family, some men felt that first they wanted to send money home, and then use what was left for themselves in Australia. Jade told me that even though her partner worked full-time, and she was on a pension, they had to eat plain spaghetti for days in a row, because he sent so much money home. Many women regarded sending money to Africa as less of a priority and did not want to sacrifice their standard of living. Such observations reflect the idea that happiness cannot be separated from the spectrum of cultural values in relation to which it becomes meaningful (Walker & Kavedžija 2015, 6–7). While for women happiness was to be found mainly in their intimate relationships, for most men, happiness was inherently linked to the wellbeing of their families back home.

4.5   Controlling Wives and the Regaining of Masculinity

Over the course of many of the relationships, power relations often became highly unbalanced. All 11 men who had separated from their partners described them as "controlling," "mean," and "bossy" women. While only three men used the words "domestic violence" and "abuse," men did elaborate on how unfairly their ex-partners treated them. As Elijah remembered, when I met him in an old-fashioned Melbourne bar, his wife was always in control, and when he would question her or go against her, she would start to shout and threaten him with breaking up, which meant that he would have to leave Australia; he said that she would threaten to call the DIBP and have him deported. While for her this could be an emotional outcry in the heat of an argument, for him, this was a very real possibility, and a reason to keep quiet, and to conform to her ways.

Not all men experienced isolation stemming from verbal and emotionally abusive behavior, but it was certainly a recurring theme. Liam confided that on one occasion, his wife pulled his hair. Another man, I was told of by one of his friends, would find the pantry and fridge locked up for days after a fight with his spouse: she would punish him for "bad behavior" by not letting him eat. Erick, a man in his early fifties and who had come to Adelaide four years ago described his situation as an abusive one. He explained that each time he did or said something that would be perceived as bad by his now ex-wife, she would correct him, by either insulting him or with physical violence. He felt as if she had total control over everything he did and if he wanted to keep his visa, he had to comply with her wishes. Eventually, he went to the police to report her abuse, and has since left her.

In the other and less extreme cases it seemed that feelings of being emasculated by the migration journey and the effects of becoming dependent on one's spouse were reasons for relationships breaking down. Lacking any form of steadiness or solidity in their lives, men started to feel inadequate as partners, too. Paul explained that he felt he could not do anything right; many small things made his partner angry. "She made me feel like a little boy all the time' " he recalled. He said that she belittled him for his alleged inadequacy for things like: forgetting to switch off a light, using the heater extensively or showering for too long. Such accusations implied careless behavior and inability or unwillingness to be mindful of the expenses of water and gas. Paul continued by explaining how he could see she was impatient with him, as she would sigh and comment on how she had to be the one that took care of everything. "As if I felt good watching TV all day, instead of working!"

Paul elaborated on this past relationship that brought him to Australia when we were driving in his new car. Although the car was second-hand, it was quite an expensive brand and model, with all sorts of upgrades and extras for comfort. While I had suggested meeting in the city for an interview over lunch, which I planned to pay for, Paul had insisted on collecting me to take me somewhere nice. Unsurprisingly, Paul also paid for lunch, even though I had been insistent about paying for the both of us. I saw such proactive, generous and chivalrous behavior with other men, too. It was in stark contrast with their stories of dependency and inadequacy, and I felt that the men particularly enjoyed opportunities such as these, when they could play more traditional roles.

Men expressed their inadequacy in comparison with their partners and ex-partners, who had their family, friends, work or pensions, and either rented or owned a home. Men explained that they had really felt useless as men and partners. It seemed that the relationship reflected, or magnified, their perceived failures. The effects of migration on manhood are further described by Juma Abuyi (2014). Abuyi narrates the experiences of Acholi refugee men from South Sudan settling in Australia, particularly in relation to service provision. Acholi men, he describes, face a range of underappreciated difficulties settling in their new surroundings. One of these difficulties is a sensed, or feared for, loss of manhood. Incidences of heavy drinking and domestic violence are reactions to feeling emasculated (Abuyi 2014).

Sometimes, for men in this study, sex and sexuality were ways of regaining a sense of their lost or diminished masculinity. As described in the previous chapter, men experienced everyday racism and othering daily, and this othering often focused on men's sexual prowess. This resonates with Morrell and Ouzgane's argument, that African men are often seen as the ultimate other (2005, 7–8). As Spronk notes, the "particular idea of men in Africa as being notoriously promiscuous and domineering ... is not a new observation: many scholars have addressed the long history of stereotyping the sexuality of Black people" (2014, 505).[15] But also, Spronk goes on to explain that among male young urban professionals in Nairobi, the "connection between sex and Africanness is a powerful one" (2014, 510). While men in her study emphasized self-control and constraint as important masculine qualities, manhood became more complex as multi-partnered sexual behavior was also seen as a cultural practice (stemming from polygamy as a cultural explanation and justification).

Some migrant men used the stereotype of hypersexual and highly promiscuous African men for their own benefits. Ezra, a man with a West African background, who did not come to Australia on a Partner visa but who had been married to an Australian woman, did not mind at all talking to me about African-Australian relationships. For years Ezra worked at a popular club attended by many migrants with African backgrounds. In general, the club was known for its multicultural atmosphere: they served food and drinks from across the globe, held weekly salsa nights, drumming performances, and on weekends DJs would play amongst other music, the newest music from the African continent. With his nightlife experience—he could be found working in the club almost every weekend—Ezra laughingly told me he could talk for hours about what he saw happening on the dance floor. But, he said, making such information public "would be disastrous for many marriages, and would go against my work ethic."

Ezra explained that what he saw on the weekends was also something he had personal experience with. He explained that when he was new to Australia, he just wanted to "play" and enjoy life as much as he could, without realizing that there were negative outcomes for his actions. "If you want your marriage

---

15   Spronk describes how a stereotype of the African man stems from not only seeing Africa as the paradigm of difference and local modes of self-representation among Africans (2014: 504), but also how it became reified by the global health discourse. African sexualities, Spronk argues, have not been studied as independent topics, but rather, as a problem relating to health, focusing on such things as: HIV/AIDS, domestic violence, as well as unwanted and abundant pregnancies. As Spronk remarks, "a dominant picture arises of men as domineering and sometimes as brutal and, hence, as perpetrators of violence and injustice against women. ... Men's sexuality is mostly studied in relation to AIDS, focusing on multi-partnered sexual behaviour, violence and the use of condoms, while hardly ever being studied in relation to intimacy, affection or sexual pleasure" (2014: 507).

to work," he explained, "you have to stay strong and not be tempted by all the availabilities, you have to be responsible." "But," he added, "the temptations are luring, especially in bars and clubs where Australian women who are interested in African men are numerous." Indeed, some Australian women I spoke to were only looking for African men, saying things like: "once you go Black, you never go back."

The way that men would sometimes express their sexualities and how this related to self-worth became particularly clear when talking to Ezra. He explained that if a man feels he is not good enough, it is very tempting to entertain advances from beautiful women in clubs. However, Ezra also emphasized that, "of course, there are men, married men; they come here [to the club] to actively chase women, and then go back to beautiful wives at home." Jacob explained that he started an affair because "that other woman made me feel good, and I did not feel good for a long time." Like one other man, Jacob only confessed his infidelity after we had established a friendship. When I first asked if he had ever been unfaithful, Jacob had denied it. Jacob met the woman he had an extramarital affair with, in a nightclub. The nightlife scene, he explained, was particularly enjoyable as "it makes you forget your sorrows," "meeting new people energizes you." and because "it was really nice to finally feel like a man again," when women showed interest in him.

Feelings of loneliness, non-belonging and problems within intimate relationships made extramarital sexual contact an attractive option. It seemed that sexual prowess made up for the loss of control and manhood experienced in intimate relationships. These findings relate to the ways in which East African men use sex to regain their sense of manhood, which is threatened by economic hardships in a rapidly changing world. As described by Margrethe Silberschmidt (2001), men's sense of self, social value and identity as breadwinners are negatively affected by unemployment, low incomes and women's increased responsibilities. Multi-partnered sexual relationships and sexually aggressive behavior are strategies to increase feelings of being a man (2001, 657). In a similar vein, some men in this study used sex and sexuality as ways to increase their masculine identity, by enjoying female attention and participating in extramarital sexual relationships.

5   Conclusion

This chapter illuminated the hardships male marriage migrants encountered after their arrival in Australia. What men imagined would be the good life, often turned out to be a concatenation of disappointments and difficulties.

Marriage migration, thus, did not deliver the promise of happiness men had anticipated, and affected men *as men*. In the above, I set out different factors that influenced men's sense of self and their perception of being a worthwhile man, and that therefore severely affected the success of their marriage migration journey. To summarize: false expectations of the relationship; unfamiliar gender roles and unbalanced gendered power relations; isolation, un/underemployment; and not being able to send home sufficient remittances were the main hurdles migrant men faced whilst settling in Australia. Men depended on their relationship for their visa status, as well as their cultural, social and economic wellbeing. Dependence on their partners to this degree was not foreseen or what men expected what life in Australia would be like.

It has become evident, then, that the model of unhappy husbands, as provided by Charsley (2005) is applicable to the everyday social worlds of migrant men in relationships with sponsoring women. My findings link in with the work of Charsley (2005) and Gallo (2006), who both pinpoint the various forms of gendered imbalances among transnational couples. Both authors describe the effects for male marriage migrants in transnational cross-border marriages and emphasize the importance of the lack of patrilocality that forms the basis of struggles for couples. While the migrant men I studied also moved away from their home countries, they did so as part of an *intercultural* relationship where men knew that their new bicultural relationships may be different from a normative relationality back home. However, what is important here is that while men did anticipate changes and differences because they moved to a new context, they generally anticipated changes to be positive in character, and the differences minimal. Men's false and overly optimistic expectations were often a complete opposite to their everyday experiences in Australia and consequently, their sense of self, their notions of masculinity were severely affected.

The complexities involved in such relationships, which may cause them to end, are generally ignored in the general discussion about marriage migration. A lack of awareness of such gendered issues among male marriage migrants leads to a lack of understanding and support for migrant men in Australia. With this chapter I aimed to emphasize that male marriage migrants face severe hardships on their journeys of marriage migration that should not be ignored, or simply brushed aside because these men are stereotyped as scam artists or insincere spouses. Furthermore, unhappiness among male migrants can easily be turned into an argument against immigration: "they are not happy here so they should return to their homes" (Verkuyten 2003, 151, cited by Tilbury 2007, 153). Such dissonance relates happiness to a geographical space in which "out of place-ness" resonates with unhappiness. But instead of the obvious solution of moving back, ideologically, migrant men should be considered as belonging *here*, in Australia. Men are unhappy here, and "action should be taken here ... to deal with the emotional impact of displacement, through a positive focus on 'emplacement'" (Tilbury 2007, 454).

But it was not only the migrant men who had unmet and unrealistic expectations of the journey of marriage migration. Also, sponsoring partners soon came to realize that marriage migration did not lead to the much anticipated happily ever after. In the next chapter, I turn to the experiences of sponsoring women with the happiness project of marriage migration.

CHAPTER 7

Sponsoring Women and Intimate Relationships

1   Introduction

This chapter narrates sponsoring women's relationship expectations and their disappointing experiences through their journey of marriage migration. It illustrates who these women are, what they hoped for, and how women's expectations of marriage migration as a pathway to everlasting happiness were often unmet.

The chapter describes how women to varying degrees are stigmatized due to their social class and aspects of their bodies, and how relationships are imagined as a way to resolve women's (feelings of) otherness. One the one hand, women occupied a privileged position due to their heterosexuality and whiteness. But on the other hand, bodies and class positions that did not match Australian ideals of appropriate femininity associated with dominant beauty ideals, and the resultant feelings of being different and not-belonging, help to explain relationship experiences. This chapter aims to illustrate the structural inequalities that are at play in the quest for happiness and argues that it seems that some bodies are bestowed more power and therefore have a better chance of finding happiness in relationships than others. The chapter reflects on multidimensionality in the intimate setting of romantic relationships: class, sexuality, gender, and race are all intrinsically related and explain certain choices that women made as they hoped such choices would lead to happiness. Relationships can be understood as a place where acceptance (of the self by the self, by the intimate partner, as well as the social group) was anticipated. However, often, relationships did not bring the anticipated acceptance and belonging, and thus happiness. Berlant's (2011) term cruel optimism is relevant here: that what was desired, the intimate relationship as a path towards happiness, turns out to actually be obstructing happiness.

I am interested in women's journeys of seeking happiness, in the directions women took that they felt would make them happy, in understanding what led them to make some decisions, and what such decisions did for them. I look at women's paths in a social and cultural context. I am therefore not interested in approaching women from a neoliberal perspective that would hold women themselves responsible for supposed failings (whatever they would be). I stress this because there is a danger in this particular focus on the paths of sponsoring women, as it runs the risk of ghettoizing white women as partners of, and who are sponsoring, migrant men, in particular Black Africa-origin men. Previous chapters illustrated that often, women are being held accountable over the migration of a (Black) foreigner and disrupting the white "pure" nation. As Moret et al. (2019, 7) explain, the "good family" is used in state politics as an idiom representing the nation, and a model for social organization. Women are often seen as guards of nation-state borders, and sexuality is controlled for women to remain "(re)producers of ... new members who fit the ethicized, racialized and even classed representations of the nation" (Moret et al. 2019, 7). Such structures work by stigmatizing women in cross-border relationships and can lead to narratives that blame women for their choices: "why can't they find an *Aussie* bloke," was a sentiment I regularly encountered during fieldwork. And so, to emphasize, I am aiming to understand women's own observations about their relationships and place them in a socio-cultural context. My observations about femininity, intimate relationships, class, and body size are not unique to sponsoring women of Black migrant men, but indeed are indicative of structures influencing the lives of all Australians.

The chapter is set up as follows. After outlining the ideal of intimate relationships as the fabric of women's expectations, I first address the ways in which some women struggled with their bodies and how such insecurities were related to relationship experiences. This section also addresses the ways in which bodies and class are intersecting, and how some women ultimately were granted less chances for happiness through intimate relationships. Hereafter, I elaborate on the notion of compatibility between partners. I discuss how some women felt that their personalities, their identities and desires regarding intimacy did not match normative ideas about Australian femininity and intimacy. In both sections, I also link discussions about gender and class to ways in which race comes into play during women's negotiations of intimacy and happiness; that women felt that they did not meet certain (normative) expectations explains some of their experiences within their relationships with migrant men. Such experiences, as well as women's choices, however, are sometimes based on stereotypical images of Africa and African men, and therefore also illustrate the ways in which women's lives and experiences are racialized in a white Australia. In the last section of the chapter, I describe women's unmet expectations and unhappy realities.

To start this chapter, I share the story of Chloë. Her experiences with settling in Australia—which I came to know of during four meetings spread over six months—illustrate how the much-anticipated new phase in the relationship can be a disheartening experience. Chloë's narrative also sheds light on the ways in which expectations and disappointments are meshed with certain expectations of intimacy and relationships, with expectations of the particular partner, and with the women's sense of self.

2   An Unhappy Wife

Chloë and her partner recently moved to Adelaide, and a new chapter of her life has begun. She wants to make sure everything is organized and that nothing will go wrong with the visa application. Right now, it is all about settling down and getting their lives on track. Chloë is originally from Adelaide and so for her, moving here feels like going back to normal. This is the place where she grew up and where her family and friends live. She also knows all the attractions, all the different beaches, the nice restaurants, the best places to go to. But right at this stage of their lives, Chloë does not feel the need to explore any of this, or to show her partner around. That can wait. Right now, it is about settling down and starting a family of their own.

Chloë made sure she had a job to go to soon after arriving in Adelaide. Luckily, her old employer had an opportunity for her. As well, she was assisting her partner to find and apply for jobs. Each time there is a vacancy, Chloë rewrites his cover letter. She says that if they sent his draft, he would never get a job: his sentences are "off," he uses too many difficult words, and his grammar is not that good either. She really tries her best to make things happen, to get his life in Australia running smoothly. But sometimes it seems as if he does not want a job at all, as if he just prefers to be lazing around at home. So right now, Chloë is the sole provider. She does not mind at all, as she understands his situation. But she does not like him going out and spending money on beer at the hotel. That is a waste of their money, which they should spend on more important things. Also, she does not like him smoking and so when he needs money for cigarettes, she does not want to give it to him. He can smoke using his own money, she reasons.

Soon after the move, she realizes that she does not recognize her partner anymore. The longer they spend together in Australia, the more they become estranged. She believes that he is the one that has changed. He used to be a "happy chatty guy," motivated and hardworking, and always with "time on his hands" to spoil her. He used to take her out, call her up, make her feel like she was the most special woman on the planet. He would never cease to amaze her, but now it seems as if he does not care about her anymore. He does not get up to help her with the household chores, and he does not even greet her in the morning. The main thing he does is talk on his phone with people from back home.

Sometimes she wonders if he really loves her, or if he has ever loved her, at all. Why did he come with her to Australia if he does not even love her? Then, sometimes, she thinks it is all a joke, and that he did not want to be with her, that he just wanted to "get out" and she was a good vehicle for moving forward. Why else would he cease showing interest in her from the moment he arrived in Australia? Thoughts like these make her feel very insecure. She wonders if she is good enough; perhaps she did something wrong. It makes her think that every time he is on his phone, he may be looking for someone else. Cheating is so easy these days! The other day, when her partner indicated that he wanted to go out with other men, without her, that made her upset, and it caused a fight. In the end he stayed home with her and they watched a movie together. On the one hand she really wants him to go out and meet with people, make some friends, to really establish himself here, but on the other hand, every time there comes an opportunity for him to go out, she gets scared.

For her, there are too many stories out there, about African men flirting and pursuing women, regardless of their marital status. She did not only hear about these things, but she also saw it with her own eyes: married men pretending to be single trying to "hit on her." And her previous partner—also an African—cheated on her, in the end. She knows that she should not generalize, but to be honest, she would rather not have a partner who likes to go out and party every night. They are too old to do such things, anyway, she thinks, and he can make friends in another way. And what is wrong with her friends?

3   White Australian Women and Relationship Expectations

Chloë's story illuminates how the hoped-for happy journey of marriage migration can be experienced as a rather unhappy reality. The narrative also illustrates how women's insecurities, as well as stereotypes about African men are subtly intertwined and influence partnerships significantly. The everyday lived reality of marriage migration, it seems, obstructs the anticipated and hoped for happily ever after. Ahmed argues that "certain objects are attributed as the conditions for happiness so that we arrive "at" them with an expectation of how we will be affected by them, which affects how they affect us, even in the moment they fail to live up to our expectations" (2008, 7). As demonstrated throughout the book, marriage, or more generally, intimate relationships, can be seen as a happiness object; and an intimate relationship as such is an ingredient for a good life. The idea or judgement that an intimate relationship brings happiness is already made, before it is encountered. This, often, is why "happiness provides the emotional setting for disappointment" (Ahmed 2008, 7).

As was the case for Chloë, other female interlocutors had formerly imagined that their cross-border loves would make them happy. Such ideas of heterosexual love and relationships leading to happiness are highly influenced by cultural constructions of femininity and normative narratives about relationships. Femininity can be "conceptualised as a script for performing cultural ideas" that are considered feminine (Rezeanu 2015, 12). In Australia, as elsewhere, culturally and sociohistorically constructed notions of femininity intersect with race and class. Not unlike other historical accounts of white femininity, early Australian ideas and ideals regarding femininity saw the ideal body as predominantly British, white, young and virginal. "Pure" Australian girls would be hard working and productive—as Australian conditions of settlement required all hands available for building this new world—but always within the patriarchal order (McPherson 1994). Moreover, the white female body was viewed as a maternal body, as colonial anxieties encouraged women to reproduce to increase the white population (Baird 2006). Such images were in stark contrast to the idea of the Black (Aboriginal) female body as "libidinous, wanton and barbaric" (Featherstone 2006, 86). After World War II, Featherstone notes, new emphasis was placed on youth, beauty and heterosexual attractiveness (2006, 234). However, for white women, "heterosexuality remained tied to reproduction rather than to sexual freedom or even sexual pleasure" (ibid.).

Women in Australia, Anne Summers (2006) notes, are socialized to believe that love and intimate relationships will validate them as women in a particular way. Summers (2006), following Jill Julius Matthews' (1984) historical mapping of Australian femininities, analyzed the conditions that shaped Australian femininities since colonization. The scarcity of white women and the unwanted presence of Indigenous women in Australia's colonial past placed an emphasis on, not only the desire for romantic and intimate relationships that culminate in marriage, but on motherhood as the only acceptable expression of femininity. Summers describes how women in Australia are consigned two possible destinies, that of a "Damned Whore" or "God's Police" (2006). Thus, women's status in society is based on stereotypes of "good" or "bad" women depending on whether women are family oriented and willing to maintain and reproduce patriarchal authority or whether they resist these scripts (Summers 2006, 255–6). Summers emphasizes that what was once constructed as essential for the survival of a "white" nation is now "not a matter of choice but a desperate necessity" for a happy life (2006, 252). The absence of choice for women, she explains, is:

> Disguised by the romantic myths of marriage, myths that are so persuasively propagated that each generation of gullible girls grows up believing

that the best thing they can do with their lives is devote them to marriage and motherhood, and that following this vocation will bestow its own rewards of satisfaction and happiness.

SUMMERS 2006, 252

Hsu-Ming Teo (2005) states that from the nineteenth century onwards, notions of romantic love influenced the way in which Australian women in particular conceive marital relationships. Teo (2005) demonstrates how women embraced gendered social scripts, often asserted through consumer capitalism that largely mirrored conceptions of romance from white middle-class values imported from the United States. In the US in the nineteenth century, romantic love was understood as private and spiritual, and its ultimate goal was to achieve intimacy in marriage. For Australians in the nineteenth century, "romantic love was an emotional, moral, physical, and spiritual attraction believed to be a necessary prerequisite to courtship, with companionate marriage as its ideal goal" (Teo 2005, 177). In this way, it was acknowledged that romantic love and by extension marriage promised "ecstasy and a feeling of empathy and completeness" but also could produce "great unhappiness, bitterness and despair" (ibid.). Bernice McPherson (1994), in her historical analysis of the works of popular writers, visual artists and photographers, explains that for women in the same century, the ideal white Australian woman was the "complete woman" with completion being reached through marriage.

Yet, throughout the twentieth century, the importing and reprinting of American advice columns, self-help books, articles and advertisements, resulted in a shift in the notion of love (Teo 2005, 173). As Australia followed in the footsteps of the US, notions of romantic love slowly transformed to incorporate the importance of sexual pleasure, especially from World War II onwards.[1] The idea that romance should bring pleasure and happiness gained ground, in particular, through the practice of "romantic consumption." For instance, dating instead of courting, as well as gift giving, became ways to express love, attraction and liking (Teo 2005). Consumer culture and advertising gradually shifted from a focus on women and domesticity, to a "nexus between women, beauty, youth, romantic love and consumption" (2005, 182). Femininity, Marilyn Lake argues, "was beginning to cast off its passivity as the

---

1   Still, during the depression-years of the 1930s and 1940s, marriage was perceived optimistically as it reflected "loyalty, commitment and obligation" and it concerned "nurturing children and sustaining stability within the family" (van Acker 2003: 16). Gender roles were clearly organized as men were breadwinners and women were wives and mothers at home (ibid.; see also Henningham 2001).

logic of the incitement to pleasure took its course (1990, 274, cited by Teo 2005, 182). In this way, new practices were instilled in women's minds through advertising and the consumption of romance novels (Teo 2005).[2]

By the 1960s, marriage had become a symbol of romantic love, and attention was paid to the quality of the relationship between husband and wife. Towards the end of the twentieth century, "true love" had become an important basis for marriage (van Acker 2003, 16). Simultaneously, intimacy became yet another layer to the idea of romantic love and replaced passion as its most important and more enduring feature. Intimacy, understood as "a deep communication, friendship, and sharing that will last beyond the passion of new love" has become an essential characteristic of the ideal marriage (Shumway 2003, 27, cited by Teo 2005, 191). Thus, in Australia, nowadays, romantic love is an important factor in choosing a partner, and places complex and "different demands on relationships" than was previously the case (van Acker 2003, 17). But while women have moved away from stereotypes of "the Australian girl" (McPherson 1994), amongst others, due to the first feminist movement and consequent waves of feminism, its legacy remains (Curthoys 1993). Marriage and motherhood still remain tied to the dominant construction of femininity in Australia (Maher 2005; Campo 2005).

Such ideas about intimate relationships leading to respectability and acceptance, as well as romance and motherhood became evident through my conversations with sponsoring women. For all interlocutors of this study, and as with all relationships, the main motivation behind commencing a cross-border relationship was the expectation of a significantly improved life (see also Williams 2010). Whereas for migrant men such improvements may have partly been geo-political or economic in character, for women, the act of being in an intimate relationship seemed to be the desired path to happiness. For sponsoring women, romantic imaginaries of love, intimacy and commitment were important factors in pursuing relationships. However, women had different expectations of romantic relationships—and in turn of their partners— and two patterns became discernible. For some women, bodily insecurities helped shape their expectations and hopes of finding acceptance in their relationships. Other women in turn, hoped to find a perceived compatibility with their culturally other partner. In the next section, I elaborate on women's romantic expectations, and what gets in the way of intimacy.

---

2 Because of advertisements mainly being directed at women, Tao argues that women first became familiar with the new ideals of romantic love. After World War II, however, this gender—as well as age—disjunction disappeared, and men were influenced by similar romantic ideals (Teo 2005: 191).

4   Experiences of Marriage Migration among Sponsoring Women

4.1   *Bodies and Relationships*

While women may be socialized to believe that marriage and intimate relationships will lead to happy lives, not all women I interviewed seemed to feel it
was easy to find love. When talking with women, a reoccurring theme relating
to relationship- and partner choice was body image and discomfort with their
bodies, in particular among women who self-identified as overweight, fat and
"thick." In this section, I elaborate on how some women understood their bodies to be obstructing their chance of romantic love, and women's strategies to
resolve such obstructions. One solution was pursuing a relationship with an
African man, who, these women believed and/or hoped, would be accepting
of women's bodies. Another path to happier lives, in some cases, was dieting
and cosmetic surgery. However, it appeared that both strategies were limited
in their success, and even then, women remained insecure in their bodies as
well as in their relationships. From my conversations with women, it became
evident that women believed that since they did not meet Australian beauty
ideals, they therefore could not enjoy a happily ever after, as this would only
be an outcome for those with "ideal" bodies. It seems, then, that it is believed
that happiness is more readily ascribed to some bodies (thinner bodies), but
not bigger bodies.

Culturally constructed notions of the body influenced women's perceived
desirability. In Australia, the ideal white female body mirrors Anglo-European
hegemonic images of the young, thin, and controlled body (see for example,
Musolino et al. 2015; Kenny & Adams 1994). That the thin body is more of an
ideal than a normative reality is implied by, for instance, by Swinburn (2003),
who observes that obesity is considered to be an epidemic in Australia. Britton
et al. note that an increasing discrepancy between cultural ideals and the reality of female bodies has led to "body dissatisfaction as a normative experience"
(2006, 247). More than half of Australian women, according to Timperio et al.,
are attempting some form of weight control, with just fewer than 3 per cent of
them actively trying to gain weight (2010, 417). It is not surprising then that half
of the 18 sponsoring women I talked to were strikingly self-conscious about
their bodies.[3] From the seven women that expressed their unhappiness with

---

3   However, not all bigger women were insecure in their bodies, and two of the most success-
    ful relationships, in which the couple had been together for over a decade, were between
    migrant men and larger women. Seven out of 18 (ex)relationships were between partners
    who both fitted within hegemonic beauty standards in Australia and with no remarkable age
    dissimilarities between the partners.

being fat, four had undergone surgery to become thinner. Two other women said they felt uncomfortable in their bodies, as they were notably older than their partners. For those women, it seemed that their inability to comply with beauty ideals produced insecurity in their own bodies that affected their perceived chances of finding love.

That bodies can be read means that bodies can express core values of a culture or society (see for example, Bordo 1993). In relation to beauty, this means "attractiveness is that which is found ideologically appealing within an overarching set of values" (Reischer & Koo 2004, 300). As Bordo observes in her book *Unbearable Weight: Feminism, Western Culture, and the Body* (1993), a body becomes the symbol for attitude. The body's size and shape appears to display a person's moral state, a person's ability for commitment and self-control. In an Anglo-European context where fat is seen as odious, a big body signals the individual's inability to comply with, or fit in with, his or her larger social world.[4] Barbara Pini and Josephine Previte (2013) argue that in Australia, normative notions of white femininity are strongly paired with class. Working-class women are depicted as the antithesis of the "naturalized standard" of the middle-class woman. Whereas the latter are perceived as "respectable" and "culturally recognizable," working class women are seen as "dirty" and "vulgar," as "excessively sexual, dirty, fat, lazy, and welfare dependent ..." (Pini & Previte 2013, 352). Except for one interlocutor, women who had issues with their bodies came from lower socioeconomic backgrounds. None of these women had tertiary education and most of them worked in aged care or were on disability pensions. These women did not talk much about their family or socioeconomic backgrounds. At times when I tried to introduce the topic of their upbringing, I got a sense that they were bored with that line of questioning. Sarah, for instance, described her family in very general terms. She stated in a matter-of-fact way that she had a few siblings who all live in Adelaide, and that they would meet each other on birthdays and at other celebrations "all the time." They would also have barbecues over the weekend, would go out for drinks, "and stuff like that." She described her family as being very close, and sometimes loud and rude.

Although Sarah's mention of loudness may provide a certain image of her family, it does not say much about her background per se. However, during the time we spent together, sometimes with her friends or family present, and

---

4   While thinness as a beauty ideal is prevalent in many sociocultural contexts, fatness is cherished as a feminine ideal among, for instance, ethnic groups in Nigeria and in the Sahara Desert (Popenoe 2004; Brink 1995). Also, among some African-American women, larger bodies are preferred over thin bodies, which can be read as resistance to hegemonic structures in society (Rubin et al. 2003; Hughes 1997).

through social media, I learned a lot about her life and lifestyle. The first time I met Sarah was at an African women's event in the summer of 2015. She was one of the few Anglo-European women present and she drew my attention because of her high heels, tattoos and the multiple chains around her neck that were dangling in her cleavage. Her runny mascara revealed she had been crying. In the middle of a speech on women's empowerment, she walked out of the relatively small but packed room. I rushed after her, as I was concerned about her wellbeing. Sarah promptly began talking about her abusive husband who was the reason for her being upset. She wanted to share her story with me but was also in a rush to get to a family gathering. We agreed to meet up for a coffee the next week. She had invited me to her house, where she greeted me with a happy face, loud music, coca cola and potato crisps. We sat and talked for about an hour about her experiences with marriage migration before her sister Naomi arrived, which made us change topics.

The next time I met Sarah, she took me out for lunch by going to the drive-through at McDonalds where she got into a fight with the girl placing our order; we had to think for a time while she waited in front of the microphone and according to the girl, we were too slow in placing our order. Consequently, Sarah gave the girl an impressive scolding which galvanized my resolve to never risk being on Sarah's bad side. When we got home, she only ate two chicken nuggets and a handful of chips. She explained that since her "stomach removal," she could not eat a lot, something she did not particularly enjoy, although she was happy with the weight loss results. Sarah told me about her plans to go out that weekend but was not sure where she would go yet. She wanted to go to a place with "lots of hot African men" and was looking for an African themed night. When I happened to meet her that weekend, she was wearing impressive high heels, bright and glamorous jewelry and bright red lipstick. She was disappointed because "there were hardly any Africans out."

As described in Chapter 4, there is a perception that only "desperate women" choose to be with African men. In informal conversations it was suggested to me that such women come in two categories: young, obese women who are desperate to belong and in search of attention, and older, larger and/or lonely women who are desperate for love and companionship. While none of the women I interviewed and who practiced marriage migration expressed any abnormal desperation or a fear of living alone, women did express their desire or preference for being in a committed relationship. Their desires fit with dominant discourses of love and marriage in Australia, as described above. They shared comments such as: "it is nicer to have dinner together," "together is just much more fun than being alone," and "I just really want to be with a man who loves me, you know?" But, none of the women directly linked their desires for romantic love to cultural ideas and opinions about their bodies.

Yet, because many women who expressed body dissatisfaction said that African men would love big women, it seemed that body size was a reason to look for a migrant partner. Women may have based such ideas on stereotypes, but also on their partners' comments that they, as African men, preferred bigger women, and in particular loved their partner's body.[5] Naomi explained that "African men just love to have a bigger woman" because, she argued, "they like someone to hold." Skinny women, she reasoned, would not have "proper asses," and in Africa, according to her, people would like body fat as it would be a sign of wealth and health.

Most self-identified fat women I interviewed who had migrant partners, regardless of practicing or not practicing marriage migration, held these beliefs. So did women who did not have a partner but were looking for relationships with African men only. They all agreed that for Africans, big bodies are considered more beautiful and a sign of prosperity. These women also had a similar lifestyle: quite a few had undergone stomach removals as they would call the procedure of having gastric sleeve surgery and they would go out looking for African men and/or be on dating sites with an eye just for African men. Diana, for instance, a woman in her late thirties who has dated only men from the continent of Africa over the last ten years, continuously remarked on how "real men love real women, and real women have a healthy booty." Almost daily, Diana posted photos of herself on social media, celebrating her body. More women would post photos of themselves on social media, posing in a way that made their "bums" look especially round and their hips well shaped. At the same time, other women regularly posted updates about their post-surgery recovery and weight loss success in order to receive compliments and encouraging replies from friends and relatives.

What struck me were the seemingly contradictive narratives: on the one hand, women were dieting and/or undergoing surgery in order to become thin, while simultaneously, they underscored how big bodies were beautiful and how African men preferred their full bodies and especially, their buttocks. At a first glance, perceptions of African beauty ideals seemed to provide women with a solution for problems they experienced with their own bodies; it provided them with a space in which their bodies could be celebrated, instead of being

---

5   People in African contexts may have different ideas and ideals regarding beautiful bodies than what is imagined about African beauty ideals in Australian or Anglo-European contexts. It furthermore seems that a general obsession with African beauty in relation to big female buttocks is related to specific colonial histories and narratives, as described by Gilman (1985).

perceived as problematic. Men's interest in larger bodies, perceived as undesirable in the wider Australian context, led initially to much greater feelings of
self-worth for women. Suddenly, women were perceived as attractive and as
sexy. This, in turn, increased women's confidence in the idea that African men
love big bodies. Men's preference for big female bodies also seemed to solve
the issue of not being able to lose enough weight, as "real men" would appreciate fuller bodies anyway. Kim Chernin (1981) argues, both anorexic as well as
obese women share a hostility and discomfort with their bodies in their cultural contexts and feel like their bodies are not accepted in their social world.
Sponsoring women, by having a migrant partner, moved from a social world
where they felt their bodies were disapproved of, to a context in which their
bodies would be desired.

But women who did not fit in with the beauty ideal of thinness and/or fit-
ness continued to consider their bodies a problematic site, despite their relationships. The significant discomfort women experienced with their body and
its place in society became clear from the number of women who underwent
gastric sleeve surgery (or similar procedures), either during or in-between relationships with migrant men. According to Sander Gilman (1998), the dramatic
rise and acceptance of aesthetic surgery mirrors the idea that "ill bodies" can
be cured easily, to fit with what is socioculturally desired. Gilman also argues
that surgery is believed to heal the mind, as a healthy and strong body reflects
a healthy and strong psyche (1998). That women took control over their bodies,
by undergoing surgery to reduce weight, and simultaneously celebrated the
voluptuous body by choosing partners accepting of their bodies, can be understood as agentive actions aimed at self-improvement both within and against a
cultural context obsessed with thinness.

However, what is presented as choice, such as to opt for surgery or a cross-
border relationship, can also be understood as a calculated necessity. Yet, such
choices did not seem to solve women's insecurities with their own bodies.
Feminist scholars, such as Avelie Stuart and Ngaire Donaghue (2011), critique
the so-called free choice women have when considering culturally constructed
ideas about beauty in their everyday life. They argue, that "choice has become
the bottom-line value of postfeminism ... so long as a woman's actions or circumstances are considered a result of her own choices, no further analysis or
problematisation of them is welcome or warranted" (2011, 99). Choice, in this
way, is portrayed as an ultimate neoliberalist achievement, all the while forgetting about or ignoring the positionality of women's bodies within larger cultural frameworks. As Stuart and Donaghue remark, "The postfeminist promise
of liberation through empowered choice is overwhelmingly packaged within

the crushingly cruel beauty images that Western women are judged against and incited to emulate" (2011, 99; see also, Gill 2006; Jeffreys 2005; Wolf 1990).[6]

Women who seemed insecure in their own bodies were actively trying to resolve such bodily issues, either by "fixing" their bodies to fit in with sociocultural beauty norms, and/or by pursuing a relationship they hoped would make them happy despite their body size. That women underwent surgery (or were actively dieting) indicated that relationships with African men did not solve their issues of self-worth. Furthermore, women might not have felt secure in their relationships, as they often remained suspicious of their partner's acceptance of their bodies, and perhaps men's motives for being in the relationships.

For Jade, her husband's younger age (he was 17 years her junior) and her role as mother of two grown-up daughters also made her very self-conscious and uncomfortable in her body. She felt that having had two children had affected her body significantly. Jade did not think of her body as beautiful, but rather ugly, and therefore never understood why her ex-partner Desmond had been attracted to her. She felt that she "looked like a cow" and wondered why a man "as gorgeous and fit as he is," would be with an "old and ugly woman like me." Jade had met Desmond online. Before he moved to Adelaide, he had complimented her continuously, said that "age is just a number" and had told her that having had children made her "extra beautiful." But as soon as he arrived in Adelaide, Jade told me, he had stopped giving her compliments, and she had instantly felt that he did not love her and did not think she was beautiful. Her partner's changed behavior had made her very insecure. From what Jade told me, it seemed that she had been afraid that this would happen all along. When I asked her why she had started a relationship with him if she was so concerned about the age gap, she explained that his persistence and romantic talk kept her intrigued. She also gave a description about his body, which was as "fit as can be" and said he had a "beautiful smile." Jade confessed that she had never seen such a beautiful body, "muscular, that chocolate color," something she felt she could only dream of. And she at first could not believe that a man this handsome was showing interest in her.

Jade's story illustrates that relationships influence self-confidence. Whereas at first relationships boosted women's sense of self, eventually, relationships

---

6   It appears that women can make choices as freely as they want, as long as it does not endanger their femininity. In fact, "the cultural privilege attached to beauty creates a compelling reason for women to engage in beauty practices" and in this way, "are a means by which women can enhance their status within the dominant social order" (Stuart & Donaghue 2011, 100). Thus, women's choice to participate in beauty rituals is not something optional, but in reality, is socially consequential.

negatively affected women's confidence. Partly, this seemed to be a consequence of men's difficulties with their migration journeys, and sometimes
because of men's decreasing attention or paying of compliments. But simultaneously, it seemed that women had hoped their partners would love them
for themselves, and that as a result, their bodily insecurities would not matter.
This was an aspiration that turned out to be too ambitious. These sometimes
younger and often exceptionally fit men complimenting them and wooing
them had made the women feel very special, a feeling they had not had in
a long time, and which was something they did not expect to experience.
Simultaneously, relationships did not seem to solve such bodily issues, but in
fact only made them reappear even stronger than before.

Often, in conversations, women who expressed dissatisfaction with their
bodies also placed a large emphasis on their partner's body.[7] The Africanness
of their partner seemed to be an important factor in the desired happiness
the relationships promised. As has been described in previous chapters, from
my own observations and interviews with white Australians, male and female,
African men, and the Black male body can be cause for uncomfortable feelings,
for sexual fears and arousals, and a general confrontation with the unknown
(See Fanon 1986; Saint-Aubin 2005). Scholarship on cross-border marriages
and relationships, sex, and romance tourism explains how race is sexualized and eroticized. For white women, especially, the *Black* male body is an
exotic and attractive site (see for instance Herold et al. 2001; Jacobs 2009; Pruitt
& LaFont 1995). Most women explained that they simply felt attracted to Black
men, as their bodies would be softer, stronger, more muscular, they would be
"well hung" and their skin tone more beautiful than men of other races.

Also, certain character traits were linked to the Africanness of the partner, and, women believed, stood in stark contrast to those of Australian men.
Some women said they fell in love with their partner because of his dominance, romantic talk and his paying of compliments. Australian men, apparently, would never be that open and sweet. It was an "African thing," women
explained, that men were clear about what they wanted and would do anything

---

7   For 12 out of the 18 women I worked with and who are or have been in relationships with
    migrant men, the African male body was desired, and was an underlying reason for starting
    the relationship. I want to emphasize that this section, as well as the next, describes wom-
    en's reasoning for pursuing relationships after I asked them specifically about their motiva-
    tions for being with their partners, or wanting to pursue a relationship with their partners at
    the time. I specifically asked about the "why" in relation to their choice for a migrant man.
    Therefore, sponsoring women's answers may be more directed towards racializations and
    stereotypes than if that question was raised outside of the frame of this study.

to conquer the heart of the woman they pursued. It made the women feel very special. For Jade, as described above, Desmond's Africanness was not only visible in the color of his skin, but also became apparent, she felt, from his "smooth talking." Even though her relationship had ended, she still felt that there are differences between African men and Australian men. African men would be more attentive, more complimentary and more macho. "They are real men, if you know what I mean, and they know how to please a woman," she explained as she winked at me and giggled. Jade felt that African men know how to make women feel beautiful and loved.

Samantha, a woman in her mid-twenties and married to Thomas, shared Jade's opinion that African men would be better partners than Australian men. Thomas had come to Australia as a student about four years before I interviewed him. The couple had met while he was still studying in Australia. After being together for just over a year, Thomas's visa was about to expire and so they decided to apply for a Partner visa. When Samantha and I met up for brunch in one of Adelaide's suburbs near the sea, we found ourselves talking about our partners. I asked her if she ever thought about the color of her partner's skin as a reason for her attraction to him. Samantha simply answered that she "just preferred African men," as they would "look better, treat women better and are better lovers." She knew this, she said, because all her boyfriends had been "great lovers," implying that all her partners had been Black. She also confessed that she could confirm the stereotype of Black men and their penis size, because whilst she had no experience with white men, all her previous partners had been "blessed in that area."

For Jo, who met her husband Robert over thirty years ago, it was no surprise she would share her life with an African man, as she recalls how she always just knew that her husband would be a Black man. When she met Robert, she knew it was *him*, even though she was a bit disappointed by his ordinary name, Robert, instead of "something African, something traditional, like Chidike or something exotic." Jo reflected on her first encounter with her husband Robert when the three of us were sitting around their kitchen table. Both Jo and Robert laughed cordially when recollecting their love story's beginning. Jo firmly believed that their relationship was meant to be, and was related to a profound experience in her youth. When in the bus with her mother as a young girl, Jo dropped her hat. It was hard for her to reach it as it had slid underneath the seat behind her. Suddenly, Jo saw a Black hand reaching out to her holding her hat. When she looked up, she saw a "dark man with a grand smile," handing her the hat. Jo felt it was that moment that she realized she would be destined to marry a Black man. However, she said she had always found that strange, since when she was young, she almost never encountered Black men.

Jo's story in particular indicates how the idea and ideal of finding one's "chosen one" to live happily ever after with can intersect with focusing on the exotic other. Women relied on stereotypes of African masculinities and preferred these men because of their bodies and perceived character traits, which included their perceived acceptance and desire of larger women's bodies. Women initially romanticized African men and felt that their bodies and traits would make them perfect partners, and that cross-border relationships would lead to a happy future not otherwise available to them. However, such idealizations of partners and expectations of relationships often did not become a reality for many of these women. In the longer-term, intimate relationships did not make women feel validated and partners did not always live up to women's expectations. In the next section, I turn to the eight women whose motivations for their relationship were different to the group above. These women stated that they were attracted to their migrant partners based on a perceived compatibility between their own interests and beliefs and their partner's cultural background.

4.2   *Cultural Compatibility*

Eight women aspired to be in loving and companionate relationships and felt that these "different" men were a good match to their own "different" identities. Compatibility is an important aspect of intimate and companionate relationships, which requires an emotional and intimate bond with an equal partner (Giddens 1992; Hirsch & Wardlow 2006). The women themselves pointed to their own otherness and "alternative" identities, which they believed would be compatible with their partner's otherness. They felt that their interests, lifestyles and life philosophies accorded better with their migrant partners' lifestyle choices and cultural background rather than with those of Australian men. Thus, even though the women felt they were different to other Australian women, they still pursued the same hopes of having a companionate relationship.

The women who placed importance on cultural compatibility, imagined or otherwise, identified themselves as "spiritual," "alternative," and "creative," traits not reflecting conventional middle-class values in Australia. Sophie, for instance, described both herself and her friend who also married an Africa-origin man, as "adventurous, against the grain and just different." These women had unique personalities and had taken many different directions in their lives. With various occupations—some were self-employed, while others worked for government institutions or universities—they seemed to be difficult to categorize. Interestingly, what they had in common was that all of them had one or more creative side projects beside their regular jobs;

these included performing music, managing a second-hand shop, or writing poetry.

These women also emphasized that compatibility, based both on women's own ideas about their partner's cultural background and otherness, as well as their partner's personality traits, were reasons for pursuing an intimate relationship. Assumptions about the prospective partner, based on background and culture, turned out to be subtle, important and sometimes decisive factors in commencing a relationship. Perceptions of Africanness as representing life moving at a slower pace, that is non-consumerist and non-capitalist, but "natural" and "spiritual" were traits women ascribed to their partners, and that women felt matched their own lifestyles.

While none of these women completely disregarded Australian men as suitable potential partners, they explained that their particular cultural backgrounds, upbringings and lifestyle choices simply corresponded more naturally with those of their migrant partner. Sophie explained that her own upbringing had led her to live an artistic and "different" lifestyle, which consequently explained her relationship choices. She described her upbringing as culturally and intellectually rich. Her parents encouraged her to read literature, visit the theatre and to be curious about the world. At home, they listened to a broad variety of music, ranging from classical and opera, to world music, including by artists from the continent of Africa. Sophie remembered that from the very beginning she always felt particularly drawn to African music genres, as well as music performed by African-American artists.

Sophie's love for music, together with her parents' stimulus provided the motivations for her travel to Africa for a drumming course. It was in that African country that Sophie realized and experienced what she thought she wanted from life and how to live it: a simple life with a focus on community and family, and an appreciation of the world as it is. This way of life was directly opposite to Sophie's sense of a typical Australian way of life, which she perceived to be mainly consumption oriented and individualistic. She had hoped to live happily ever after with Anthony, her now ex-husband, whom she met during that trip. Unfortunately, when they settled in Australia Anthony had not turned out to be the man that she hoped he would be. Anthony, who back home had been charismatic, charming, and dominant, had become a quiet and disengaged man. He seemed to be a different person. When the marriage ended, Sophie sought a new partner. She felt that an artistic Australian man could certainly be a potential match. However, she married Lucas, another Africa-origin man, and explained that his love for nature, simple life, his interests in music, food and family—their commonalities—were more encompassing and that her personal interests and lifestyle choices would be shared more readily with him.

These eight women seemed more adventurous and showed broader interests in art, cultural activities such as attending festivals, dance performances
and museums, and global issues, compared to other women. Charlotte, for
instance, ran her NGO in Africa. She travelled back and forth on a regular
basis but preferred to move there permanently. "What would I do then, with
an Australian partner," she explained, "who is not interested in that country,
my cause, and who does not know about anything I am interested in and passionate about!" To her, it made sense that she is together with her Zachary.
Similarly, Eileen, who had met her husband when she attended a drumming
course in Africa, described being together with her partner Mark as a logical
result of their shared interest in African drumming. As they both loved the
music and shared their passion for rhythm, she felt that it was unlikely she
would find this connection with an Australian man.

Emma reasoned that her individuality, spirituality and political outlook
were interests she shared with her partner Matthew. Emma explained that she
had always felt herself to be a free-spirited person, following her own path.
When she was younger, her parents and siblings always knew that she would
go about things differently. It therefore came as no surprise to any of them that
she decided to travel overseas by herself, even though she described the decision for her to go as an unaccompanied woman was "quite rare at the time." In
her early twenties, Emma travelled through southern Europe for a few months,
to explore her roots. It was there where she met her husband, Matthew. Emma
felt that her being different explained why she does not have a "mainstream-
looking or culturally similar husband." She emphasized that while they may
look different, the norms, values and personality of her and her husband are
very similar. Both Emma and Sophie had a strong connection with their families, and valued family significantly. During my fieldwork, they would often
express how present their families were in their lives. Perhaps, this importance
placed on the family, rather than the individual was another real or perceived
commonality they shared with their partners.

Such narratives illustrate how not only women were looking for a mate, a
likeminded partner to share their lives with, but also how a cultural match subtly becomes racialized. Women sometimes simplified, idealized, and romanticized the continent of Africa and its imagined way of living. Such general
stereotypes about Africa were sought after and ascribed to their partners in a
way that was meaningful for them.

Within social psychology, stereotypes are understood in various ways.
Generally, they are viewed as "an inevitable consequence of the psycholog-
ical and cognitive need to categorize and simplify a complex social world"
(Augoustinos & Walker 1998, 629). Discursive psychology emphasizes that such

categorization is not merely a cognitive process, but rather a "social establishment," through which categories are socially constructed (1998, 640–1). Some of these constructions, Martha Augoustinos and Iain Walker argue, "are so familiar, pervasive and common-sensical that they 'give an effect of realism' or fact" (1998, 641). In this way, people "come to regard some constructions not as versions of reality, but as direct representations of reality itself" (ibid.). Likewise, the women I spoke to often hinted at how African men would be different from Australian men, and when I asked about their reasons for being with their partners, they often gave answers describing their perception of Africans in general, rather than of their specific partners; they were relying on stereotypes.

But while women were sometimes overtly positive about Africa and tended to overlook the heterogeneity of the continent, simultaneously, women who were still with their migrant partners evidently shared many commonalities. These women, while idealizing the continent and romanticizing its way of living, were with partners who matched their lifestyle choices, and were not necessarily with an African for the sake of being with an African.

Some of the women described in this section also placed a large emphasis on their partner's body and style of masculinity. Anne, for example, expressed how she had imagined her now ex-partner Boris to be her protector, with whom she could feel safe. When she met her partner in Africa, he showed her the way; he had been her cultural broker, the one who made sure nothing bad would happen to her. Anne explained how Boris played a vital role in the way she experienced the country she had travelled to for her drumming course. Boris, an excellent drummer himself, had been one of the students' supervisors at the drumming camp. The students—all young, mostly female and all from Anglo-European countries—were allocated a guest family in the village where the music school was located. In Anne's case, Boris chaperoned her from her house to the school and back, every day. He had showed her around the village, to the music halls, the beaches and the markets. Thanks to Boris, the village had become a comfortable place for Anne. And not only had Boris been very helpful, Anne remembered him too as an exceptionally handsome and romantic man. She described his "dark and sweaty skin," his "big arms and shoulders" and his "dreadlocks bouncing up and down," during his drumming performances. She added, grinning, that "of course a young girl falls in love with such an appearance!"

Stories such as Anne's indicate that while a pattern was observable, the dataset consists of specific women with individual stories and experiences and unique relationships with partners. Despite this, what they had in common, more often than not, was a shared feeling of being disappointed by the reality of their cross-border relationship. Women were disappointed not only because their partners failed to meet their expectations, but they were often saddened because they found themselves acting in ways that they had not anticipated. In the next section, I look at my dataset on all female interlocutors to analyze the ways in which relationships turned out to be disappointing rather than what they had hoped for.

4.3   Unhappy Relationships

Disappointments in women's relationships can partly be explained by the perception of romantic love as being mysterious, intuitive and unique, and leading to a happy future (van Acker 2003). In Australia, as outlined earlier, romantic love is currently seen as a necessary basis for marriage. Women are socialized to believe that marriage—or a de facto relationship—is the only acceptable way to womanhood, and romance is the vehicle towards this much coveted goal. At the same time, romance is not easily reconcilable with long-term relationships. As van Acker argues, "Romance is culturally constructed as a private or personal emotion that mysteriously manifests as 'chemistry', as an unexplainable but natural emotion" (2003, 17). Such feelings are "disconnected from reality," she continues, but simultaneously "elevate the couple to the status of unique and exclusive, bestowed with the mantle of 'chosen one' or 'one and only' from 'now until forever'" (ibid.; see also Ingraham 1999). But such ideas of romance and true love contradict the responsibility that is attached to long-term commitment, whether this is in marriage or a de facto partnership. The ultimate celebration of true love and romance ideally results in marriage, which in itself can be seen as a construct "taming" that love. Popular imaginings of romance and true love, for instance, "rarely raise issues about how the couple will adapt and negotiate domestic duties, care for children and tackle work and financial commitments" (van Acker 2003, 17).

For my female interlocutors, disappointments in relationships were even more complex, as they were also strongly related to their often-hasty decisions to marry and/or migrate due to visa regulations, and due to the influence of the migration journey on their migrant partners. Because of the journey of marriage migration, relationship dynamics became uncomfortable for both partners. Men turned out to be different than women had hoped for them to be and as men had initially portrayed themselves. As illustrated in the previous chapter, settling in Australia made it hard—if not impossible—for men to retain their identity as strong and caring partners. Just as men were negatively affected by their everyday dependency (Williams 2010) on their partners, so too were women suffering from their newly gained burden of responsibility as it directly opposed the ideal of a companionate relationship. Dragojlovic analyses Balinese-Dutch relationships in the Netherlands and describes two points in their narratives that negatively influence relationships:

> The first is class, educational differences, and access to citizenship rights, which place partners in different positions during their initial life in the Netherlands. The second is women's desire for a companionate marriage.
>
> DRAGOJLOVIC 2008, 336

Often, Australian women, like Dutch women, had imagined their partners to be good partners and husbands, but the often-difficult reality of everyday life after marriage migration, combined with women's unmet expectations, left women disappointed with what they had hoped would be a lasting companionship among equal partners. In most cases, men's new dependency, passivity and insecurity was not what women expected from their partners. Women did not necessarily enjoy this new dynamic and felt disappointed that men seemingly had lost their once proactive and self-confident attitude. Thus, the imagination and idealization of romantic relationships and *the* African partner turned out to be very different from the lived reality of everyday life with a migrant partner.

After settling in Adelaide and Melbourne, the intimacy and equality women had hoped would continue, disappeared. That women now had greater economic, social and cultural capital than the men, made it self-evident that women took the lead. This, in turn, could easily be interpreted as controlling behavior. Women experienced great pressure as they felt they had to take care of everything by themselves, without much help from their partners. In this new context, according to the women in my study, men would have to learn many new things—from household duties such as cleaning, cooking and administration on the one hand— to being a provider as well as regaining or retaining a chivalrous attitude, on the other. Women lamented that regardless of how they acted, reacted or dealt with any issues faced by the couple, their husband's dependency put them in a very difficult position. Even though women sincerely tried their best to accommodate their partners, the result was often counterproductive.

Some women described their partners as "big babies" or as an extra child they had to look after. Lauren stated that her ex-husband constantly claimed that she was belittling him each time she made a suggestion or gave advice. While she did not mean it that way, her comments were construed as a "lecture," once again reminding him of his inadequacy. Consequently, she tried not to share her opinion on things he was doing, but also found it difficult and not always sensible to do so: "When I saw something going wrong, it was really hard for me not to come to the rescue." Lauren went on to describe how at one point her husband lacked motivation. Although he never admitted to it, Lauren strongly suspected he suffered from depression after he moved to Australia. When she gave birth to their daughter, she said that he did not "step up" at all. As a result, she had to take full care of their small baby and the household, while recovering from childbirth, and leaving her with little rest prior to her return to work. The only thing he was capable of, she felt, was "laying on the floor and wailing."

Sophie had been in a similar position. She recounted that soon after her previous partner Anthony arrived in Australia, it seemed that almost everything was difficult for him—things like: doing the shopping, eating Australian food and using a computer. While this made her feel disappointed and annoyed, as it meant she had to do everything herself and for two people, she also understood that he did not behave in this way on purpose. She tried her best to make him feel at home in Australia, to help him settle in, but always in vain. When looking back, she understands that perhaps she was mothering him too much, that there was "no space for him to breath." Maybe, she reasoned, if she had withdrawn from her newly adopted role of carrying all responsibility, it would have encouraged him to accept some. But at the same time, she explained that it was because of his idleness that she simply had to take on all the responsibilities of everyday life. Sophie felt that his difficulties with adjusting, his depressive moods and unwillingness to work on their issues made her feel as if she had made a mistake by marrying him. She felt that there was just nothing left of his charismatic identity and strong demeanor she had fallen in love with, in Africa. Both Lauren and Sophie where the ones to end their relationships; they realized they could not continue in this way without suffering from a breakdown themselves. The pressure they felt to take care of their new-born babies, as well as their depressed partners, was too much to bear.

For both women, it was the changed character of their partners, and the changed character of their relationships once they were united in Adelaide, which inevitably made them reconsider their relationships. The circumstances made men seem less masculine and thus less desirable. This new reality was also the exact opposite of what they had searched for in a relationship, and of their expectations of intimacy and companionship (Giddens 1992; Hirsch & Wardlow 2006). It also made women feel like mothers instead of wives or lovers, and thus undesirable themselves. Their relationships were not the happy ones they had hoped for.

While women realized that men failed to be ideal partners, women also recognized that they themselves had changed in ways they had not anticipated, nor liked. Some women could see their behavior as unhealthy and too controlling; Emma, described herself, fifteen years ago, as an "obsessed mothering bitch." It seemed that women wanted their partner to thrive in Australia, and at first assumed that their own cultural script of what married life is supposed to be like was the only legitimate one to follow. Yet, some women soon realized that they could not expect their partner to do everything exactly the way the women themselves were used to doing it, especially since their partners were not used to living in Australia. Eileen, for instance, remembers their argument about cheese, and stated that she could now see where she went wrong. She acknowledged that her request for a particular cheese "must have sounded like Russian to him." "How does he know where I buy my cheese, let alone the difference between young and aged cheese, and cheddar and Gouda?" Eileen, who is still together with her partner, explained that she learnt to be more flexible about cheese, as well as her other requests.

It becomes evident that the process of settling in Australia had a negative effect on both men and women. Migrant men were not familiar with the local cultural repertoire (Nowicka 2018) or habitus and did not have the durable dispositions (Bourdieu 1984) that their partners had. This caused difficulties for both partners. Whereas most women recognized this issue sooner or later, it was also not easy or even possible to solve. In this way, migration journeys had an insidious effect on relationships that couples had not anticipated, but that were also outside of their control. Men's lack of cultural, economic, and social capital in Australia changed partnerships and resulted in a burden shared by both partners. As a result, the equal partnerships that women felt were achievable through marriage migration were obstructed by the very process of marriage migration (Dragojlovic 2008).

Expectations and disappointments about their partner were sometimes influenced by stereotypes of the other. Assumptions about their partners, based on sex, race, background and culture turned out to be subtle, important, and sometimes decisive factors, not only for starting off a relationship, but also for conflicts within relationships. Disappointments were sometimes explained to me by women in racialized terms. At times, when I heard complaints about men not living up to their partner's expectations, women would directly link this to their partners being African. For example, they would say: "African men would not be used to cooking," "African men would refuse to perform household duties," or "African men would not want to be seen shopping." Everyday quarrels and misunderstandings among couples were explained by or seemed to stem from the fact that their partners were African, instead of deriving from difficulties in interpersonal relationships.

This became particularly clear when talking to Alice and Vivian one day. I had driven southwards to one of Adelaide's beach suburbs to meet up with the two women at Alice's house for a coffee. We did this every now and then, and the three of us all enjoyed these occasions as they offered us time to reflect on things that had happened since our last meeting. According to Alice and Vivian, African men were not even capable of buying the right groceries. Alice explained that the one time she sent her now ex-partner to the supermarket, he came home with only meat instead of the products on the shopping list she had given him. She argued that "Africans only eat meat," which was according to her "unhealthy, and way too expensive." But, she reasoned, "He did not have a clue because he was not working, and just spending my money."

The alleged "stupidity" of African partners also became clear when listening to Vivian. Like Alice, Vivian had met her now ex-partner in Adelaide where he had come as a student. She explained that he would just "sit around." When she asked him to help her with household duties, he would do it, but he would also be visibly annoyed. She felt that he would never do anything around the house based on his own initiative. And if he cleaned, it would not be thorough enough, and she would have to start the cleaning all over again. She explained away his apparent inability as, "African men, you know?" She continued about his ineptitude by elaborating on his practice of doing the grocery shopping. He would come home with margarine, when she had asked for butter, for instance, and he would not even know the difference between full-cream and skimmed milk.

It thus appeared that some women based the disappointing realities of their relationships on the fact that their ex-partners were African. Such categorizations of African men's character traits indicate how stereotypes are often inconsistent and are dependent on the context in which categorization takes place (Augoustinos & Walker 1998, 641). When asking women what they liked about their partners, they often indicated positive traits related to their partner being African. But now, when discussing relationship problems, women also used their partner's African identity as an explanatory factor for their lack of "know-how," and to frame their frustration with their partner and their now difficult relationship.

Women's frustrations and resentment, as well as their controlling behavior sometimes crossed over into social spheres, too, with women telling men when they could go out and how much money they were allowed to spend. While the controlling behavior might be attributed to women's additional burden as the sole breadwinner or the main provider, and the person who had the most knowledge of their budget, the line between a fair negotiation and telling the other partner what to do turned out to be easily crossed. Many women told me that while they really did not want to be giving orders to their partner, they had to because their partner did not understand the value of Australian dollars and what bills had to be paid. Other women, however, felt this had been the only option, as men would always misuse their limited funds. For instance, Jade explained that her partner would send most of their money home, if he could, and Chloë complained that her partner would spend too much of their money on beer.

Women's tendencies to control were sometimes related to trust issues. Some women expressed that their partners were difficult to trust and how they had difficulty understanding why men had to go out socializing without them. They wondered if wanting to go out alone was a sign of him pursuing other women. For some women I interviewed, their distrust was explained by instances of infidelity and/or dishonesty in their relationships with their partners. While some women now refused to allow their husbands to go out without them, others explained that their partner would disappear for hours—sometimes days—without telling them where they went. Jade, for instance, described her relationship with her now ex-husband as a constant struggle from her side to find out where he went and with whom (as opposed to what he told her). She felt that it would be wrong of him to talk to another woman, just as it would be wrong to be an hour late, or to not pick up the phone when she called. It was unclear to me if he ever really had been unfaithful, which could have explained her extreme jealousy. However, it became apparent from her story that her partner did lie about his whereabouts, and did disappear for long periods of time, sometimes overnight. Jade explained this behavior as something African men did rather than as an individual trait.

It seemed that some women generalized about African men based on their own experiences with their partners. By reducing their partners to a stereotype, women presented and processed relationship problems as being outside of their control. When listening to women who had been treated badly by their ex-partners, I was often presented with the idea of African men as "players going around," as always being "on the hunt," and hypersexual. It thus appeared that among some of the women there was general consent on a narrative regarding African men as a specific type, in need of some sort of specific treatment. African men would need time for themselves and certainly could not stand women asking about their whereabouts and the associated details. Not only sponsoring women explained this to me, but some men and women with an African background, as well, elaborated on how a woman should never ask too many questions about where her partner goes when he leaves the house. The lack of communication—whether or not this was explained as a cultural or racialized matter—not only seemed to cause anxiety among women, but it also acted against women's idealization of the companionate relationship, in which couples should communicate and share their emotions (Teo 2005).

Some women I interviewed seemed to have created a narrative of African men as hypersexual, incapable of commitment, and unable to communicate their experiences or whereabouts with their female partners. However, such ideas were also influenced by other factors. Views about men's perceived fidelity can be explained partly by media images, visa procedures and stereotypes encountered in everyday life. But also, it seemed that women's friends, who often had Africa-origin partners too, influenced women's mistrust in African men. For instance, what Sarah heard from her girlfriends about African men influenced her ideas about her ex-partner's behavior. She told me about her friend who had installed a Detective-app on her partner's phone, which is how she found out about his "cheating on her" with several women. Sarah, with feeling, told me: "You see, they are all cheating scumbags."

As described by Dragojlovic (2008), the desire or need for communication can be a source of conflict for intercultural couples. The author describes how for Dutch women, the sharing of emotions was a taken for granted requirement for a relationship, something that their Balinese spouses did not deem that important, and consequently left Dutch women disappointed (2008, 341). Yet, women I interviewed who were in good relationships with their partners, like Lillian and Jo, never brought up discourses of uncommunicative, "bad" African men. Other migrant men as well as couples such as Charlotte and Zachary, and Sophie and Lucas also, did not agree with the suggestion that African men did not communicate, and argued that when living together, it only makes sense to communicate, to keep one's partner updated on where one is going, with whom, and their expected return time. Emma, married to her partner for over fifteen years, specified that migrant men, like other men and women, need time for socializing. "And this does not equal sleeping with other women per definition," she emphasized. She felt that there were some women in Adelaide who imagined that the moment their partners stepped outside, they would only be looking for other women to have sexual contact with. Trust in one's partner, as well as communication, Emma felt, were vital aspects of relationships.

In eleven cases, women's intimate relationships had ended. These relationships did not work because they were not functional or romantic partnerships, even though some partners may have still been attracted to, or cared for, each other. As a result, many found it hard to let go. The story of Sarah illustrates how complicated separations can be. Two weeks after their separation, I visited Sarah for a coffee. When I arrived, she told me that her ex-partner would be stopping by to pick up his laundry, which she was still doing for him. She mentioned that he came over every now and then, also to just "hang out." They often got intimate during such visits. Sarah's ex-partner had been violent with her on multiple occasions. She had sometimes showed me the marks on her skin from when he had beaten her or bitten her. Yet it was difficult for her to break up with him, as she often thought it was better to be with him than to be alone, better to have *a* relationship, than *no* relationship at all. This is consistent with Summer's (2006) argument that Australian women are socialized to believe that marriage is the only path to happiness and acceptability.

Yet, Sarah's ex-partner also had told her she was too ugly to be loved, and that she was lucky to have him, and she had believed him. Whether Sarah's ex-partner was aware of it before he settled in Adelaide or not, he seemingly used his knowledge that her body was not socially considered desirable as a weapon to re-gain power in their relationship. While he depended on the relationship for his visa status, emotional, verbal and physical abuse might have been ways for him to re-balance the power in their relationship. According to others, the relationship was abusive on both sides, as he had also suffered from Sarah's emotionally abusive behavior. While their relationship had clearly been bad for both parties, now that they had separated, they seemed to get along a little bit better.

Sarah seemed both nervous and excited about his appearance, and said she was curious to see if he would be on his best behavior "to charm me." She implied that he was going to try to impress me in order to pursue me. She had complained about him using her to do things for him, and how in this way he dominated her and mistreated her, even though they were not together anymore. Sarah portrayed him in a very bad way prior to his arrival. Surprisingly, her attitude changed completely when he came in, and she started acting amusingly and sweetly, instead of showing the more serious and comfortable Sarah I had seen just before. Sarah did seem to enjoy his company. While actively flirting with him, she seemingly made sure to make the necessary mean comment every now and then, too. I felt as if she wanted to show him, in front of me—a guest, and a "classy" friend as she always called me—that she was in control of the situation, too. I did not understand what she was doing: Why would she provoke him like that? Was she showing me how she still had power over this man she had just described as a brute? This instance can be explained in relation to the limited subject positions available to Sarah. She may have wanted to be perceived as a desirable woman to feel a sense of worth, and simultaneously she wanted to show both me and him that she is aware of his limitations.

But also, her ex-partner behaved in ways that I had not anticipated. I had never met him before; I had only heard about him, mainly from Sarah, and what I had heard about him was mostly negative. Although he was just as physically fit as Sarah had described, he was also nicer and calmer than I had expected; based on her stories about him I had been nervous about meeting him from the moment she mentioned him visiting. While it was clear that the two had a toxic relationship, it now also dawned on me that the two might still feel affectionate towards each other. Sarah was doing his laundry for him because she still liked him. And possibly, his approval and the continued contact legitimated her partner choice, while simultaneously reminding her why the relationship did not work. And maybe, he came to visit Sarah because he liked being around her.

Although this relationship was extremely complicated, the example illustrates that while partnerships did not work out in the way couples had hoped for, it was still possible for the partners to have some sort of relationship with each other. The example also indicates that when relationships become dysfunctional, separations do follow, no matter how hard such splits can be for both partners. This is in line with the current notion that the idea of an everlasting union—whether this is through marriage or a de facto relationship—has lost its significance (Coontz 2005). As described in Chapter 3, instead of one lasting marriage, people can opt for a number of consecutive intimate relationships. When romance and emotional intimacy fades in one relationship, it might be found in a new one (see Coontz 2005; Giddens 1992). For the interlocutors, like Sarah, who had separated from their partners, the journey of marriage migration, in which relationship dynamics are being turned upside down, when individual partner traits come to the fore and through which partners change significantly, has not led to the expected outcome. Their experiences of romance and intimacy have been upset, and their great expectations for the future not met.

5   Conclusion

This chapter provides extensive evidence of how women perceived their relationships with their migrant partners. Where relationships ended and regardless of which partner was seen as most responsible for its break-up, women were extremely unhappy prior to the relationship ending. I have shown that this is due to the great expectations placed on their partners and limited foresight about practical realities. Unhappy relationships had a lot to do with the ways that the women projected a happily-ever-after future onto their partners because they hoped that their partners would help to validate them—either their bodies or their lifestyles—in ways that they had not found in Adelaide or Melbourne. They also realized that they had been complicit in entering into a relationship based on assumptions of either pure body/physical acceptance and/or presumptions of compatibility. This led to either feelings of distrust and/or disappointment and resulted in some surprising outcomes. One of these was that many women found themselves exerting power over their relationship, and their partners, in ways that could be described as overbearing, distrustful or controlling. This was also a source of unhappiness for the women as they saw themselves transformed in ways that they did not expect and did not particularly like.

Unfortunately, the hoped for happily ever after often did not materialize. For the various reasons discussed in this chapter, relationships did not befit women as well as they hoped. But often, for a long time, women preferred their unhappy relationships over the alternative of being single. This relates back to the normative idea that love and intimate relationships validate women *as women* (Summers 2006). Yet, such narratives are not unique to African-Australian couples: more generally, the prefabricated idea that an intimate relationship brings happiness provides the emotional setting for disappointment (Ahmed 2008). Intimate relationships in this way can be seen as examples of cruel optimism. As Berlant explains, "a relationship of cruel optimism exists when something you desire is actually an obstacle to your flourishing" (2011, 1). While marriage can be perceived as the marker of happiness, marriage itself is set up for crisis, as becomes evident for instance by the significant divorce rates in Australia and elsewhere.

The dominant narrative provided by both government and media discourses about cross-border relationships describes them as sham—focusing on the amount of money naïve women ostensibly lose, and their manipulation by foreign men. This chapter has shown that such a narrative is far from realistic. Women were not victims who were tricked by "evil men." Instead, the grand hopes for romance and acceptance, as well as difficult migration journeys influenced relationships and their endings. And, women as well as men ended relationships. While the number of separations can be seen as high—11 out of the 18 women I worked with separated from their migrant partners—in Australia, more than 45 per cent of marriages end in divorce (van Acker 2003, 15). Given the various obstacles cross-border couples face throughout their journey of marriage migration, as I have described throughout this work, this number of separations should not come as a surprise but could actually be interpreted as commendable.

For some of the women I interviewed, the romantic and intimate love that they were looking for in their migrant partner—and that would validate their femininity in Australian society—did not materialize. For women who were still with their partner, love was not only perceived as romantic and happy, but also required much work. This concurs with van Acker's observation, that "the construction of romance overlooks the contradictions between the allure of passion and the responsibility of long-term commitment" (2003, 17). Women's pursuit of lasting happiness, either remained unmet or demanded effort to attain their desired relationship outcomes. This indicates that achieving happiness is a process and remains directed towards the future (Ahmed 2010). While some of the personal changes required have been flagged in this chapter, the concluding chapter adds more evidence of the long-term transformations that intimate partners underwent—both female and male. In that concluding chapter, I also discuss partners' experiences of life in Australia after migrant men gained permanent residency.

CHAPTER 8

Conclusion

Life after Permanent Residency

This study illuminated how for African-Australian cross-border couples, marriage migration is envisioned as a happiness project (Ahmed 2010), but simultaneously is experienced as a path faced with multiple obstructions. It showed how sponsoring women and migrant men, with high expectations, imagined a good and happy life in Australia, and how they actively tried to build hopeful futures. A happy future in Australia served as the purpose, the horizon, that couples and partners aimed towards. Happiness, viewed in this way, becomes a motive in people's everyday lives (Ahmed 2010; Gardner 2016).

How people pursue happiness can reveal much about the values they hold dear (Walker & Kavedžija 2016, 1; Gardner 2016). For the interlocutors of this study, embarking on journeys of marriage migration was related to their hopes of finding happiness through love and intimate long-term relationships. For the partners whose experiences I studied, their relationships created opportunities to become happier men and women. For the migrant men, happiness was to be found not only in their intimate relationships, but also in migration. Settling in Australia, men hoped, would lead to upwards socioeconomic mobility, an increased status, and a better life for those they left behind. For sponsoring women, the relationship itself promised to make them happy. Experiencing romance and intimacy were seen as ways to increase their status as women in their particular locality. Such different values indicate that happiness is inherently subjective. As Walker and Kavedžija argue, happiness "says much about the social, economic, and political conditions in which it emerges" (2016, 2).

While all interlocutors envisioned their journeys of marriage migration as happiness projects, for almost all, the much-anticipated happiness and fulfilment did not materialize. By combining a dark anthropological framework with a focus on happiness, I aimed to illustrate how several intertwining obstructions interfered with aspirations for happy lives. Each chapter of this book elaborated on different hurdles on the path to happiness. The net result was that marriage migration did not always lead to happiness. Instead, the journey often left couples and partners disappointed.

Aspirations of, and movements towards, happiness are influenced by dominant structures and values (Walker & Kavedžija 2016). Throughout the book I have illuminated this while using a Critical Race Theory lens to focus on the ways in which, for cross-border couples, the pursuit of happiness was obstructed by various instances of racism and exclusion. The visa application procedure, with its focus on demonstrating the genuineness of relationships was the first obstruction to couples' happiness projects. Such bureaucratic hurdles have the intention of avoiding sham marriages—those serving to secure visas or obtain money, rather than recognizing sincere love—thus protecting the nation-state and its citizens from insincere others (Andrikopoulos 2019; Scheel & Gutekunst 2019; Eggebø 2013; Fernandez 2013; Lavanchy 2014). For the partners and couples I interviewed, this process was often experienced as intrusive. They felt targeted because of the migrant partner's background, and that this was the only reason their intimate relationships were being questioned. The mistrust couples experienced, as well as the lengthiness of the procedure, was considered by interlocutors as hindering their desired happy futures.

Experiences of everyday racism (Essed 1991), combined with the implicit normative authority of whiteness in Australia (Ramsay 2017), made it hard for couples to enjoy their everyday lives as a cross-border couple after settling in Australia. Migrant men experienced various instances of sometimes blatant and at other times subtle racism and prejudice that significantly impacted on them as well as their partners. And because of the otherness of the migrant partner, sponsoring women, through their cross-border relationships, also experienced racialized encounters. It appeared that instances of racism were not only encountered in Australian contexts, but also in contexts that were predominantly African, such as among migrant men's families back home, as well as among African community organizations. The everyday racism couples encountered included biases, stereotypes and instances of protectionism, as well as well-intended warnings of relatives and friends stemming from fears of other men (Dragojlovic 2008; Lavanchy 2014).

Combined with racism, the experiences of homesickness and isolation, as well as liminality in the visa application process, left men feeling emasculated, and turned men into unhappy husbands (Charsley 2005). For many of the women, the anticipated happiness that would come by means of their intimate relationships never materialized. Partnerships were not as intimate as women wished for, and partners were not what women thought they would be once in Australia. These women hoped their relationships would improve the quality of their life, but this did not happen. Instead, women continued to struggle with insecurities, and acted in ways they did not anticipate, nor like. Such obstructions to happiness indicate that hardships, suffering, and sadness are part and parcel of pursuing happy lives. As Gardner suggests, "to get to the promised happiness takes time and may involve other emotions and states of being" along the way (2015, 200). In fact, happiness, this study illustrates, often remains a promise, a future state (Ahmed 2010, Gardner 2015).

Thus far, the discussion has demonstrated that there is no single pursuit of happiness, and that ideas of what makes people happy change over the course of the journey of marriage migration. In the remaining pages, I will look beyond the initial project of marriage migration. In so doing, I add more evidence of the long-term transformations that people underwent—both female and male. I also discuss partners' experiences of life in Australia after migrant men gained permanent residency. This allows me to situate the arc of the experiences that my interlocutors underwent in a wider context. It also allows me to show the variation and heterogeneity of experiences that are possible when one engages in love and/or marriage migration. For all interlocutors, the pursuit of happiness continued, albeit in various ways. Whether or not couples stayed together or separated, interlocutors adjusted their previously held imaginaries of the future. I first describe the often-difficult experiences of "moving on" for men and women who separated from their partners. After that, I focus on couples that surmounted the barriers of the journey of marriage migration.

1 Migrant Men: Separations and Moving On

In many cases, cross-border relationships did not last. The timing of separations—often right after migrant men obtained permanent residencies—seems to suggest that migrant men separated from their Australian spouses as soon as they had the opportunity. However, most migrant men explained how hard this decision to leave had been. It is difficult to convey the depth of their feelings of despair in writing. The unfamiliar context, in which the men's partners were their only real support, played a significant role in making the break-up a huge step to take. In Australia, men felt, that a lack of cultural, economic and social capital made leaving hard. Men, as newly arrived migrants, and without any established network except for their partner's family, found it hard to consider leaving that family. Peter, for instance, summed up his main worries: "Where would I go? With what money? And all alone?"

Moreover, reasons for leaving felt irrational, contradicting, and confusing. Men wanted to leave their partners because of their everyday experiences—the control, being told what to do, being shouted at and sometimes being verbally and emotionally abused. Yet, men often described their gratitude for what their sponsoring partners had done to help them. Sponsoring partners not only spent considerable amounts of money on the visa application and on staying in touch during the visa processing period, but also, they spent their time and energy providing for their migrant partners during the first months after arrival. The care that women extended to them made men very confused when thinking about their reasons for wanting to leave.

All of the men who separated from their Australian partner had left their now ex-partner with everything they had acquired as a couple. Some couples had bought a house while they had been together, but the men moved out without disagreement. Men said that it was easier for them, as "young and strong men" to start anew, than it would be for their ex-partners, especially when there were children involved. Perhaps men felt guilty that women had invested so much in them by sponsoring their journey and therefore considered leaving with nothing as a way to repay their ex-partners for their efforts, or as a way of reducing their own sense of guilt. While men never expressed this directly, it seemed that statements like: "having nothing to lose," "she deserves to have everything" and "I am the one leaving" also meant that leaving in this way, men did not owe their ex-partners anything. Or, at least it meant that men felt they repaid just a tiny bit of the debt—both financial and emotional—they had. Feelings of guilt were suggested by other behaviors as well. Jacob, for instance, kept visiting his ex-partner every time she called, and did anything she asked. According to him, it was impossible to refuse his ex-partner. Such repayments seemingly also helped men to feel like "real men" again. By taking responsibility, where possible, men seemed to create a sense of co-dependency despite the separation, as opposed to the previously experienced dependency.

Men found this period after the separation hard as they started on another journey towards happiness. Paul, when looking back at that period, told me it was the hardest part of his new life in Australia. He said how he felt homesick and defeated, wanting to party, to go out and forget his sorrows by drinking and meeting women. Yet, he also wanted to meet his responsibilities as a new father, as well as to continue sending remittances back home. Although he tried his best to fulfil all requests, he felt that he was a continual failure. Paul, like other men, had to reinvent himself whilst simultaneously having to meet the responsibilities of everyday life. Many men who had migrated relatively recently expressed how they were still very stressed, as they worried about the direction their life would take. They all struggled with the fact that their expectations and hopes of life in Australia were still very different from their lived realities.

Living a healthy and balanced life seemed difficult and energy consuming for many. Jacob elaborated on his health and lifestyle when we sat together for dinner in a restaurant. By this time, Jacob had moved out of his apartment and to save money was temporarily living with a friend whilst looking for another apartment to rent. I had wanted to treat Jacob and take him out for dinner but was surprised that he was not impressed with the menu, which mainly consisted of meat options. Jacob explained that a healthy vegetable dish is a luxury. "All I have been eating lately is McDonalds, I just crave some greens," and he sighed as he took a sip of his beer. While I had thought that Jacob would have been happy to go out for dinner, I now realized that he may have preferred a simple but nutritious home-cooked meal. He felt relieved that he could stay with his friend, but he also knew that he needed his own accommodation. "I need my daughter to be able to come visit me." But it was hard for him, as he did not have any money and still had debts to pay off. In the meantime, his ex-partner kept nagging him that he should spend more time with their daughter. Jacob was thinking of getting an apprenticeship in a trade, so that he could earn significantly more in the future. But this would mean that for the time being he would have less money, and so he was unsure of what to do. He felt as if he was "back at scratch," as if he was "standing still instead of moving ahead." He continued by mentioning that his friends back home all had good jobs now. They surely also thought he was "living the life in the west," but, "look at me," Jacob downheartedly said. He added that he also needed to keep sending remittances to his family back home. "I want to buy a house, settle down, and get my sister over, but I really do not see any of this happening any day soon."

My interviews and ethnographic observations with male interlocutors made it clear that for various reasons, staying in Australia was often perceived as the best option for them. Even though these men experienced sincere hardships, such as racism, a lack of opportunities, isolation, little sense of community and homesickness for friends and family, they all named the living conditions and opportunities for future happiness as important reasons for staying in Australia. Here, men could obtain more and/or better education, had access to health care and could rely on the state if they needed help.

One exception was Elijah, who concluded that his move had only brought positive change. Elijah clearly expressed how happy his life in Australia had made him and never felt homesick or defeated. "I will never move back," he convincingly proclaimed, as "my country has never been good to me." Elijah explained that his father had left the family when Elijah was still young, and that his mother had struggled to survive. He himself had never finished high school, as he had to help provide for his family. Therefore, when he had met his ex-wife, he did not hesitate about moving to Australia. He emphasized that he never regretted moving to Australia, even though the relationship did not turn out to be good for him. Although he experienced racism daily, he did enjoy his hometown of Melbourne as here "I can make money and I have the freedom to do whatever I want to do." For Elijah, the lifestyle he was able to live was something he felt was not possible back home.

Also, most men seemed well aware of "losing face" if they returned home permanently. To move back to their African country would be constructed as a failure by relatives and friends back home, and in a way, it would be a failure. These men had moved to Australia mostly aged in their twenties and thirties and spent a few years here. In the meantime, their peers back home had moved on, moved away, found jobs, and started families. As such, single men moving back would be seen to be lagging behind. This was quite the opposite to the perception of their life in Australia held by those back home: namely, that they were well ahead and high up on the socioeconomic ladder. Men all seemed to agree that with their hopes of becoming successful in Australia, it was better to stay here than to move back to their original home.

Children were another important reason for men to stay in Australia. Men who had children with their now ex-partners, explained that maybe if they did not have children here, they would have ended their relationships before being granted permanent residency. This would have meant that they then had to leave Australia as soon as possible, as their visas were based on their relationship status. But they felt that having had children removed that option, as leaving Australia would mean that the men would not be able to be in their children's lives. Saleem, for instance, explained that "honestly, my relationship ended already a year after I arrived in Australia." Even though he had known for a long time that his wife was having an affair, he had decided to "sit it out." He "counted the days" until he obtained permanent residency. "Because we have a daughter, you see?" He explained that if he had left his wife, this would have meant that he had to leave Australia straight away. If Saleem had done that, he reasoned that he probably would have never seen his daughter again. He explained that in his home country, with a regular job it was almost impossible to earn enough money for a flight ticket. And, he added, "even if I would have that money, I would not get a visa, because they [the Australian Government] do not give tourist visas to Africans." Even though Saleem continuously felt homesick and "like shit," being able to see his daughter grow up was reason enough for him to stay in Australia.

Paul elaborated further on this topic. He explained that even though having children in Australia meant a break from his African family and homeland, it also meant that the children would grow up with many opportunities that were not available in his country of origin. Here, opportunities for a better life for future generations abound, he emphasized. While maybe men did not enjoy life as much as they would have done back home, raising children in Australia meant that they would have access to good education. Men also appreciated the access to social security, which they found to be very important. For these men, moving to Australia represented a turn-around from having few prospects for advancement in life, to having many opportunities for socioeconomic development.

Thus, while most men did not feel entirely at home in Australia, they all preferred to stay, as eventually for them, and certainly for their young families, life here would be better. In Australia, men saw more opportunities, a better income and more money to share with their family back home, freedom, a higher socioeconomic status (at least from the perspective of their African home), and they would not need to experience the shame of returning. As such, men seemed to be accepting of the hardships as they felt they served a purpose—that life for them and their children would be good in the long-run. It becomes clear, thus, how imaginaries of happiness shift, are adjusted to current circumstances, and in the case of migrant men, happiness remained something in the future. While first men imagined they would be happy upon arrival in Australia, now they realized that only when they finally managed to settle and feel at home in Australia, sometime in a far-away future, will they be happy.[1]

2   Sponsoring Women: Separations and Moving On

By the time of separation, relationships had often become untenable for both partners. While both men and women initiated break-ups, for some women a break-up, coinciding with the man obtaining permanent residency, represented an "ultimate betrayal" by the man. Their first reaction was to think that he could have used her just to obtain a visa. This thought had sometimes been lingering in the back of women's minds due to the messaging they received through visa application procedures, media coverage of unsuccessful marriages involving migration, and warnings by family, friends, and acquaintances. However, most women explained that after a first moment of emotional upheaval, they also realized that it was much more complicated than that.

While most women were balanced and rational in their recollections, I sometimes listened for hours to other women full of anger, expressing how terrible African men were. Women explained to me how "African men are all the same," "cheaters," "liars," have "no manners," and are "just so selfish."[2] While

---

1   Most men even expressed a view that the ultimate happiness would stem from retirement in their homeland, in their own house they will have built over the (future) years. However, this ideal seemed so very far away from the situation they were in at this moment in time, that it was not a serious topic of discussion for most men.

2   These were often women who had separated from their partners in the not-so-distant past. Their recollections, then, were often especially emotionally laden.

such alleged behavior could have much to do with the emotional journey of marriage migration, which affected both men and women, these women linked such behaviors to their partner's visa status. They explained that men's behavior always turned worse the moment they saw their legal rights increased—a sign of men having used their female sponsors.

Some women recalled a sudden change in their partner's behavior that coincided with a milestone in his migration journey. Sarah's husband left her just days after he obtained his permanent residency. According to her, he would just have been waiting for this moment all along. She explained that her ex-partner had treated her badly from the moment he had arrived in Australia. They had sometimes separated for short periods, but he would then always "smooth talk" her back into the relationship. He would exclaim how he could not live without her, and how she should give him "one last shot." A few months before he would be eligible for permanent residency, the couple had broken up again, only to reunite about three weeks before the deadline for the approval to come through. Sarah explained that this time, "he literally begged me to give him another chance." Those weeks, she felt, had actually been very good. He had behaved at his best and she actually started to believe again in his genuineness. However, two days after the couple had been together for two years—and thus when he became eligible for residency—he had left Sarah. Immediately, Sarah recalls, "he went to Centrelink to ask for some sort of pension." Because the staff member at the office had thought it looked suspicious, they had contacted Sarah, as well as the DIBP. "You can see it clearly now, he just used me all this time," Sarah concluded. In this and one other case, it was obvious to the women that they had been used for visa purposes.

For other women, separations were far more ambiguous. Sophie's and Lauren's stories in Chapter 6 illustrate this. Both women had seen their partners change from confident and happy men, to becoming despondent and low-spirited once in Australia. When looking back on their relationships, both women could clearly see how the journey of marriage migration had affected their partners' self-confidence. They acknowledged that their relationships had resulted in some good outcomes for their ex-partners as it granted them many opportunities for betterment, and both Lauren and Sophie felt that their partners had loved and cared about them. They thought that if the journey of marriage migration had been easier for both the men and for them as a couple, their intimate partnerships might have continued successfully.

In Lauren's case, her marriage migration journey with her first husband had not turned out as well as she had hoped. She had been married to her first Africa-origin husband about twenty years ago. After having been together for about two years, Lauren found out that he was married and had a family in his home country. The woman he would always call his ex-partner appeared to still be his wife. When he separated from Lauren, he brought his family to Australia. While at the time this had affected Lauren greatly, she since had come to terms with what happened. She explained that she understood why he did what he did. "At the time," she reasoned, "a kind of a general powerlessness, his inability to gain any sort of successes" in his home country had influenced his decisions. Lauren thought that for her ex-partner, marrying her was "a way of safeguarding his life, his future." But he also loved her, she was very sure, "as much as he could." Lauren felt that "he wanted to have this, our child, me, as a fresh start." "But," she added, "his [real] ability to love was back home, where he left it, with his family." While it had been very hard on her, Lauren had also tried to understand the situation and had helped her ex-partner bring his family to live in Australia. This example illustrates the importance of cultural contexts when analyzing chosen pathways to happiness, as described by Robbins (2013). It also indicates how the pursuit of happiness is fluid rather than static, with happiness continuously serving as an object on the horizon rather than something to be found in the present.

After relationships ended, women often experienced new relationships with their now ex-partners as ongoing, yet dysfunctional. Women expressed surprise at how much they still meant to their ex-partners. Men seemed to continue to act as though they were still in the mother-child relationship that had developed throughout their intimate relationships, and which had often contributed to the separation itself. Men often relied on their ex-partners for help and advice, and women felt they needed to have some sort of contact, even though the relationship had ended years ago. Because they had been through so much together, letting go of everything was hard. While men felt guilty and indebted to their Australian ex-partners, it seemed that some women could not yet see clearly how significant their role in their ex-partners lives had been. Jade, for instance, could only stop being angry with her ex-partner after he called her crying, to say he was sorry, and she eventually understood that she was now like a mother figure to him. It was only after that call that she realized how indebted he felt towards her, and thus how much he actually respected her, even though he had never showed this respect to her before. For her, this phone call had given her a way to reconcile, to accept what had happened, and was an action that brought her peace of mind.

While the life changing character of the unions was a reason for continuing at least some sort of relationship after a separation, children were also a very important reason for attempts to keep in contact. Women's experiences with the fathers of their children varied. While Naomi thought her ex-partner was a terrible man for what he did to her, she was "very impressed, very happy" with his involvement with their daughter. Naomi emphasized that he never missed a chance to see his daughter. Also, she felt her ex-partner was very reliable, and helped out financially when needed. She said that "it is obvious he loves his daughter a lot and I am lucky it is this way, you know." Also, Eileen was happy to see that their divorce did not stop her ex-partner from seeing his children. Even though he now lived far away from her and the children, she said that "he manages to come and spend time with his kids every week, and sometimes has them to stay the night or a weekend at his."

For other women, children were solely their responsibility, as it appeared that fathers had decided not to be involved. Sophie explained how she tried—and was still trying—to have Anthony as involved in their daughter's life as much as possible. She would ask him to come to visit, join them on excursions or pay child support, but generally Anthony ignored such requests. Sophie also said that even if he did agree, that would not mean that he would keep to the arrangement. While such behavior was very disappointing for Sophie and their daughter, and I am not aware of his reasons for his unreliable and hurtful behavior, the stories I captured of the men I interviewed may explain at least part of the reasons behind Anthony's conduct. Perhaps he did not feel he had anything to contribute and therefore preferred to keep his distance until some future day when he might have a more stable life.

After separations, women slowly came to terms with the tumultuous years of marriage migration. Even though women had realized their relationships were not particularly good or healthy, and often felt the exhaustion and stress deriving from such relationships, they had also been extremely reluctant to break up with their partner. Women expressed how incredibly hard it had been for them, how long it had taken them to accept the break-up, and how much time it had taken before they were able to move on with their lives. Alice for instance had suffered from a severe depression after the break-up. And Jade had attempted suicide after her partner left her straight after he received his permanent residency. Also, Sophie felt depressed and visited a psychologist for some time after her separation from Anthony. It seemed that for women, marriage migration made partners especially connected to each other, giving them an extra layer of commitment in their relationship. For women, because their romantic relationship failed, so did their marriage migration project, increasing the seriousness of the effects on them. For women, it took time to embark on new pathways to happiness. For men, on the other hand, migration-related happiness projects continued as they were more easily able to shift the project's aims.

Yet, as women "picked up the pieces" after a failed relationship, they often stated that it was important for them to work on themselves and/or to find another relationship built on more stable foundations. Lauren focused on what she felt "makes me happy," which were her children, her involvement with the community and her poetry. Sophie found love in her new partner Lucas. She told me that she had learnt a lot from her previous marriage migration project. Her new partner, she felt, was much more compatible, and she insisted on more independence for herself and her partner. She also thought that she had become calmer herself, and more comfortable in her role as wife and mother, which made the new relationship easier. Such examples indicate that happiness projects evolve. It also illustrates that moments of loss, grief and sadness are part of projects—lives are hardly ever just happy, and that such feelings help women to make way for new or altered pursuits of happiness.

3   The Happy Ones: Narratives of Companionship

Despite many undesired and unhappy outcomes, there were happy outcomes for some of my interlocutors. As should be expected, these are not the fairy-tale happily-ever-afters from children's books, as that is not in the spirit of the nature of happiness, which as discussed is a process and a pursuit (Ahmed 2010). Eight couples I interviewed were still together by the end of my field-work. The youngest relationships had lasted for about three years, whereas Jo and Robert had been together for over thirty years. All of these couples, while having successfully managed their marriage migration journeys, also acknowledged the difficulties of the realities of marriage migration, and how the obstructions they faced had been influential in shaping their partnerships.

Partners were well aware that African-Australian couples often separated or divorced. All partners, male and female, said that they were just very lucky with their partners. Nevertheless, some did offer suggestions about things which they felt made their relationship healthier and happier. Most women pinpointed a high level of independency within their relationship and felt they had managed to create a healthy balance between teamwork and allowing each partner to remain an independent individual. Anne for instance explained that it was more important for her husband to visit his home country than it was for her. Therefore, they decided that he would travel as often as he could and that she would not join him on every single journey. She said that continually travelling to Africa would leave her frustrated—mainly due to the geographical distance and language barriers—and would eventually make her "resent his background." Instead, when he travelled by himself, she would stay in Melbourne with their daughter. She felt there were some advantages to this arrangement. For example, she explained that "When he goes for Christmas,

we are happy because we can have a real tree when he is not there." Her partner hated all the needles on the ground and would demand a fake tree. She
said that other people did not always understand that she did not mind him
being away for weeks at a time. But she enjoyed the time apart. She felt it was
"healthy for personal development" and did not think that people "need to be
together all the time to have a good relationship."

Like Anne, other women emphasized the importance of having men not
being dependent on them, which had been difficult to achieve, given the visa
regulations and experiences of settling in Australia. Men and women suggested
that equality and mutual respect were important for healthy relationships.
Both male and female partners explained that if there is space for both partners to develop themselves in Australia, and be responsible adults, the relationship will not fail. This had not always been easy to achieve. As described in
the previous chapter, women in lasting relationships admitted to being guilty
of mothering their partners too much early on in their relationships. Emma
recalled how much better their relationship became when she decided to
really stop interfering with her partner Mathew's business. But she also had
seen him change in Australia. It was clear to her that the migration journey had
been hard on him. "Especially in the early years, he struggled," she recalled. Not
being able to get a respectable job, nor to pursue his music career in "sleepy
Adelaide," as he could have in Europe, had changed Matthew's uplifted spirit
into a somewhat downhearted demeanor. While Emma had done what she
could to support her partner, she emphasized that the journey of marriage
migration had affected him greatly. Their case, like others, exemplifies how
marriage migration, with its institutional and everyday racism and other hurdles along the way transforming men into unhappy partners, as well as the
disappointments experienced by women, is a journey to happiness inflicted
with hardships.

Lillian, on the other hand, recalled no problems with her partner settling
in Adelaide. Right from the start, her husband sought to connect with other
African migrants from his region. "William," she argued, "never stopped being
independent," and "I have always considered him to be the head of our household." She also explained, while laughing out loud, that she often complimented William on his looks, his clothing, on anything that came to mind, as it
would be good for him to feel valued, to feel like a good man and partner. While
no other women stressed complimenting their partners as a key to happy relationships, on social media women did praise their partners on special occasions, or shared photos of the couple happily in love, adding words of praise
for their partners. Such instances of commendation and admiration seemed

important ways to keep relationships intimate. They also may have improved men's self-confidence in an otherwise rather harsh environment.

While men, as well as women, mentioned companionship as reasons for their successful relationships, they mainly reflected on the way in which a sense of purpose would lead to better outcomes. Men felt that a feeling of purpose in Australia, and freedom and confidence to explore, as well as compatibility with one's partner, were crucial to healthy relationships. As a relationship counsellor who often worked with Africa-origin partners of Australian women explained, both marriage and migration are life changing events, and to combine the two often leads to crisis. Even when men have very good intentions, the counsellor argued, the double reinvention of the self after marriage *and* migration was often too much to tolerate. Especially in situations in which the local female spouse had practically all the power and would use it, too, the counsellor said, it would be almost impossible for the man to retain a sense of meaning in his life, a good sense of self.

Women described their partners as their best friends, and often their soul mates. Women would use the idea of having found their soul mate as a way to explain why she and her partner made such a successful couple. But being suited to each other and sharing common interests and aspirations did not mean that there were not difficulties in their relationship. Anne, for instance, who said she had found her soul mate in Dylan, did express disappointment in the way the couple brought up their children. Whereas she had held romantic imaginaries of their future together—she for instance had pictured them together in the park, with their baby—such hopes turned out too "rose-colored." In reality, her husband left major parts of the child rearing to her, something she was not particularly happy with. She felt that this was due to his cultural background, as she thought that in his home country, women were the prime carers of children, which was at odds with her own expectations. Thus, while she felt she was living the happily ever after with her partner, their relationship in practical and everyday matters had not-so-happy and rather disappointing aspects. But such disappointments, she felt, were part of life, and normal. This example also—and again—makes it evident that this work describes the journeys of real people, with different stories and different personalities and outlooks. Anne had her own ideas and expectations of relationships, just like all the other interlocutors.

Generally, though, companionship, as described by Giddens (1992), could be considered a fitting model of lasting relationships. Women and men named the following as reasons their relationships were successful and lasting: intellectual compatibility; shared future plans; similar lifestyle; keeping to themselves; retaining some privacy in their individual lives; respect for the other person; friendship; complimenting and honoring the partner in private as well as in public; showing interest in the partner's family; good communication with the partner and adhering to their rules; and being responsible and available for the nuclear family first.

What such reflections indicate is that marriage migration could be a meaningful, worthwhile and positive experience for some. And, even the unsuccessful relationships provided separated partners with reasons for appreciating the experience of marriage migration—even as the memories of that experience could still bring back hurt and pain. This indicates that the search for happiness—the happiness projects of my interlocutors—continues even though their orientations and horizons have shifted. This shows that happiness is future oriented, something illusive that can bring a sense of purpose to the mundane everyday (Walker & Kavedžija 2015; Ahmed 2010). As Gardner states, and following on from Ahmed (2010, 31), "the point of the promise of happiness is to travel, not to arrive. In this sense, it is easier to anticipate happiness than to actually have it" (2015, 209). While couples and partners were not always particularly happy during their relationships or after they formally ended, the experiences they encountered have now informed their current and future happiness projects.

Seeing marriage migration as a happiness project counters the narrative provided by the media, and evident in government visa application processes, about sham marriages, how much money women ostensibly lose, and how evil foreign men are. Both migrant men and sponsoring women were looking for happy relationships and happy lives in Australia, but the obstructions of institutional and everyday racism, as well as the gendered expectations of relationships interfered with their desired happy endings. Such obstructions met during their journeys of marriage migration were often the reasons for separations, not the ill intentions often presumed and described by the media. By looking at the nuances of couples' experiences with marriage migration, it becomes evident that despite the best of intentions, the hardships met along the way have an insidious effect on happy outcomes. Such findings also help to situate the importance of an anthropological effort to reflect on both the light and dark experiences of marriage migration.

References

Abu-Lughod, L. (1986). Shifting politics in Bedouin love poetry. In C. Lutz & L. Abu-Lughod (Eds.), *Language and the politics of emotion* (pp. 24–45). Cambridge: Cambridge University Press.

Abuyi, J. (2014). *African men's experiences in Australia: Resettlement processes and the impact of service provision*. Tasmania: Mercy Refugee Project.

Acharya, M. (2017, February 8). An Indian migration agent along with his wife has been accused of running fake marriage scams for visa in Australia. SBS. Retrieved from https://www.sbs.com.au/yourlanguage/hindi/en/article/2017/02/08/marriage-visa-scam-i-love-curries-says-fake-bride-who-married-indian-man, 22 January 2016.

Adepoju, A. (1995). Migration in Africa: An overview. In J. Baker & T. Akin Aida (Eds.), *The migration experience in Africa* (pp. 87–108). Uppsala, Sweden: Nordiska Afrikainstitutet.

Ahearn, L. (2001). *Invitations to love: Literacy, love letters, and social change in Nepal*. Ann Arbor: University of Michigan Press.

Ahmed, S. (2007/08) The happiness turn, *New Formations, 63*, 7–14.

Ahmed, S. (2008) Sociable happiness. *Emotion, Space and Society, 1*, 10–13.

Ahmed, S. (2010). *The promise of happiness*. Durham and London: Duke University Press.

Akin Aina, T. (1995). Internal non-metropolitan migration and the development process in Africa. In J. Baker & T. Akin Aida (Eds.), *The migration experience in Africa* (pp. 41–64). Uppsala, Sweden: Nordiska Afrikainstitutet.

Akokpari, J. (1999). The political economy of migration in Sub-Saharan Africa. *African Sociological Review, 3*(1), 75–93.

Alberoni, F. (1983). *Falling in love*. New York: Random House.

Ali, L., & Sonn, C. (2010). Constructing identity as a second-generation Cypriot Turkish in Australia: The multi-hyphenated Other. *Culture & Psychology, 16*(3), 416–436.

Allen, W. S. (2019). "I had Missionary Grandparents for Christ's Sakes!": White Women in Transracial/Cultural Families Bearing Witness to Whiteness. *Journal of Ethnic and Cultural Studies, 6*(1), 130–141.

Allport, G.W. (1954). *The Nature of Prejudice*. Reading, MA: Addison-Wesley.

Amin, S. (1995). Migrations in contemporary Africa: A retrospective view. In J. Baker & T. Akin Aida (Eds.), *The migration experience in Africa* (pp. 29–40). Uppsala, Sweden: Nordiska Afrikainstitutet.

Andikopoulos, A. (2019) Love, money and papers in the affective circuits of cross-border marriages: beyond the 'sham'/'genuine' dichotomy. *Journal of Ethnic and Migration Studies*, DOI: 10.1080/1369183X.2019.1625129.

Ang, I. (2001). *On not speaking Chinese: Living between Asia and the West*. London: Routledge.

Appadurai, A. (2016). Moodswings in the anthropology of the emerging future. *HAU: Journal of Ethnographic Theory, 6*(2), 1–4.

Arnfred, S. (2004). Re-thinking sexualities in Africa: Introduction. In Arnfred, S. (Eds.), *Re-thinking sexualities in Africa* (pp. 7–29). Uppsala, Sweden: Almqvist & Wiksell Tryckeri AB.

Augoustinos, M., & Reynolds, K. (2001). Prejudice, racism, and social psychology. In M. Augoustinos & K. Reynolds (Eds.), *Understanding prejudice, racism and social conflict* (pp. 1–23). London: SAGE.

Augoustinos, M., & Walker, I. (1998). The construction of stereotypes within social psychology. *Theory & Psychology, 8*(5), 629–652.

Australian Bureau of Statistics (2016a). *BPLP country of birth of person by persons, VISAP visa type and SEXP sex.* ABS, Australian Census and Migrants Integrated Dataset, 2016.

Australian Bureau of Statistics (2016b). *ANCiP of person by persons.* ABS, Australian Census and Migrants Integrated Dataset, 2016.

Australian Bureau of Statistics (2016c). *Australia: population and growth.* Cat. No. 3101.0—Australian Demographic Statistics.

Australian Bureau of Statistics (2016d). *Greater Adelaide and Melbourne: Sub-Saharan Africa-born persons by visa category, 2016.* ABS, Australian Migrants and Census Integrated Dataset, 2016.

Australian Competition and Consumer Commission (2015, February 13). Australians lose $75,000 every day to romance scams. Retrieved from https://www.accc.gov.au/media-release/australians-lose-75000-every-day-to-romance-scams, 22 January 2016.

Australian Government (n.d.) Our country. Retrieved from https://www.australia.gov.au/about-australia/our-country, 15 May 2018.

Baird, B. (2006). Maternity, whiteness and national identity. *Australian Feminist Studies, 21*(50), 197–221.

Barn, R. & Harman, V. (2013). Mothering across racialized boundaries: introduction to the special issue, *Ethnic and Racial Studies, 36*(8), 1265–1272, DOI: 10.1080/01419870.2013.791400.

Bashford, A. (2014). Immigration restriction: rethinking period and place from settler colonies to postcolonial nations, *Journal of Global History, 9*(1), 26–48.

Beasley, C. (2008). Rethinking hegemonic masculinity in a globalizing world. *Men and Masculinities, 11*(1), 86–103.

Beck-Gernsheim, E. (2007). Transnational lives, transnational marriages: a review of the evidence from migrants' communities in Europe. *Global Networks, 7*(3), 271–288.

Berlant, L. (2011). *Cruel optimism.* Durham & London: Duke University Press.

Betts, K. (2003). Immigration policy under the Howard Government. *Australian Journal of Social Issues, 38*(2), 169–192.

Block, L. (2019): '(Im-)proper' members with '(im-)proper' families?—Framing spousal migration policies in Germany, *Journal of Ethnic and Migration Studies*, DOI: 10.1080/1369183X.2019.1625132.

Bochow, A., & van Dijk, R. (2012). Christian creations of new spaces of sexuality, reproduction and relationships in Africa: Exploring faith and religious heterotopia. *Journal of Religion in Africa, 42*(4), 325–344.

Bonjour, S., & de Hart, B. (2013). A proper wife, a proper marriage: Constructions of 'us' and 'them' in Dutch family migration policy. *European Journal of Women's Studies, 20*(61), 61–76.

Bordo, S. (1993). *Unbearable weight: Feminism, western culture, and the body*. Berkeley; Los Angeles; London: University of California Press.

Borelli, J., Rasmussen, H., Burkhart, M., & Sbarra, D. (2014). Relational savoring in long-distance romantic relationships. *Journal of Social and Personal Relationships, 32*(8), 1083–1108.

Bourdieu, P. (1984). *Distinction. A social critique of the judgement of taste*. Cambridge: Harvard University Press.

Bourdieu, P. (1993). *The weight of the world: Social suffering in contemporary society*. (P. P. Ferguson et al., Trans.). Stanford, CA: Stanford University Press.

Brennan. D. (2004). *What's love got to do with it?: Transnational desires and sex tourism in the Dominican Republic*. Durham, London: Duke University Press.

Brettel, C. (2017) Marriage and migration. *Annual Review of Anthropology, 46*, 81–97.

Brink, P. (1995). Fertility and fat: The Annang fattening room. In I. de Garine & N. Pollack (Eds.), *Social aspects of obesity* (pp. 71–86). London, New York: Taylor & Francis.

Britton, J. (2013). Researching white mothers of mixed-parentage children: the significance of investigating whiteness, *Ethnic and Racial Studies, 36*(8), 1311–1322.

Britton, L., Martz, D., Bazzini, D., Curtin, L., & LeaShomb, A. (2006). Fat talk and self-presentation of body image: Is there a social norm for women to self-degrade? *Body Image, 3*, 247–254.

Campo, N. (2005). 'Having it all' or 'had enough'? Blaming feminism in the Age and the Sydney Morning Herald, 1980–2004, *Journal of Australian Studies, 28*(84), 63–72.

Carrier-Moisan, M. (2015). 'Putting femininity to work': Negotiating hypersexuality and respectability in sex tourism, Brazil. *Sexualities, 18*(4), 499–518.

Chant, S., & Radcliffe, S. (1992). Migration and development: The importance of gender. In S. Chant (Ed.), *Gender and migration in developing countries* (pp. 1–29) London: Belhaven Press.

Charsley, K. (2005). Unhappy husbands: Masculinity and migration in transnational Pakistani marriages. *Journal of the Royal Anthropological Institute, 11*(1), 85–105.

Charsley, K. (Ed.) (2012) *Transnational marriage: New perspectives from Europe and beyond*. New York & London: Routledge.

Chen, W., Ling, L. & Renzaho, A.M. (2017). Building a new life in Australia: an analysis of the first wave of the longitudinal study of humanitarian migrants in Australia to assess the association between social integration and self-rated health, *BMJ Open*, 7(3), DOI: 10.1136/ bmjopen-2016-014313.

Chernin, K. (1981). *The obsession: Reflections on the tyranny of slenderness*. New York: Harper and Row.

Childs, E.C. (2019). Mixed matters in Australia, *Social Identities*, 25(3), 424–438.

Chivaura, R.S. (2020). *Blackness as a defining identity: Mediated representations and the lived experiences of African immigrants in Australia*. Springer, DOI: 10.1007/ 978-981-32-9543-8.

Clarke, M.B. (2019). Introduction. In: M.B. Clarke (Ed.) *Growing up African in Australia* (pp. 1–3). Carlton, Victoria: Black Inc.

Cole, J. (2009). Love, money and economics of intimacy in Tamatave, Madagascar. In J. Cole & L. M. Thomas (Eds.), *Love in Africa* (pp. 109–134). Chicago: University of Chicago Press.

Cole, J. (2014). Working mis/understandings: The tangled relationships between kinship, Franco-Malagasy binational marriages, and the French state. *Cultural Anthropology*, 29(3), 527–551.

Cole, J., & Thomas, L. M. (Eds.). (2009). *Love in Africa*. Chicago: University of Chicago Press.

Connell, R. (1995). *Masculinities*. Cambridge: Polity.

Connell, R. (2014). Margin becoming Centre: For a world-centered rethinking of masculinities. *NOMRA: International Journal for Masculinity Studies*, 9(4), 217–231.

Constable, N. (2003). *Romance on a global stage: Pen pals, virtual ethnography, and 'mail order marriages'.* Berkeley: University of California Press.

Constable, N. (2009). The commodification of intimacy: Marriage, sex, and reproductive labor. *Annual Review of Anthropology*, 38, 49–64.

Coontz, S. (2005). *Marriage, a history: From obedience to intimacy, or how love conquered marriage*. New York: Penguin Group.

Cordell, D., Gregory, V., & Piché, V. (1996). *Hoe and wage. A social history of a circular migration system in West Africa*. Boulder: Westview Press.

Cornwall, A. (2002). Spending power: Love, money and the reconfiguration of gender relations in Ado-Obo, southwestern Nigeria. *American Ethnologist*, 29(4), 963–980.

Crapanzano, V. (2004). *Imaginative horizons: An essay in literary-philosophical anthropology*. Chicago: University Press.

Curthoys, A. (1993). Feminism, citizenship and national identity. *Feminist Review*, 44, 19–38.

Da Col, G. (Ed.) (2015). Happiness: Horizons of purpose [special issue]. *HAU: Journal of Ethnographic Theory*, 5(3).

Dafler, J.R. (2005). Social Darwinism and the language of racial oppression: Australia's stolen generations, *ETC: A Review of General Semantics, 62*(2), 137–150.

De Hart, B. (2007). The right to domicile of women with a migrant partner in European immigration law. In S. van Walsum & T. Spijkerbroek (Eds.), *Women and immigration law: New variations on classical feminist themes* (pp. 142–159). New York: Routledge Cavendish.

de Munck, V. (1988). The economics of love: An examination of Sri Lanka Muslim marriage practices. *South Asia: Journal of South Asian Studies, 11*(1), 25–38.

Deeb, L. (2009). Emulating and/or embodying the ideal: the gendering of temporal frameworks and Islamic role models in Shi'i Lebanon. *American Ethnologist, 34,* 242–257.

Delgado Bernal, D. (2002). Critical race theory, Latino critical theory, and critical raced-gendered epistemologies: Recognising students of color as holders and creators of knowledge. *Qualitative Inquiry, 8*(1), 105–126.

Department of Immigration and Border Protection (2017). Partner Migration. Retrieved from https://www.glitf.org/pdfs/booklet.pdf, 23 July 2021.

Dion, K., & Dion, K. (1996). Cultural perspectives on romantic love. *Personal Relationships, 3,* 5–17.

Dixson, A. (2018). "What's going on?": A critical race theory perspective on Black Lives Matter and activism in education. *Urban Education, 53*(2), 231–247.

Donaldson, M., Hibbins, R., Howson, R., & Pease, B. (Eds.). (2009). *Migrant men: Critical studies of masculinities and the migration experience.* New York, London: Routledge.

Dragojlovic, A. (2008). Dutch women and Balinese men: Intimacies, popular discourses and citizenship rights. *The Asia Pacific Journal of Anthropology, 9*(4), 332–345.

Duncan Owen, J. (2002). Mixed matches: interracial marriage in Australia. Sydney: UNSW Press.

Eggebø, H. (2013). A real marriage? Applying for marriage migration to Norway. *Journal of Ethnic and Migration Studies, 39*(5), 773–789.

Essed, P. (1991). *Understanding everyday racism: An interdisciplinary theory.* Newbury Park: Sage.

Essed, P., & Hoving, I. (Eds.). (2014). *Dutch Racism.* Leiden: Brill Publishers.

Essed, P., & Triekekens, S. (2008). 'Who wants to feel white?' Race, Dutch culture and contested identities. *Ethnic and Racial Studies, 31*(1), 52–72.

Faier, L. (2007). Filipina migrants in rural Japan and their professions of love. *American Ethnologist, 34*(1), 148–162.

Fair, L. (2009). Making love in the Indian Ocean: Hindi films, Zanzibari audiences, and the construction of romance in the 1950s and 1960s. In J. Cole & L. M. Thomas (Eds.), *Love in Africa* (pp. 58–82). Chicago: University of Chicago Press.

Fanon, F. (1986). *Black skin, white masks.* New York: Grove Press.

Fassin, D. (2011). Policing borders, producing boundaries. The governmentality of immigration in dark times. *Annual Review of Anthropology, 40,* 213–226.

Featherstone, L. (2006). Imagining the black body: Race, gender and gynaecology in late colonial Australia. *Lillith: A Feminist History Journal, Annual, 15,* 86–96.

Fechter, M. (2007). Living in a bubble: Expatriates' transnational spaces. In V. Amit (Ed.), *Going first class? New approaches to privileged travel and movement* (pp. 33–52). Oxford: Berghahn Books.

Ferguson, J. (1999). *Expectations of modernity: Myths and meanings of urban life on the Zambian copperbelt.* Berkeley: University of California Press.

Ferguson, J. (2006). *Global shadows: Africa and the neoliberal world order.* Durham, NC: Duke University Press.

Fernandez, N. T. (2013). Moral boundaries and national borders: Cuban marriage migration to Denmark. *Identities: Global Studies in Culture and Power, 20*(3), 270–287.

Fernandez, N.T. (2018) The masculine and moral self: Migration narratives of Cuban husbands in Scandinavia. In C. Green & N.T. Fernandez (eds.), *Intimate mobilities: Sexual economies, marriage and migration in a disparate world* (213–230). New York & Berghahn: Berghahn Books.

Fernandez, N. T. (2019). Tourist brides and migrant grooms: Cuban-Danish couples and family-reunification policies, *Journal of Ethnic and Migration Studies,* DOI: 10.1080/1369183X.2018.1547025.

Fischer, E. (2014). *The good life: Aspiration, dignity, and the anthropology of wellbeing.* Stanford: Stanford University Press.

Foucault, M. (2008). *The birth of biopolitics: Lectures at the College de France, 1978–79.* (G. Burchell, Trans.). Houndmills, UK: Palgrave Macmillan.

Frankenberg, R. (1993). *White women, race matters: The social construction of whiteness.* Minneapolis: The University of Minneapolis Press.

Freeman, C. (2005). Marrying up and marrying down: the paradoxes of marital mobility for Chosonjok brides in South Korea. In N. Constable (Ed.), *Cross-border marriages: Gender and mobility in transnational Asia* (pp. 80–100). Philadelphia: University of Philadelphia Press.

Frohlick, S. (2013). Intimate tourism markets: Money, gender, and the complexity of erotic exchange in a Costa Rican Caribbean town, *Anthropological Quarterly, 86*(1), 133–162.

Gaffey, J. (2019). Melbourne's "African gangs" and media narratives, *Salus Journal, 7*(2), 68–84.

Gallo, E. (2006). Italy is not a good place for men: Narratives of place, marriage and masculinity among Malayali migrants. *Global Networks, 6*(4), 357–371.

Gallo, E. & Scrinzi, F. (2016). *Migration, masculinities and reproductive labour: Men of the home.* London: Palgrave MacMillan.

Galloway, A. (2018, November 29). Love (not) Actually. *Herald Sun*. Melbourne, Australia.

Garcia, A. (2010). *The pastoral clinic: Addiction and dispossession along the Rio Grande*. Berkeley: University of California Press.

García, S. (2017). Bridging critical race theory and migration: Moving beyond assimilation theories. *Sociology Compass, 11*, 1–10.

Gardner, K. (2016). The path to happiness?: Prosperity, suffering, and transnational migration in Britain and Sylhet. In I. Kavedžija & H. Walker (Eds.), *Values of happiness: Toward an anthropology of purpose in life* (pp. 191–214). Chicago: Hau Books.

Giddens, A. (1990). *The consequences of modernity*. Cambridge: Polity.

Giddens, A. (1992). *The transformation of intimacy: Sexuality, love, and eroticism in modern societies*. Stanford California: Stanford University Press.

Gill, R. (2006). *Gender and the media*. Cambridge: Polity Press.

Gilman, S. (1985)., Black bodies, white bodies: Toward an iconography of female sexuality in late nineteenth-century art, medicine, and literature. *Critical Inquiry, 12*(1), 204–42.

Gilman, S. (1998). *Creating beauty to cure the soul*. Durham: Duke University Press.

Glick Schiller, N., & Fouron, G. (1990). "Everywhere we go, we are in danger": Ti Manno Annu. *Annual Review of Anthropology, 24*, 47–74.

Goode, W. (1959). The theoretical importance of love. *American Sociological Review, 24*(1), 38–47.

Greaber, D. (2001). *Towards an anthropological theory of value: The false coin of our dreams*. New York: Palgrave.

Groes, C. & Fernandez, N.T. (2018). Introduction: Intimate mobilities and mobile intimacies. In C. Green & N.T. Fernandez (eds.), *Intimate mobilities: Sexual economies, marriage and migration in a disparate world* (1–27). New York & Berghahn: Berghahn Books.

Groes-Green, C. (2014). Journeys of patronage: Moral economies of transactional sex, kinship, and female migration from Mozambique to Europe. *Journal of the Royal Anthropological Institute, 20*, 237–255.

Gugler, J., & Ludwar-Ene, G. (1995). Gender and migration in Africa south of the Sahara. In J. Baker & T. Akin Aida (Eds.), *The migration experience in Africa* (pp. 257–268). Uppsala, Sweden: Nordiska Afrikainstitutet.

Hage, G. (1998). *White nation: Fantasies of white supremacy in a multicultural society*. London: Routledge.

Hage, G. (2002). Multiculturalism and white paranoia in Australia. *Journal of International Migration and Integration, 3*(3–4), 417–437.

Hage, G. (2010). The affective politics of racial mis-interpellation. *Theory, Culture & Society, 27*(7–8), 112–129.

Hannaford, D. (2016). Intimate remittances: Marriage, migration and MoneyGram in Senegal. *Africa Today, 62*(3), 92–109.

Hannaford, D. (2020). *Marriage without borders: Transnational spouses in neoliberal Senegal.* Philadelphia: The University of Pennsylvania Press.

Harman, V. (2010). Experiences of racism and the changing nature of white privilege among lone white mothers of mixed-parentage children in the UK, *Ethnic and Racial Studies, 33*(2), 176–194, DOI: 10.1080/01419870903023652.

Harman, V. (2013). Social capital and the informal support networks of lone white mothers of mixed-parentage children, *Ethnic and Racial Studies, 36*(8), 1323–1341.

Harrison, F. (1995). The persistent power of 'race' in the cultural and political economy of racism. *The Annual Review of Anthropology, 24,* 41–74.

Helle-Valle, J. (2004). Understanding sexuality in Africa: Diversity and contextualised dividuality. In S. Arnfred (Ed.), *Rethinking sexualities in Africa* (pp. 195–210). Uppsala: Nordiska Afrikainstitutet.

Henningham, N. (2001). 'Hats off, gentlemen, to our Australian Mothers!' Representations of white femininity in north Queensland in the early twentieth century. *Australian Historical Studies, 32*(117), 311–321.

Herold, E., Garcia, R., & DeMoya, T. (2001). Female tourists and beach boys: Romance or sex tourism? *Annuals of Tourism Research, 28*(4), 978–997.

Hibbins, R., & Pease, B. (2009). Men and masculinities on the move. In M. Donaldson, R. Hibbins, R. Howson & B. Pease (Eds.), *Migrant men: Critical studies of masculinities and the migration experience* (pp. 96–114). New York, London: Routledge.

Hill Collins, P. (1992). Book review of 'Understanding everyday racism: An interdisciplinary theory' by Philomena Essed. *Contemporary Sociology, 21*(6), 790–791.

Hirsch, J. S. (2003). *A courtship after marriage: Sexuality and love in Mexican transnational families.* Berkeley and Los Angeles: University of California Press.

Hirsch, J. S., & Wardlow, H. (Eds.) (2006). *Modern loves: The anthropology of romantic courtship & companionate marriage.* Michigan: University of Michigan Press.

Hoch, P. (1979). *White hero, black beast: Racism, sexism and the mask of masculinity.* London: Pluto Press.

Hollan, D., & Throop, C. (Eds.). (2011). *The anthropology of empathy: Experiencing the lives of others in Pacific societies.* New York: Berghahn.

Hondagneu-Sotelo, P. (1999). Introduction: Gender and contemporary U.S. migration. *The American Behavioural Scientist, 42*(4), 565–576.

Hoogenraad, H. (2012). Men at play: Freedom and alternative ordering through (romantic) intercultural relationships at the beach in Zanzibar. Master thesis, Faculty of Humanities, Leiden University.

Horne, D. (1964). *The lucky country.* Camberwell, Victoria: Penguin Books.

Howson, R. (2005). *Challenging hegemonic masculinity.* London, New York: Routledge.

Hughes, M. (1997). Soul, black women and food. In C. Counihan & P. van Esterik (Eds.), *Food and culture: A reader* (pp. 272–280). London, New York: Routledge.

Hugo, G. (2009). *Migration between Africa and Australia: A demographic perspective.* Sydney: Australian Human Rights Commission.

Hunter, M. (2009). Providing love: Sex and exchange in twentieth-century South Africa. In J. Cole & L. M. Thomas (Eds.), *Love in Africa* (pp. 135–156). Chicago: University of Chicago Press.

Hunter, M. (2016). Introduction: New insights on marriage in Africa. *Africa Today, 62*(3), vii-xv.

Illouz, E. (1997). *Consuming the romantic utopia: Love and the cultural contradictions of capitalism.* Berkeley: University of California Press.

Illouz, E. (1998). The lost innocence of love: Romance as a postmodern condition. *Theory, Culture and Society, 15*(3–4), 161–186.

Ingraham, C. (1999). *White weddings: Romancing heterosexuality in popular culture.* New York: Routledge.

Iredale, R. (1994). Patterns of spouse/fiancé sponsorship to Australia. *Asian and Pacific Migration Journal, 3*(4), 547–566.

Jacobs, J. (2009). Have sex will travel: romantic 'sex tourism' and women negotiating modernity in the Sinai. *Gender, Place & Culture: A Journal of Feminist Geography, 16*, 43–61.

Jankowiak, W., & Fischer, E. (1992). A cross-cultural perspective on romantic love. *Ethnology, 31*(2), 149–155.

Jankowiak, W., & Paladino, T. (2008). Desiring sex, longing for love: A tripartite conundrum. In W. Jankowiak (Ed.), *Intimacies: Love and sex across cultures* (pp. 1–36) New York: University of Columbia Press.

Jeffreys, S. (2005). *Beauty and misogyny: Harmful cultural practices in the West.* London and New York: Routledge.

Johnson, P. (2005). *Love, heterosexuality and society.* London: Routledge.

Jones, F., & Luijkx, R. (1996). Post-war patterns of intermarriage in Australia: The Mediterranean experience. *European Sociological Review, 12*(1), 67–86.

Jørgensen, M. (2012). Danish regulations on marriage migration. In K. Charsley (Ed.), *Transnational marriage: New perspectives from Europe and beyond* (pp. 60–78.) New York & London: Routledge.

Jupp, J. (2002). *From white Australia to Woomera: The story of Australian immigration.* Canberra: Cambridge University Press.

Kavedžija, I. & Walker, H. (Eds.) (2016) *Values of happiness: Toward an anthropology of purpose in life.* Chicago: Hau Books.

Kenny, D., & Adams, R. (1994). The relationship between eating attitudes, body mass index, age, and gender in Australian university students. *Australian Psychologist, 29*(2), 128–134.

Khan, S. & Pedersen, A. (2010). Black African immigrants to Australia: Prejudice and the function of attitudes, *Journal of Pacific Rim Psychology, 4*(2), 116–129.

Khoo, S. (2001). The context of spouse migration to Australia. *International Migration, 39*(1), 111–132.

Kimmel, M. (2005). *Gender of desire: Essays on male sexuality*. New York: State University of New York Press.

Kofman, E. (2004). Family-related migration: a critical review of European studies. *Journal of Ethnic and Migration Studies, 30*(2), 243–262.

Krause, K. (2008). Transnational therapy networks among Ghanaians in London. *Journal of Ethnic and Migration Studies, 34*(2), 235–251.

Laidlaw, J. (2002). For an anthropology of ethics and freedom. *Journal of the Royal Anthropological Institute, 8,* 311–332.

Lake, M. (1990). Female Desires: The Meaning of World War II. *Australian Historical Studies, 24*(5), 267–248.

Lambek, M. (Ed.). (2010). *Ordinary ethics: Anthropology, language, and action*. New York: Fordham University Press.

Lambek, M. (2016). Le Bonheur Suisse, again. In I. Kavedžija & H. Walker (Eds.), *Values of happiness: Toward an anthropology of purpose in life* (pp. 237–266). Chicago: Hau Books.

Lavanchy, A. (2014). *How does 'race' matter in Switzerland?* Université de Neuchatel, Maison D'Analyse des Processus Sociaux, Working Paper 7.

Lindholm, C. (1988). Lovers and leaders: A comparison of social and psychological models of romance and charisma. *Social Science Information, 27,* 3–45.

Lindholm, C. (1995). Love as an experience of transcendence. In W. Jankowiak (Ed.), *Romantic passion: A universal experience?* (pp. 57–71). New York: Columbia University Press.

Lindholm, C. (1998a). The future of love. In V. de Munck (Ed.), *Romantic love and sexual behaviour: Perspectives from the social sciences* (pp. 17–32). Westport: Praeger.

Lindholm, C. (1998b). Love and structure. *Theory, Culture and Society, 15*(3–4), 243–263.

Lindholm, C. (2001). *Culture and identity: The history, theory and practice of psychological anthropology*. New York: McGraw-Hill.

Lindholm, C. (2006). Romantic love and anthropology. *Etnofoor, 19*(1), 5–21.

Lipset, D. (2004). Modernity without romance? Masculinity and desire in courtship stories told by young Papua New Guinean men. *American Ethnologist, 31*(2), 205–224.

Littlely, B. (2012, May 14). 'He just married me for a visa': Adelaide woman outraged after African man leaves. *The Advertiser*. Retrieved from https://www.perthnow.com.au/news/he-just-married-me-for-a-visa-adelaide-woman-outraged-after-african-man-leaves-ng-31ec53e58e298713cd59dbb0bc465ecc, 23 July 2021.

Lohman, R. (Ed.) (2010). Special Issue: Creations: Imagination and innovation. *Anthropological Forum, 20,* 3.

Luke, C., & Luke, A. (1998). Interracial families: difference within difference. *Ethnic and Racial Studies, 21*(4), 728–754.

Lutz, C., & White, G. (1986). The anthropology of emotions. *Annual Review of Anthropology, 15*, 405–436.

Madison, D. (2005). *Critical ethnography: Method, ethics, and performance.* Thousand Oaks; London; New Delhi: SAGE.

Maher, J. (2005). A mother by trade: Australian women reflecting mothering as activity, not identity. *Australian Feminist Studies, 20*(46), 17–29.

Mahler, S., & Pessar, P. (2006). Gender matters: Ethnographers bring gender from the periphery toward the core of migration studies. *International Migration Review, 40*, 127:63.

Mai, N., & King, R. (2009). Love, sexuality and migration: Mapping the issue(s). *Mobilities, 4*(3), 295–307.

Malkki, L. (1992). National Geographic: The Rooting of Peoples and the Territorialization of National Identity among Scholars and Refugees. *Cultural Anthropology, 7*(1), 24–44.

Masanauskas, J. and Minear, T. (2017, February 26) Partner Visa Anger. *The Herald Sun.* Melbourne, Australia.

Maskens, M. (2015). Bordering intimacy: The fight against marriages of convenience in Brussels. *The Cambridge Journal of Anthropology, 33*(2), 42–58.

Maskens, M. (2018). Screening for romance and compatibility in the Brussels civil registrar office: Practical norms of bureaucratic feminism. In C. Green & N.T. Fernandez (eds.), *Intimate mobilities: Sexual economies, marriage and migration in a disparate world* (74–97). New York & Berghahn: Berghahn Books.

Mathews, G., & Izquierdo, C. (Eds.). (2009). *Pursuits of happiness: Well-being in anthropological perspective.* New York: Berghahn Books.

Matthews, J. (1984). *Good and mad women: The historical construction of femininity in twentieth century Australia.* Sydney & London: George Allen & Unwin.

Mbembe, A. (2001). *On the Postcolony.* Berkeley & Los Angeles, CA: University of California Press.

McEwen, H. (2009). Fauna, flora and fucking: Female sex safaris in South Africa. In M. Steyn & M. van Zijl (Eds.), *The Prize and the price: Shaping sexualities in South Africa* (pp. 112–128). Cape Town: HSRC Press.

McKenzie, L. (2015). *Age-dissimilar couples and romantic relationships: Ageless love?* Basingstoke, UK: Palgrave MacMillan.

McPherson, B. (1994). A colonial feminine ideal: Femininity and representation. *Journal of Australian Studies, 18*(42), 5–17.

Meaney, N. (1995). The end of 'white Australia' and Australia's changing perceptions of Asia, 1945–1990, *Australian Journal of International Affairs, 49*(2), 171–189.

Miles, R. & Small, S. (1999). Racism and Ethnicity. In Taylor, S. (Ed.) *Sociology: Issues and Debates* (PP. 136–157). New York, NY: Palgrave Macmillan.

Moran, A. (2011). Multiculturalism as nation-building in Australia: Inclusive national identity and the embrace of diversity. *Ethnic and Racial Studies*, *34*(12), 2153–2172.

Moret, J., Andrikopoulos, A. & Dahinden, J. (2019). Contesting categories: cross-border marriages from the perspectives of the state, spouses and researchers, *Journal of Ethnic and Migration Studies*, DOI: 10.1080/1369183X.2019.1625124.

Moreton-Robinson, A. (2000). *Talkin' up to the white woman: Aboriginal women and feminism*. St. Lucia: University of Queensland Press.

Moreton-Robinson, A. (2009). Imagining the good indigenous citizen: Race war and the pathology of patriarchal white sovereignty, *Cultural Studies Peer Review*, *15*(2), 61–79.

Morrell, R. (1998). Of boys and men: Masculinity and gender in southern African studies. *Journal of Southern African Studies*, *24*(4), 605–630.

Morrell, R. (Ed.), (2001). *Changing men in southern Africa*. London, New York: Zed Books.

Morrell, R., & Ouzgane, L. (2005). African Masculinities: An Introduction. In L. Ouzgane, & R. Morrell (Eds.) *African masculinities: Men in Africa from the late nineteenth century to the present* (pp. 1–20). New York, NY: Palgrave MacMillan.

Morrell, R., & Swart, S. (2005). Men in the third world: Postcolonial perspectives on masculinity. In M. Kimmel, J. Hearn, & R. Connell (Eds.) *Handbook of studies on men and masculinities* (pp. 90–113). Thousand Oaks, CA: Sage.

Muchoki, S. (2014). *Migration, sexuality and sexual health: Exploring the experiences of Horn of Africa men with refugee backgrounds*. Thesis submitted for the degree of Doctor of Philosophy, Australian Research Centre in Sex, Health & Society, School of Public Health and Human Bioscience, Faculty of Health Science, La Trobe University, Victoria, Australia.

Mullings L. (2005). Interrogating racism: Toward an antiracist anthropology. *Annual Review of Anthropology*, *34*, 667–693.

Musolino, C., Warin, M., Wade, T., & Gilchrist, P. (2015). 'Healthly anorexia': The complexity of care in disordered eating. *Social Science & Medicine*, *139*, 18–25.

Ndholvu, F. (2011). Post-refugee African Australians' perceptions about being and becoming Australian: Language, discourse, and participation. *African Identities*, *9*(4), 435–453.

Neveu Kringelbach, H. (2013). 'Mixed marriage': citizenship and the policing of intimacy in contemporary France. International Migration Institute/University of Oxford, Working Paper 77.

Noble, G. (2005). The discomfort of strangers: Racism, incivility and ontological security in a relaxed and comfortable nation. *Journal of Intercultural Studies*, *26*(1), 107–120.

Noble, G., & Poynting, S. (2010). White lines: The intercultural politics of everyday movement in social spaces. *Journal of Intercultural Studies*, *31*(5), 489–505.

Nowicka, M. (2018). "I don't mean to sound racist but …": Transforming racism in transnational Europe. *Ethnic and Racial Studies,* *41*(5), 824–841.

Objects, money and meaning in contemporary African marriage [special issue] (2016). *Africa Today 62*, 3.

Ong, A. (2006). *Neoliberalism as exception: Mutations in citizenship and sovereignty.* Durham, NC: Duke University Press.

Ortner, S. (2016). Dark anthropology and its others: Theory since the eighties. *HAU: Journal of Ethnographic Theory, 6*(1), 47–73.

Ouzgane, L., & Morrell, R. (Eds.). (2005). *African masculinities: Men in Africa from the late nineteenth century to the present.* New York, NY: Palgrave MacMillan.

Padilla, M. B., Hirsch, J. S., Munos-Laboy, M., Sember, R. E., & Parker, R. E. (Eds.) (2007). *Love and globalization: Transformations of intimacy in the contemporary world.* Nashville: Vanderbilt University Press.

Palumbo-Liu, D. (1999). *Asian/American: Historical crossings of a racial frontier.* Stanford, CA: Stanford University Press.

Patico, J. (2009). For love, money, or normalcy: Meanings of strategy and sentiment in the Russian-American matchmaking industry. *Ethnos, 74*(3), 307–330.

Pellander, S. (2019). Buy me love: entanglements of citizenship, income and emotions in regulating marriage migration, *Journal of Ethnic and Migration Studies*, DOI: 10.1080/1369183X.2019.1625141.

Pessar, P. (1999). Engendering migration studies: The case of new immigrants in the United States. *The American Behavioral Scientist, 42*(4), 577–600.

Pessar, P., & Mahler, S. (2001). *Gender and transnational migration.* Paper presented at the Conference on Transnational Migration: Comparative Perspectives, Princeton University, NJ.

Pini, B., & Previte, J. (2013). Gender, class and sexuality in contemporary Australia. *Australian Feminist Studies, 28*(78), 348–363.

Popenoe, R. (2004). *Feeding desire: Fatness, beauty, and sexuality among a Saharan people.* London: Routledge.

Povinelli, E. A. (2002). Notes on gridlock: genealogy, intimacy, sexuality. *Public Culture, 14*(1), 215–238.

Povinelli, E. A. (2006). *The empire of love: Toward a theory of intimacy, genealogy, and carnality.* Durham: Duke University Press.

Powell, G. (2013, March 4). Woman believed victim of online scam found dead. ABC News. Retrieved from http://www.abc.net.au/news/2013-03-04/woman-believed -victim-of-online-scam-found-dead/4551050, 22 January 2016.

Pruitt, D., & LaFont, S. (1995). For love and money: Romance tourism in Jamaica. *Annals of Tourism Research, 2*(22), 422–440.

Pybus, C. (2006). *Black founders: The unknown story of Australia's first black settlers.* Sydney: University of New South Wales.

Ramsay, G. (2017). Central African refugee women resettled in Australia: Colonial legacies and the civilising process. *Journal of Intercultural Studies, 38*(2), 170–188.

Ratele, R. (2004). Kinky politics. In Arnfred, S. (Ed.) *Rethinking sexualities in Africa* (pp. 139–156). Uppsala: Nordiska Afrikainstitutet.

Ratele, R. (2013). Masculinities without tradition. *Politikon: South African Journal of Political Studies, 40*, 33–156.

Rauktis, M.E., Fusco, R.A., Goodkind, S. & Bradley-King, C. (2016). Motherhood in liminal spaces: White mothers' parenting Black/White children, *Affilia, 31*(4), 434–449.

Rawsthorne, S. (2019, August 4) 'Easy money' for sham marriage: The women targeted by global syndicate. The Sydney Morning Herald. Retrieved from https://www.smh.com.au/national/nsw/easy-money-for-sham-marriage-the-women-targeted-by-global-syndicate-20190729-p52bto.html, 15 June 2020.

Rebhun, L. (1999). *The heart is unknown country: Love in the changing economy of northeast Brazil.* Stanford: University of Stanford Press.

Reischer, E., & Koo, K. (2004). The body beautiful: Symbolism and agency in the social world. The *Annual Review of Anthropology, 33*, 297–317.

Rezeanu, C. (2015). The relationship between domestic space and gender identity. *Journal of Comparative Research in Anthropology and Sociology, 6*(2), 9–29.

Riccio, B. (2008). West African transnationalisms compared: Ghanaians and Senegalese in Italy. *Journal of Ethnic and Migration Studies, 34*(2), 217–234.

Richards, E. (2015, August 12). Migration. *Adelaidia*. Retrieved from http://adelaidia.sa.gov.au/subjects/migration-0, 15 May 2018.

Robbins, J. (2013). Beyond the suffering subject: toward an anthropology of the good. *Journal of the Royal Anthropological Institute, 19*, 447–462.

Robbins, J. (2015). On happiness, values, and time: The long and the short of it. *HAU: Journal of Ethnographic Theory, 5*(3), 215–233.

Robinson, K. (1996). Of mail-order brides and "boys' own" tales: Representations of Asian-Australian marriages. *Feminist Review, 52*, 53–68.

Rodríguez-García, D. (2006). Mixed marriages and transnational families in the intercultural context: A case study of African-Spanish couples in Catalonia. *Journal of Ethnic and Migration Studies, 32*(3), 403–433.

Rosenthal, D. A., Bell, R., Demetriou, A., & Efklides, A. (1989). From collectivism to individualism? The acculturation of Greek immigrants in Australia. *International Journal of Psychology 24*(1–5), 57–71.

Rubin, L., Fitts, M., & Becker, A. (2003). 'Whatever feels good in my soul': Body ethics and aesthetics among African American and Latina women. *Culture, Medicine and Psychiatry, 27*(1), 49–75.

Rytter, M. (2012). The semi-legal family life: Pakistani couples in the borderlands of Denmark and Sweden. *Global Networks, 12*(1), 91–108.

Saint-Aubin, A. F. (2005). A grammar of black masculinity: A body of science. In L. Ouzgane & R Morrell (Eds.), *African masculinities: Men in Africa from the late nineteenth century to the present* (pp. 23–42). New York/Schotsville: Palgrave Macmillan/University of KwaZulu-Natal Press.

Saraiva, C. (2008). Transnational migrants and transnational spirits: An African religion in Lisbon. *Journal of Ethnic and Migration Studies, 34*(2), 253–269.

Sayad, A. (1999). A displaced family. In P. Bourdieu et al. *The weight of the world* (pp. 23–36). Cambridge: Polity.

Scheel, S., & Gutekunst, M. (2019). Studying marriage migration to Europe from below: Informal practices of government, border struggles and multiple entanglements, *Gender, Place and Culture*, DOI: 10.1080/0966369X. 2018.1489375.

Schmidt, G. (2011). Law & identity: transnational arranged marriages and the boundaries of Danishness. *Journal of Ethnic and Migration Studies, 37*(2), 257–275.

Selänniemi, T. (2003). On holiday in the liminoid playground: Place, time, and self in tourism. In T. Bauer &B. McKercher (Eds.), *Sex and tourism: Journeys of romance, love and lust* (pp. 19–32). Binghamton NY: The Haworth Press.

Shabbar, F. (2012). Protecting our non-citizens: Iraqi women on Australian temporary spouse visas. *The Sociological Review, 60*(1), 149–168.

Shaw, A., & Charsley, K. (2006). *Rishtas*: Adding emotion to strategy in understanding British Pakistani transnational marriages. *Global Networks, 6*(4), 405–421.

Shumway, D.R. (2003). *Modern Love: Romance, Intimacy and the Marriage Crisis*. New York, NY: New York University Press.

Silberschmidt, M. (2001). Disempowerment of men in rural and urban East Africa: Implications for male identity and sexual behavior. *World Development, 29*(4), 657–671.

Silberschmidt, M. (2005). Poverty, male disempowerment, and male sexuality: Rethinking men and masculinities in rural and urban East Africa. In L. Ouzgane & R. Morrell (Eds.), *African masculinities: Men in Africa from the late nineteenth century to the present* (pp. 189–204). New York: Palgrave Macmillan.

Silverstein, P. (2005). Immigrant racialization and the new savage slot: Race, migration, and immigration in the new Europe. *The Annual Review of Anthropology, 34*, 363–384.

Simons, M. (2006). (Re)-forming marriage in Australia? *Family Matters, 73*, 46–51.

Smid, K. (2010). Resting at creation and afterlife: Distant times in the ordinary strategies of Muslim women in Fouta Djallon, Guinea. *American Ethnologist, 37*, 36–52.

Smith, A. (2016). *Racism and everyday life: Social theory, history and 'race'*. Hampshire; New York: Palgrave Macmillan.

Smith, D. (2009). Managing men, marriage, and modern love: Women's perspectives on intimacy and male infidelity in Southeastern Nigeria. In J. Cole & L. M. Thomas (Eds.), *Love in Africa* (pp. 157–180). Chicago: University of Chicago Press.

Smith, D. (2010). Promiscuous girls, good wives, and cheating husbands: Gender inequality, transitions to marriage, and infidelity in Southeastern Nigeria. *Anthropological Quarterly, 83*(1), 123–152.

Smith, D. (2017). *To be a man is not a one day job: Masculinity, money and intimacy in Nigeria*. Chicago, IL: The University of Chicago Press.

Smolicz, J. J., Secombe, M. J., & Hudson, D. M. (2001). Family collectivism and minority languages as core values of culture among ethnic groups in Australia. *Journal of Multilingual and Multicultural Development 22*(2), 152–172.

Solivetti, L. (1994). Family, marriage and divorce in a Hausa community: A sociological model. *Africa: Journal of the International African Institute, 64*(2), 252–271.

Spanger, M. (2013). Doing love in the borderland of transnational sex work: Female Thai migrants in Denmark. *NORA—Nordic Journal of Feminist and Gender Research, 21*(2), 92–107.

Spronk, R. (2002). Looking at love: Hollywood romance and shifting notions of gender and relating in Nairobi. *Etnofoor, 15*(1–2), 229–239.

Spronk, R. (2006). *Ambiguous pleasures: Sexuality and new self-definitions in Nairobi.* Academisch proefschrift, Faculteit der Maatschappij- en Gedragswetenschappen, Universiteit van Amsterdam.

Spronk, R. (2009a). Media and the therapeutic ethos of romantic love in middle class Nairobi. In J. Cole & L. M. Thomas (Eds.), *Love in Africa.* (pp. 181–203). Chicago: University of Chicago Press.

Spronk, R. (2009b). Sex, sexuality and negotiating Africanness in Nairobi. *Africa, 79*(4), 500–519.

Spronk, R. (2014). The idea of African men: Dealing with the cultural contradictions of sex in academia and in Kenya. *Culture, Health & Sexuality, 16*(5), 504–517.

Stafford, L., & Merolla, A. (2007). Idealization, reunions, and stability in long-distance relationships. *Journal of Social and Personal Relationships, 24*(1), 37–54.

Stiles, E. (2005). 'There is no stranger to marriage here!': Muslim women and divorce in rural Zanzibar. *Africa: Journal of the International African Institute, 75*(4), 582–598.

Stuart, A., & Donaghue, N. (2011). Choosing to conform: The discursive complexities of choice in relation to feminine beauty practices. *Feminism & Psychology, 22*(1), 98–121.

Summers, A. (2006). *Damned whores and God's police: The colonisation of women in Australia.* Sydney: NewSouth Publishing.

Svašek, M. (2005). Introduction: Emotions in anthropology. In K. Milton & M. Svasek (Eds.), *Mixed emotions: Anthropological studies of feeling* (pp. 1–23). Oxford: Berg Publishers.

Swinburn, B. (2003). The obesity epidemic in Australia: Can public health interventions work? *The Asia Pacific Journal of Clinical Nutrition, 12*, S7.

Sykes, K. (2005). *Arguing with anthropology: an introduction to critical theories of the gift.* London: Routledge.

Teo, H. (2005). The Americanisation of romantic love in Australia. In A. Curthoys & M. Lake (Eds.), *Connected worlds: History in transnational perspective* (pp. 171–192) Canberra: ANU E Press.

Thomas, D., & Clarke, M. (2013). Globalization and race: Structures of inequality, new sovereignties, and citizenship in a neoliberal era. *Annual Review of Anthropology*, *42*, 305–325.

Thomas, L., & Cole, J. (2009). Introduction: Thinking through love in Africa. In J. Cole & L. M. Thomas (Eds.), *Love in Africa* (pp. 1–30). Chicago: University of Chicago Press.

Thompson, A.E., & O'Sullivan, L.F. (2012). Gender Differences in Associations of Sexual and Romantic Stimuli: Do Young Men Really Prefer Sex over Romance? *Archives of Sexual Behavior*, *41*(4), 949–957.

Thompson, K. (2013). Strategies for taming a Swahili husband: Zanzibari women's talk about love in Islamic marriages. *Agenda: Empowering Women for Gender Equality*, *27*(2), 65–75.

Tilbury, F. (2007). "I feel I am a bird without wings": Discourses of sadness and loss among East Africans in Western Australia. *Identities*, *14*(4), 433–458.

Timperio, A., Cameron-Smith, D., Burns, C., & Crawford, D. (2010). The public's response to the obesity epidemic in Australia: weight concerns and weight control practices of men and women. *Public Health Nutrition*, *3*(4), 417–424.

Tolson, A. (1977). *The limits of masculinity*. London: Tavistock.

Trouillot, M.R. (2003). *Global Transformations: Anthropology and the Modern World*. New York, NY: Palgrave Macmillan.

Turner, G. (2008). The cosmopolitan city and its other: The ethnicizing of the Australian suburb. *Inter-Asia Cultural Studies*, *9*(4), 568–582.

Twine, F.W. (1997). The white mother, *Transition*, *73*, 144–154.

Twine, F.W. (2010). White like who? The value of whiteness in British interracial families, *Ethnicities*, *10*(3), 292–312.

Twine, F.W. & Steinbugler (2006). The gap between whites and whiteness: Interracial intimacy and racial literacy, *Du Bois Review*, *3*(2), 341–363.

Uchendu, E. (Ed.), (2008). *Masculinities in contemporary Africa*. Dakar: CODESRIA.

Udah, H. & Singh, P. (2010). Identity, othering and belonging: Toward an understanding of difference and the experiences of African immigrants to Australia, *Social Identities*, *25*(6), 843–859.

Udah, H., Singh, P., Hiruy, K. & Mwanri, L. (2019). African immigrants to Australia: Barriers and challenges to labor market success, *Journal of Asian and African Studies*, *54*(8), 1159–1174.

Vaa, M., Findley, S., & Diallo, A. (1989). The gift economy: A study of women migrants' survival strategies in a low-income Bamako neighbourhood. *Labour, Capital and Society*, *22*, 234–260.

Valdes, F., McCristal Culp, J., & Harris, A. (2014). Battles waged, won, and lost: Critical race theory at the turn of the millennium. In F. Valdes (Ed.), *Crossroads, directions, and a new critical race theory* (pp. 1–6). Philadelphia: Temple University Press.

Valentine, G., Piekut, A., Winiarska, A., Harris, C., & Jackson, L. (2015). Mapping the meaning of 'difference' in Europe: A social topography of prejudice. *Ethnicities, 15*(4), 568–585.

van Acker, E. (2003) Administering romance: Government policies concerning pre-marriage education programs. *Australian Journal of Public Administration, 62*(1), 15–23.

van Dijk, H., Foeken, D., & van Til, K. (2001). Population mobility in Africa: An overview. In M. de Bruijn, R. van Dijk & D. Foeken (Eds.) *Mobile Africa: Changing patterns of movement in Africa and beyond* (1–21) Boston, Leiden: Brill.

Van Dijk, R. (2015). A romantic zone of transference? Botswana, Ghanaian migrants and marital social mobility. In A. Akinyinka Akinyoade & J. Gewald (Eds.), *African roads to prosperity: People en route to socio-cultural and economic transformations* (pp. 111–138). Leiden, Boston: Brill.

van Tilburg, M., & Vingerhoets, A. (Eds.). (2005). *Psychological aspects of geographical moves: Homesickness and acculturation stress.* Amsterdam: Amsterdam University Press.

Vannier, S., & O'Sullivan, L. (2017). Passion, connection and destiny: How romantic expectations help predict satisfaction and commitment in young adults' dating relationships. *Journal of Social and Personal Relationships, 34*(2), 235–257.

Verkuyten, M. (2003). Racism, Happiness and Ideology. In Van den Berg, H., Wetherell, M., & Houtkoop-Steenstra, H. (Eds.) *Analyzing Race Talk* (PP. 138–155). Cambridge: Cambridge University Press.

Vigh, H. (2009). Wayward migration: On imagined futures and technological voids. *Ethnos, 74*(1), 91–109.

wa Mungai, N., & Pease, B. (2009). Rethinking masculinities in the African diaspora. In M. Donaldson, R. Hibbins, R. Howson & B. Pease (Eds.), *Migrant men: Critical studies of masculinities and the migration experience* (pp. 96–114). New York, London: Routledge.

Wagner, R. (2015) Family life across borders: Strategies and obstacles to integration. *Journal of Family Issues, 36*(11), 1509–1528.

Walker, H., & Kavedžija, I. (2016). Introduction: Values of happiness. In I. Kavedžija & H. Walker (Eds.), *Values of happiness: Toward an anthropology of purpose in life* (pp. 1–28). Chicago: Hau Books.

Wardlow, H., & Hirsch, J. (2006). Introduction. In J. Hirsch & H. Wardlow (Eds.), *Modern loves: The anthropology of romantic courtship & companionate marriage* (pp. 1–33). Michigan: University of Michigan Press page.

Waxman, P. (2000). The shaping of Australia's immigration and refugee policy, *Immigrants & Minorities, 19*(1), 53–78.

Wekker, G. (2016). *White Innocence: Paradoxes of Colonialism and Race.* Durham, NC: Duke University Press.

Williams, L. (2010). *Global marriage: Cross-border marriage migration in global context.* New York: Palgrave MacMillan.

Wise, A. (2005). Hope and belonging in a multicultural suburb. *Journal of Intercultural Studies, 26*(1–2), 171–186.

Wolf, N. (1990). *The beauty myth.* London: Vintage.

Wray, H. (2012). Any time, any place, anywhere: Entry clearance, marriage migration and the border. In K. Charsley (Ed.), *Transnational marriage: New perspectives from Europe and beyond* (pp. 41–59). New York & London: Routledge.

Zelizer, V. (2005). *The purchase of intimacy.* Princeton: Princeton University Press.

Index

CPSIA information can be obtained
at www.ICGtesting.com
Printed in the USA
JSHW052244050822
28933JS00005B/9

9 781642 597943